GABRIEL BEN-TASGAL

300 QUESTIONS in 300 WORDS

Myths and Realities
about the Israeli-Palestinian Conflict

English version by Deborah Bigio and Sara Fernandez-Bigio
Revision by Sammy Eppel
Cover and design by Carolina Rosenthal
Photo of Gabriel Ben Tasgal by Fred Braunstein

FOREWORD

Gabriel Ben Tasgal is part philosopher, journalist, Zionist, political analyst and humorist, among other interesting personal and personality traits, the most striking and in my opinion most important, is that he is an educator. And what makes a good educator is the ability to communicate, in this respect, Gabriel simply excels. After more than ten years of continuous travel giving lectures, interviews, presentations and workshops to tens of thousands of Jews and Christians, while becoming the driving force of the premier public diplomacy organization Hatzad Hasheni together with Roby Croitorescu and a small group of helpers, he now embarks in a groundbreaking educational endeavor with the publishing of this book.

With profound knowledge and moral integrity, he takes the reader on a learning adventure seldom seen. Using simple language, he deploys an amazing amount of 100% unadulterated facts in a most curious way, he formulates 300 questions that he has gathered from hundreds of sessions of Q&A and proceeds to answer them in a clear and didactic way, not easily found when dealing with sometimes intractable subjects, such as anti-Semitism and the Israeli-Palestinian conflict.

Gabriel has an encyclopedic knowledge which he delivers in a clear, concise and engaging manner that directly targets the new manifestations of Judeophobia, like BDS, that are now taking hold in many universities all over the world.

To those in search of knowledge and the truth in a subject that so far has defied and mystified clarity and understanding, you have in your hands the "key" that will unlock decades, maybe centuries, of myths and misinformation in Judeophobic attitudes and politics.

Sammy Eppel

The Israeli-Palestinian conflict is relatively simple to understand if you study the codes of the Middle East. At the same time, it is a conflict in which countless spokespeople hoist the most misbegotten interpretations. There is somewhat of impunity on this subject. Nobody would dare to write about the disputes in Africa or the conflict in Ukraine, without delving deeply into the subject. However, "we all express our opinion about Israel" (as the brilliant Jorge Marirrodriga would say, in reference to the excess babble when dealing with the Israeli-Palestinian conflict). Finally, it's about a conflict that encourages the use of liters of ink, not necessarily because of true concern about the future of the Palestinian people, but because the Jews are part of it.

Since the origin of Christianity, there has been an obsession concerning this small group of people that didn't accept Jesus as their Messiah. This obsession has been joined by an adverse theology (from the Theory of Replacement or Substitution to the accusation of deicide), translated into violent actions and forced conversions against Jews, and that – during the XX Century – became planned murders of European Jews (and North-African communities) during the Shoah.

Anti-Semitism has twenty-one centuries of experience and has evolved during its destructive genealogy, appearing in different myths and conceptions. During the Middle Ages many "were convinced" that Jews kidnapped children to prepare unleavened bread, or that they contaminated the waters on purpose to bring on Black Death. In modern times, many people were "convinced" that Jews were racially non-human beings, a non-creative pariah race that had to be eliminated. Many were convinced in Europe, and throughout the world, there were more that did nothing to refute such an abomination or to prevent the genocide, at least by opening their frontiers for those Jews in need of refuge.

Currently, Anti-Semitism appears in three forms. These are mutations of the XX and XXI centuries awaiting new myths. First, a modern Judeophobe will affirm that the Holocaust did not happen and will try to mask his hatred with an illegitimate "scientific" question.

Second, the current Judeophobe will assure that Jews (or the Mossad) are behind all crises, be them anarchists, vulture funds, political crises or unfortunate events of nature. For the modern Anti-Semite, Jews are behind all evil, and they blindly trust the "Protocols of the Elders of Zion, or its tropical Argentinean version "The Andinia Plan".

Third, the modern Judeophobe understands that it is discriminatory and unacceptable to declare himself as an Anti-Semite, and therefore opts to hate "the Jew" among nations (Israel) and will do so obsessively, in a Manichaean and demonizing way.

Criticizing Israel is a legitimate act. In fact, the harshest critics are the Israelis themselves. However, obsessive demonization against Israel by the media and other institutions, from certain academics to political parties, is so evident and clear that it has to be qualified for what it is: Anti-Semitism or Judeophobia.

This book was written for those who enjoy good moral health, for those who try to understand the Middle East in its original language and for those with honest intellectual inclinations.

In times when many falsehoods are sheltered under "this is my narrative and it's as valid as yours", we want to offer verifiable data, processes and interpretations that will allow opting for a constructive posture instead of a demonizing one.

In general terms, the interpretation framework of the Palestinian-Israeli conflict in Europe is influenced by the fact that this continent is the birthplace of Anti-Semitism. We can see endless manifestations of Anti-Semitism in Spanish precisely in Spain, a country that has suffered this illness for hundreds of years, even though for centuries it hardly has had Jews among its citizens.

Latin America is influenced in its interpretation of the Middle East by central-peripheral theories, anti-Yankee feelings and "materialistic" ideologies, many times quite strongly. It is common to listen to Spanish-speaking spokespeople arguing out loud that "Israel is an imperialist and colonialist State just like the North-Americans with our countries, and therefore we must oppose both of them"

If the interpretation in Europe is influenced by being the birthplace of Anti-Semitism and in Latin America by materialistic interpretations, it becomes impossible to understand the Middle East without specializing in tribal or clan identities, and above all in the dominant religion: Islam. Considering that the base of the identity of the Middle-Eastern peoples is their tribal belonging (clan) and their religious identity, any text on these topics that lacks depth is like a "translation" from one reality to another that loses its essence on the way.

In Argentina, we can find journalistic work that DOES NOT help to understand the Palestinian-Israeli conflict. An example is Pedro Brieger's The Palestinian-Israeli Conflict: 100 Questions and Answers (El conflicto palestino-israelí: 100 preguntas y respuestas. 2007) When a person is so involved in a materialistic pattern, conflicts are always explained as disputes for power and use of resources (water, land, oil). Analyzing the Middle East in this way will promote the dismissal or even the exclusion of fundamental religious elements to understand the region. In words of the world-wide eminence, specialized in the Middle East, Bernard Lewis (author of "Faith and Power", among others), religion is a fundamental part of the local identity. In the framework of the classic "materialistic" pattern, the conflict between Palestinians and Israelis is obsessively explained by the occupation (of territories), and the rest of the factors are of secondary or tertiary importance. Certainly, some extreme-left newspapers in Israel think the same way, and even the Palestinian narrative is similar, but this is an unacceptable principle among specialists.

Since the main materialistic argument is that "it's all about the occupation", it is not good or desirable, although intellectually correct, to explain the reality of the Israeli presence in Judea-Samaria (the West Bank) and Gaza. It is worrying and even surrealistic the almost absent description and deep explanation of that author about the consequences of the division of Oslo II (1995) in Territories A, B, and C and the disengagement of Israel from the Gaza Strip in 2005.

Throughout his book, Zionism is shown as a movement created with the sole purpose of having Jews living in Israel, and therefore, it deducts that Palestinians were "expelled" in 1948. Zionist leadership, even right-wing revisionists, always assumed that if Arabs lived in Israel and would continue to do so, they would live as a minority, just as Jewish minorities inhabited other countries. Moreover, for decades Zionism was led by its socialist branch that advocated for an identity without classes (including Arabs), as they also requested a bi-national State with

Arabs. There are no deep foundations, not in texts or in declarations, that Zionism is what is argued.

Many consider that the Israelis are to blame for the lack of peace in the region. To support such a statement, they discard or minimize peace proposals by Prime Ministers Ehud Olmert (2007-2008) and Ehud Barak (2000) and the ideas brought forth by Bill Clinton to end the conflict. The Israelis' desire for peace is usually faded as well as the total lack of will of the Palestinians to even propose counter-offers for peace to solve the territorial aspects of the conflict. Explaining both things from an academic-intellectual standpoint would be correct, although it would damage consistency when promoting preconceptions.

The conflict is easy to understand in its essence, but more complex in its details. A demonizing analysis of Israel serves as an excuse to increase the "stigmatization" of the only state with an absolute Jewish majority in the world (Israel).

In light of these considerations, the purpose of this book is to answer dozens of honest and legitimate questions in only 300 words. Not one more, not one less. This our attempt to provide students an investigators a brief but useful tool, that will hopefully serve as a stepping stone to increase studies on the Palestinian-Israeli conflict.

May peace be with each of you and your families!

My gratitude to Sergio Pikholtz, President of the Argentinean Zionist Organization for his trust and encouragement; to Roby Croitorescu, President of Hatzad Hasheni (The face of Truth); to Anabella and Oscar Jaroslavsky, for introducing me to the world of the dialectic defense of Israel; to my invaluable friends from Jewish and Christian communities of the continent; to Dori Lustron and Israel (Issi) Winicki for their revision of the Spanish manuscript and their advice; to Sammy Eppel for his revision of the English version; to Judge Franco M. Fiumara for his friendship and suggestions… and of course to Eva Ben-Tasgal, Eitan and Galit, for allowing me to rob their time to explain things that I am absolutely convinced of (although they may laugh at me and say: "you didn't leave us much choice!")

Yours, Gabriel Ben-Tasgal

Hatzad Hasheni (The Face of Truth) is an educational program founded in 2010 by Roby Croitorescu, at the time the President of CLAM (The Latin American Maccabean Confederation) in collaboration with all the leading institutions of the Spanish-speaking world. By producing educational material, we hope to position Israel as a state that loves peace, that fosters the progress of humanity and that is unjustly defamed by disinformation that at times masks anti-Semitic remnants. The main information is broadcasted via www.hatzadhasheni.com and online university-level courses can be taken free of charge at www.academiajs.com

CONTENIDO

Part One - Present Imperfect -

1. Why is there a conflict between Palestinians and Israelis?
2. Why are there authors and journalists, even from Israel, that state that the conflict between Palestinians and Israelis is about "occupation"?
3. What territories are currently (2019) dominated by Palestinians and Israelis?
4. Is it true that the Jewish settlements in the West Bank are so expanded that a territorial solution is impossible?
5. What are the Jewish settlements located in the "Territorial Blocks"?
6. Is there a sound and executable solution to the Palestinian-Israeli conflict?
7. Does Mahmoud Abbas – President of the Palestinian Authority – dominate effectively Territories A and B in the West Bank (2019)
8. Why do Mahmoud Abbas and other spokespeople of the Palestinian Authority complain about Israeli soldiers entering and acting on the territory that they dominate?
9. Why is the Palestinian Authority such an unstable government?
10. Are there specific examples of alarming corruption cases from the Palestinian Authority?
11. Is it true that the Palestinian Authority pays those who murder civilian Israeli Jews from its national budget?
12. Is it legal that the Palestinian Authority pays the salaries of terrorists from their budget?
13. How do Palestinians incite violence among their civilians?
14. Is the Israeli government (2019) interested in reaching a peaceful agreement with the Palestinians?
15. Are there radical Jewish forces that attack Palestinians?
16. Do the Intelligence Services of Israel act to control their radicals?
17. What is the Gaza Strip?
18. What is the Gaza Strip Blockade?

19. *Is it true that Israel does not allow Palestinian civilians from the Gaza Strip to enter its territory?*

20. *Is Israel guilty of the lack of development in the Gaza Strip?*

21. *Is it true that the Gaza Strip is currently (2019) undergoing a deep economic crisis?*

22. *When did Israel withdraw from the Gaza Strip?*

23. *Is Israel still occupying the Gaza Strip? When does the foreign occupation end?*

Part Two - Past Explanatory -

24. *What is the Zionist movement?*

25. *Are all Jews identified with Zionism?*

26. *When it emerged... were all the Jews supportive of Zionism?*

27. *What is the relation between the rebirth of the Hebrew language and Zionism?*

28. *Is Zionism a consequence of European anti-Semitism?*

29. *Who was Theodore Hertzl and what was the Dreyfuss case?*

30. *Was Zionism an invention from the colonialism to occupy "Palestine"?*

31. *What is anti-Zionism?*

32. *Why have the extreme left, and part of the moderated left, raised quite firmly an anti-Zionist flag?*

33. *Are there other anti-Zionists in modern times?*

34. *Can you be anti-Zionist without being anti-Semitic?*

35. *How can we recognize a modern Judeophobe?*

36. *Is every person who criticizes Israel an anti-Semite?*

37. *Can a person be Jewish and at the same time an anti-Semite (Judeophobe)?*

38. *But... is the term "anti-Semitic" properly used?*

39. *Why did Jews choose Palestine to develop their State?*

40. *When Zionism began, did the Palestinian people exist?*

41. *What happened in 1834 and when did the Palestine national identity develop?*

42. *Is it correct to say that the Jews stole the land from the Palestinians before 1948?*

43. Was the phrase "a land without a people for a people without a land" true?
44. Why are there so many testimonies that affirm that Israel was abandoned before the arrival of the Zionists and the British?
45. Did the Zionist ideologists consider the possibility of a confrontation with the local Arabs?
46. So, does a Palestinian people exist (2019)?
47. Is it true that Zionism planned for a State "only for Jews" and that this created the conflict?
48. Why did the British and French divide up the Middle East in 1916?
49. What is the secret Sykes-Picot Agreement of 1916?
50. What do the promises to the Arabs or the letters of McMahon-Hussein from 1915 mean?
51. What is the importance of the Balfour Declaration?
52. Why did the British issue the Balfour Declaration?
53. What was the British Mandate of Palestine?
54. Is it true that the British created an artificial state called Jordan?
55. Is it true that the Zionist leaders met with the Arabs in order to achieve a coexistence agreement in the Middle East in 1919?
56. At what point did the physical confrontations occur between Jews and Arabs?
57. Is it true that Zionist Jews wanted to create a state "only for them", based on what Yosef Weitz said?
58. What did Yosef Weitz really say?
59. Is it true that throughout history Jews and Muslims coexisted in harmony and that only "Zionism" ruptured such an idyll?
60. Did the Arabs and the Jews agree on the British occupying Palestine?
61. What happened during the Arab massacres of 1920?
62. How did the Jews and Arabs react to the massacre of 1920?7
63. How did the British react to the Massacre of 1920?
64. What happened in the Arab massacre from 1921?
65. How did the British react to the massacre of 1921?

66. What are the British White Papers of 1922?

67. What happened during the Arab massacres of 1929?

68. Are there testimonies of the Arab massacre in 1929?

69. Is it true that in 1929 the Jewish community of Hebron was massacred?

70. What was the Jewish people's reaction to the 1929 massacre?

71. What did the British decide after this new wave of Arab violence of 1929?

72. What role did Hajj Amin Al-Husseini play in the conflict?

73. Is it true that the Palestinian Mufti of Jerusalem, Hajj Amin Al-Husseini, was Hitler's ally?

74. What happened to the Mufti Al-Husseini after World War II and his Alliance to the Nazis?

76. What does it mean when the Palestinian narrative transforms the order of the facts?

77. What were the causes of the outburst of violence in 1936-1939?

78. What military actions did the Palestinian-Arabs perform between 1936 and 1939?

79. What did the British do to repress the Arab violence against them?

80. How did the Jews react to the outrage of 1936-1939?

81. What were the consequences for the Palestinian Arabs of the failure of their revolt?

82. Who was Izz Adin Al-Qassam?

83. What was the Peel Commission?

84. What is the McDonald White Paper of 1939?

85. What was the reaction of Arabs and Jews to the McDonald White Paper of 1939?

86. Did the Jews respect the boundaries of immigration stated in the White Papers of 1939?

87. What was the Exodus ship?

88. What did the British do to stop Jewish illegal immigrants?

89. Is it true that the Jews from British Palestine collaborated with the Nazis?

90. What was the Jews' reaction to the Transfer Agreement of 1933?

91. Is it true that Mahmoud Abbas, President of the Palestinian Authority (2019) denied the Holocaust and accused the Jews of collaborating with the Nazis?

92. What did the Jews do to become the majority in the Palestinian territory after being a minority?

93. Is it true that Jews had a "solid military structure" for the War of Independence of 1948?
94. Is it true that the Jewish clandestine forces cooperated normally to foster common objectives?
95. How institutionalized were the Jews near the War of Independence of 1948?
96. What was the institutional level of the Palestinians regarding the Independence War of 1948?
97. Is it possible to compare Arab-Palestinian and Jewish terrorism before 1948?
98. What happened at the King David Hotel in 1946?
99. Why did the United Nations decide the partition of Palestine in 1947?

Part Three - Fluctuating Modernity -

100. What was the UNSCOP and what did it decide?
101. What did the General Assembly of the UN decide on November 29th, 1947?
102. How did the Latin American countries vote on this Partition Plan?
103. What is the legal value of Declaration 181 of the United Nations General Assembly?
103. If Declaration 181 lacks legal strength, why did the UN accept the State of Israel as a member in 1949?
105. How did the Arabs respond to the Palestine Partition Plan?
106. How did the Jews respond to the Partition Plan of Palestine?
107. Was the partition of Palestine fair – Declaration 181?
108. Up to what point was the creation of Israel a compensation for the suffering in the Holocaust?
109. Is it fair to say that the "guilt" for the Holocaust explains the current indulgence towards the State of Israel?
110. Is it true that between Declaration 181 and Israel's Independence they lived through a civil war?
111. What is Plan Dalet?
112. Were there terrorist attacks during the civil war before May 1948?

113. What happened to the Arab village Deir Yassin?

114. What was the Trust Plan to postpone the Independence of Israel?

115. Why did Israel declare its Independence on May 14 of 1948?

116. What does the Israeli Declaration of Independence state?

117. Is the Declaration of Independence of Israel considered a law?

118. Why didn't Israel write a constitution? What is the Basic Law?

119. How did the War of Independence of 1948 develop?

120. Why did Israel defeat the invading Arab armies during the 1948 War?

121. Is it true that the Arabs were expelled intentionally during the war of 1948, and became refugees?

122. Are there testimonies from Arab leaders that confirm that their previous leadership caused the problem of the Palestine refugees?

123. Are there more testimonials of Arab leaders that recognize their faults for the Palestinian refugee problem?

124. Are there individual testimonies that corroborate that the Palestinian Arabs were not expelled in 1948?

125. Are there more testimonials about the Arab-Palestinians not being expelled in 1948?

126. Can we get "more confirmations" that the Palestinian Arabs were not expelled in 1948?

127. What are the differences between a world refugee and a Palestinian refugee?

128. Is it true that the Palestinians have an organization for eternalizing the refugee status?

129. Are there relations and connections between UNRWA and terrorist groups?

130. How many Palestinian-Arabs abandoned the combat zone in 1948?

131. What does the term Nakba Palestine mean?

132. Is it true that Jewish communities in Arab countries were destroyed during the 1948 War?

133. Is it true that there were more Jews than Arab-Palestinians displaced during the War of Independence of 1948?

134. How much money worth of goods and properties are the Jews claiming from the

Arab countries?

135. When did the War of Independence of 1948 end in territorial terms?
136. What is Declaration 194 of the General Assembly of the UN?
137. What is the situation of the Palestinian refugees in the Arab countries?
138. Can we say there was an ethnic cleansing on Palestine?
139. Can a Palestinian that abandoned his land in 1947 return to it?
140. Is it true that Israel accepted compensation payment from Germany?
141. What is the Law of Return for the Jews?
142. What principles does Pan-Arabism defend?
143. Who was Gamal Abdel Nasser and what was his role in the Arab-Israeli conflict?
144. Why were the Christians strong drivers of the Pan-Arab ideals?
145. Who were the Fedayeen?
146. Why was Unit 101 of Ariel Sharon so important?
147. Why did Great Britain, France and Israel join to weaken Nasser?
148. What happened during Operation Kadesh – Sinai War of 1956?
149. Is it true that France helped Israel to develop a nuclear plant with military purposes?
150. What is Israel's policy regarding the use of nuclear weaponry?
151. Is the situation of Israel comparable to the plans of Iran to develop non-conventional weapons (2019)?
152. What is the Palestine Liberation Organization (PLO)?
153. What is the National Charter of Palestine (1968)?
154. Who was Yasser Arafat?
155. Why did Palestinians resort to violence?
156. Why did the Six-Day War begin in 1967?
157. What territories did Israel conquer in the War of 1967?
158. Why was the Six-Day War in 1967 so important?
159. What was the position of the United Nations in reference to the War of 1967? What is Resolution 242 of the UN Security Council?

160. What was the attitude of the Israeli population towards the conquest of the West Bank and the Gaza Strip?
161. What did the Israeli government decide to do with the conquered territories of the War of 1967?
162. Do all Palestinians live in territories that were once occupied by Israel in 1967?
163. What is the situation of the Palestinians living in Israel?
164. What was the Attrition War? What do we refer to when we talk about the "Country of Persecutions"?
165. What is Black September?
166. What happened in the 1972 Munich Olympic Games?
167. What is the importance of the War of Yom Kippur of 1973 for the Palestinian-Israeli conflict?
168. Why do all the Jewish people in the world feel so linked to Israel?
169. How can the US support to Israel be explained? Is it because of the Jewish lobby?
170. What is the Interim Agreement between Israel and Egypt?
171. Why did nationalism defeat socialism in Israel in the 1977 elections?
172. What did the Egypt-Israel Peace Agreement of Camp David mean to the Palestinians?
173. What ideology replaced Pan-Arabism and why is Pan-Islamism so important today?
174. How can we differentiate and analyze Islam schools?
175. What deep factors motivated the rise of Islamic radicalism?
176. How many Muslims feel close to the ideas of the Islamic radicalism (2019)?
177. What does it mean to a radical Islamist that all the west is Yahiliyah?
178. How does an Islamic radical divide the world?
179. How does a radical Islamist divide humanity?
180. Is it true that there are no universal values for Islamic radicals?
181. Is it true that imitating Mohammed in all his actions and sayings increases the tendency towards radicalism?
182. What is the Jihad Islamic Organization for Palestine?
183. Why did Israel invade Lebanon in 1982?

184. What are the baseless interpretations of the reasons for the 1982 Lebanon War?

185. What was the strategy of Israel in Lebanon in 1982?

186. What happened in the refugee camps of Sabra and Shatila in Beirut?

187. When did the Hezbollah arise in Lebanon?

188. What is the Security Strip in the South of Lebanon and the Southern Lebanese Army?

189. Is it true that Israel created Hamas?

190. When was Hamas founded?

191. Does Hamas defend anti-Semitic arguments in their political platform?

192. Why did a Palestinian revolt begin in 1987, known as Intifada?

193. What influence did the Persian Gulf War 1990-1991 have over the Palestinians?

194. What was the meaning of the Madrid Peace Conference of 1991?

195. What were the reasons that made Yitzhak Rabin and Yasser Arafat recognize each other?

196. What are the Oslo Accords? What is the Palestinian Authority?

197. What was the Palestinian reaction to the Oslo Accords?

198. What was the Jewish reaction in Israel to the Oslo Accords?

199. What is Israel's legal basis to build settlements in the West Bank and in Gaza?

200. What are the Oslo B Accords?

201. How did the assassination of Yitzhak Rabin destroy the peace process with the Palestinians?

Part Four - Intifada And Disarray -

202. Is it true that Israel and Syria were about to sign a peace agreement?

203. What was the unilateral withdrawal of Israel from the south of Lebanon?

204. What peace plan was negotiated by Ehud Barak and Yasser Arafat at Camp David in 2000?

205. What was the main negotiators' opinion over the failure of Camp David 2000?

206. What was the reason for the Al-Aqsa Intifada?

207. Is it true that Ariel Sharon's visit to the Temple Mount began the Intifada?

208. What were the consequences for Palestinians and Israelis after the Al-Aqsa Intifada?

209. Why did Israel build a security barrier between Israel and the West Bank?

210. Why didn't Israel build the fence on the Green Line? Is it true that the fence is illegal?

211. Why do some people qualify the fence as a "Wall" and refer to the Berlin Wall?

212. Why did Hamas win the elections of 2006?

213. What was the Second Lebanon War of 2006?

214. What are the practical consequences of the coup of Hamas against the Palestinian Authority?

215. What weapons does Hamas use against the Israeli population?

216. What are the tunnels that Hamas and Hezbollah build to attack Israel?

217. Since when have the Palestinians recognized the State of Israel?

218. Does Hamas acknowledge the State of Israel?

219. Why did an ex-Prime Minister from Israel say that "if I would have been born Palestinian I would have joined a terrorist organization"?

220. Are the Palestinian suicidal attacks the main obstacle for peace?

221. What is the Palestinian position regarding violence and suicidal attacks?
  209

222. How does Palestinian violence affect Israelis?

223. Why would a Palestinian decide to commit suicide to murder Israelis?

224. How does Israeli violence affect the Palestinians?

225. Is it true that there are Palestinian cities surrounded by a wall?

226. Who is Gilad Shalit?

227. How does Israel control the West Bank?

228. Is it true that Israel steals water from the Palestinians in the West Bank?

229. Do Palestinians use their citizens as "human shields"?

230. What are the selective killings practiced by Israel?

231. Do innocent civilians die when Israel kills a Palestinian terrorist?

232. Why do Palestinians and Israelis accuse each other of terrorist practices?

233. Why did Israel carry out Operation Cast Lead in the Gaza Strip in December 2008?

234. Is it true that Israel violates International Law by using "white phosphorus"?

235. Why was Operation Cast Lead so harshly criticized in the media?

236. Why is Israel generally so harshly criticized in the media?

237. Is it true that Palestinians violate international laws with their war actions?

238. What are the legal approaches to fight against Islamic terrorism (including the Palestinian)?

239. Is it true that Israelis violate international laws by using disproportionate force?

240. What happened with the UN schools (UNRWA) during Operation Protective Edge 2014?

241. What is the Human Rights Council of the United Nations?

242. What is the Goldstone Report?

243. What was the Flotilla to the Gaza Strip?

244. What was Operation Pillar of Defense 2012?

245. What was Operation Protective Edge 2014?

246. What narrative was imposed during Operation Protective Edge 2014?

247. Why is the United States so influential in the Middle East?

248. What was the strategy of Barack Hussein Obama for the Palestinian-Israeli conflict?

249. What is Resolution 2334 of the UN Security Council? What role does it play in the Palestinian-Israeli conflict?

250. Are the territories of Judea and Samaria (West Bank) "Occupied Territories"?

251. How do the Oslo Accords and the Disconnection from Gaza 2005 coexist with the "Occupied Territories"?

252. What is the strategy of Donald Trump for the Palestinian-Israeli conflict?

253. Why is Jerusalem so important for Jews, Muslims and Christians?

254. Does the relocation of the US Embassy to Jerusalem improve or diminishes the peace process?
255. Who are the Sunni and their most radical referents?
256. What is Qatar and to what extent is their radicalism influencing the world?
257. Why has Israel approached the non-radical Sunni Muslim countries?
258. Who are the Shiites and how do they express their radicalism?
259. What is the influence of the Shiites on Latin America?
260. Is there a relation between Hezbollah in Latin America and drug traffic?
261. Why are there few doubts about the responsibility of Iran for the attack on AMIA?
262. What were Israel's complaints about the 6+1 agreement with Iran?
263. How did the civil war in Syria favor the penetration of Iran? Can we assume that there will be confrontations there?
264. Did the Arab Spring favor the Palestinian national aspirations?
265. How has Donald Trump punished the Palestinian intransigence?
266. Who are the so-called "new Israeli historians"?
267. Why are there people who cite Ilan Pappe or Shlomo Sand?
268. What is BDS?
269. How was BDS born?
270. Why has BDS been forbidden in so many democratic states?
271. Who promotes BDS in Spanish-speaking countries and what have been the judicial issues?
272. What is the relation between the BDS members and terrorist groups?
273. What are the six modern techniques to demonize Israel and promote its destruction?
274. Can the treatment of Israelis to Palestinians be compared to the treatment of Nazis to Jews?
275. Can it be said that Israel conducts an Apartheid policy?
276. I don't hate Israel or the Jews. Why is the Israel-Apartheid comparison misbegotten?
277. Is Israel the only democracy of the Middle East?
278. What type of modern polyarchy is Israel?

279. What does being right- or left-wing mean in Israel?

280. What other topics are crucial to understand the political map of Israel?

281. Do the Palestinian Authority and the Gaza Strip live in a democracy?

282. What is the Basic Law of the Jewish State?

283. Is it true that there is an alternative to the principle of "two states for two peoples"?

284. How is anti-Semitism expressed in Spain?

285. Why is anti-Semitism in Chile a matter of concern?

286. How is anti-Semitism expressed in Argentina?

287. What is Plan Andinia?

288. What does it mean that peace is not possible but a Hudna (Truce) is?

289. What has been the role of Europe in the Palestinian-Israeli conflict?

290. What has been the role of Russia in the Palestinian-Israeli conflict?

291. What has been the role of Latin America in the Palestinian-Israeli conflict?

292. Why does Israel mistrust the United Nations?

293. Are there specific numbers to justify Israel's lack of trust in the UN? 294. What Declaration compares Zionism to Racism?

295. Why do countries that are close to Israel vote against it in the United Nations?

296. What is the peace initiative of Saudi Arabia? Do the Arab countries want peace with Israel?

297. What "bottom-up" peace initiatives can be highlighted in the framework of the Palestinian-Israeli conflict?

298. Why has Israel become a creative power?

299. Is the implosion of Iran possible (2019)?

300. Does time play in favor of Palestinians or Israelis?.

PART ONE
- PRESENT IMPERFECT -

1. Why is there a conflict between Palestinians and Israelis?

The Israeli-Palestinian conflict is quite easy to understand. For the vast majority of the Jews that live in the State of Israel, where Jews represent almost 80% of the population, **the conflict is about territory**. According to Jewish beliefs, the land is less important than life, therefore it is justified to give up territories that are considered as "national" in order to attain peace. Certainly, there are Israeli Jews that consider land as sacred and that it may not be surrendered under any circumstance, but they are a minority in Israel.

For most of the Palestinian people, highly influenced by the Muslim values and rhetoric, **the conflict is about religion**. In the traditional Islam, Judaism is a false religion (Din Batel); Jews are not a people but only a religion (a false one), Jews occupy properties inherited from the Islam (Waqf Al-Islamiyah) and occupy part of the Islamic holy land that must never be surrendered (Dar El-Islam). Of course, there are those among the Palestinians that believe that the conflict is about territory, but they do not stand out among the decision-makers, or those who impose the local rhetoric.

For the Jews in Israel, the conflict is about territory and for the Palestinians, the conflict is essentially religious. There is, undoubtedly, a territorial conflict, but it is secondary to the main motivation. Furthermore, there are proposals for specific and implementable solutions to solve territorial disputes.

Those who impose the nature and the root causes of the conflict are the aggressors. How do we know that the aggressors are the Islamic radicals and the leadership of the Palestinian people? The answer can be inferred logically: if Israelis abandon the use of physical force, they will be eliminated by groups such as Hamas (and others) because this is the way they act and even announce their intentions. If, on the other hand, Palestinians abandon the use of physical force, no one would attack them, and this would radically increase the possibilities of achieving an agreement.

2. Why are there authors and journalists, even from Israel, that state that the conflict between Palestinians and Israelis is about "occupation"?

There is no unique and complete answer. Among Israelis, there are those who consider that Israel should give up all control of the territory in the West Bank (Judea and Samaria) for their own benefit. They believe that direct or indirect control over the Palestinians provokes a moral degradation or because they consider that if Israel is not "disconnected" from the Palestinians, it will result in a bi-national state with a Jewish minority. In these Israelis' speech, the term "occupation" is commonly used as a clear show of the Jewish tradition of considering land as something less important than life or human values.

For others who discuss the Palestinian-Israeli conflict (where certain journalists and academics stand out), the conflict is presented as "territorial" ("occupation") to not provoke a discord with their "dialectical materialist conceptual training. The dialectical materialism (offered by Engels and Marx) defines matter as the substrate of all reality, whether it is concrete or abstract (ideology, philosophy). For a materialist, conflicts are always about oil, land ("occupation"), water, gas, power, etc.

When analyzing the Palestinian-Israeli conflict, materialistic analysts adopt two postures. The most radical posture will argue that all Jewish presence in Israel is an "occupation" since they say that Zionism is a manifestation of European Imperialism. One can notice their anti-Semitic DNA when we ascertain that they promote the elimination of a "sole state" in the land, "the Jewish state among nations".

Others will argue that the conflict explains itself with the "West Bank occupation" by Israel after the Six-Day War (1967). The fact that the majority of the Palestinians live under a Palestinian government or that the Palestinian-A-rabs murdered Jews long before 1967 is an anecdotal fact that cannot contradict the materialistic dogma.

3. What territories are currently (2019) dominated by Palestinians and Israelis?

The State of Israel decided to "disconnect", and withdraw all military and civilian presence in the Gaza Strip. From Sep 12/2005 until June/2007 the territory was under the control of the Palestinian Authority and later ousted by a military coup by the terrorist group Hamas. Since then, the Gaza Strip is governed by the Islamists of Hamas and the Palestinian Authority is claiming its return. Meanwhile, Israel imposes a legal military blockage over Gaza since early 2009.

The Gaza Strip
(Source: The CIA World Factbook)

The situation in the West Bank (Judea-Samaria) is different. The Oslo B Accords (Sep/28/1995, signed in Washington), also known as the "Interim Agreement on the West Bank and the Gaza Strip", state that Palestinians would take over the autonomous government of the Palestinian cities and 450 villages.

The territories would be divided into Areas A, under the civilian and military control of the Palestinian Authority. Israeli civilians cannot enter these territories by express order of their government because they fear their citizens may be murdered, as has happened in the past. Areas A include Ramallah, Bethlehem, Jericho, Jenin, Tulkarem, Kalkilya, Nablus and the Arab portion of Hebron. Areas B are under civilian and police administration of the Palestinian Authority, and the safety of the perimeter is in hands of Israel. Areas C are under the civilian and military control of Israel until an agreement is reached on its final status.

Oslo B division *(Source: Wikipedia)*

Currently, 100% of the Palestinian citizens of Gaza live under the Palestinian government (Hamas) while 91% of the Palestinians of the West Bank live under the government of the Palestinian Authority in Areas A or B.

Areas A and B comprise 40% of the 5,790 km2. Areas C, under Israeli control, comprise 60% of the territory.

4. Is it true that the Jewish settlements in the West Bank are so expanded that a territorial solution is impossible?

False. Such a statement is used to reaffirm the "materialistic" concept of the conflict. Currently, the Israelis that live beyond the Green Line (the separation line - it was never a border - between Israel and Jordan from Apr/3/1949), add up to 649,872 souls next to a not certified number in the census of 2,700,000 Palestinians.

In 2018, the Judea and Samaria Council published data stating that 201,200 Israelis live in the Jewish neighborhoods of Jerusalem built after the 1967 war (there is a consensus that they will remain as part of Israel in a future agreement). These neighborhoods are Gillo, Pizgat Zeev, Armon HaNatziv, and others.

The other 448,672 Israelis that live behind the Green Line are located only in Territory C (60% of the West Bank).

We can divide the Jewish colonies beyond the Green Line into four types: **Brown**—settled by socialist governments within the Alon Plan framework. These include 6,000 people located in the Jordan Valley on the Jordan border. **Red**—Orthodox Jewish colonies that settled there encouraged, mainly, by housing prices. **Green**—Big cities like Maale Adumim or Ariel where religious and secular Jews live. **Blue**—Neo-orthodox Jewish settlements (national religious), some of them isolated as small colonies with only about 100 families.

The majority of the Jewish settlers are not dispersed in the midst of the Palestinian cities but concentrated in blocks of settlements next to the Green Line.

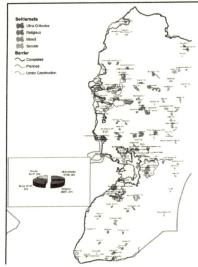

Distribution of the settlements beyond the Green Line
(Source: https://www.shaularieli.com)

To understand the possible territorial solution to the Palestinian-Israeli conflict, it is important to understand that an "isolated" Jewish settlement is not the same as another one located in the "territorial blocks". The construction of settlements has been concentrated in territorial blocks.

5. What are the Jewish settlements located in the "Territorial Blocks"?

The territorial blocks are the areas with a large Jewish presence and little or no Palestinian presence. The blocks are joined or united to the Green Line. These are:

- **Maale Adumim Block** – 52,000 Israelis spread in a 60 km2 municipality.
- **Givat Zeev Block** – Located north-east of Jerusalem, with a 25 km2 extension, inhabited by 20,000 Israelis.
- **Gush Etzion Block** – 72 km2, with 48,000 Israelis living in 9 cities.
- **Modiin-Illit Block** – A land of 11 km2 with 70,000 Israelis in 4 colonies.
- **Ariel Block** – About 60,000 settlers in 13 villages in an area of 80 km2.
- **Karnei Shomron Block** – 20,000 people in a 78 km2 territory.

In the large territorial blocks of Jewish settlements of Judea and Samaria, there are 270,000-290,000 Israelis, comprising 65% of the 448,672 Israelis that live in 326 km2 (5.70% of all the West Bank). According to this information, Israelis that live beyond the Green Line and in Jerusalem or in the Territorial Blocks, comprise 75.58% of the total.

In his article "How Many Settlers Need to be Evacuated to Make Way for a Palestinian State?" Ori Mark (Haaretz) explains that there are 33 "isolated" settlements with 46,000 people, about 9,800 families, a number that can be compared to a large Israeli neighborhood.

In 2018, Israeli novelist A.B. Yehoshua wrote in Haaretz: "The solution of two states is disappearing because of the constant expansion of the settlements in Judea and Samaria". In October 2015, writer Gideon Levy (Haaretz) stated that the solution of having two states "was lost" because of the expansion of the settlements. However, and according to sound data, both Yehoshua and Levy are wrong.

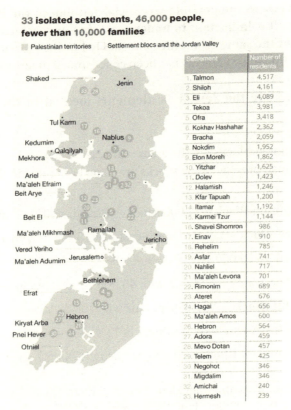

Source: Haaretz, Article by Ori Mark

6.   Is there a sound and executable solution to the Palestinian-Israeli conflict?

In September 2008, Israeli Prime Minister, Ehud Olmert, offered the President of the Palestinian Authority, Mahmoud Abbas, a definite solution in which Israel was annexed to the Territorial Blocks (in blue, 6.2%), but it compensated the Palestinians with a 5.8% of territories located within Israel before 1967 (marked in red). An internationally recognized Palestinian State would be created, also recognized by Israel (in the yellow territories). The logic of Ehud Olmert was clear: "Israel will keep the majority of the Israeli citizens but renounces to the majority of the territory in question and even compensates by the annexed blocks". **The principle of territorial exchange is known as "Swap" and has been transformed into the base of any future agreement.**

The Olmert Plan
(Source: jewishpublicaffairs.org)

To unite the Gaza Strip to the West Bank, the Israelis offered a secure 4-lane route located in the Israeli territory, where "only" Palestinian cars could circulate.

The solution for Jerusalem would be based on the premise that the Jewish neighborhoods would be for Israel while the Arab ones would be for the Palestinian State. The Old City of Jerusalem would be divided in two: the Arab-Christian and Muslim neighborhoods would belong to the Palestinian while the Armenian and the Jewish would belong to Israel. Everything on the Temple Mount would be for Palestine and the Wailing Wall would continue being Jewish.

The President of the Palestinian Authority, Mahmoud Abbas, rejected the opportunity to finalize the territorial conflict and did not respond to the offer. His excuse was that Ehud Olmert was about to quit, which is why there was "no time". Abbas, like Arafat in the past, did not propose a counter-offer.

The Olmert Proposal demonstrated that there are territorial alternatives to finalize the conflict. The fact that the Palestinians believe that the conflict is not territorial results in not having a solution.

7. Does Mahmoud Abbas – President of the Palestinian Authority – dominate effectively Territories A and B in the West Bank (2019)?

Mahmoud Abbas, President of the Palestinian Authority, DOES NOT dominate the Gaza Strip, because his forces were expelled in a coup by Hamas in 2007. According to the Oslo Accords B (1995), Israel legally controls Territory C in the West Bank until a final agreement is reached.

What is happening in Territories A and B in the West Bank? **At present, the extreme levels of hostility by the parties and tribes within the Palestinian Authority are shocking**. Political and armed rivalries exist among the Fatah leadership (Muhammad Dahlan against Marwan Barghouti versus G'ibril Rajoub, etc.) in cities and villages. **The situation seems more like a dispute among "mafias"**. Whole neighborhoods in Nablus or Hebron receive direct orders from Gaza (Hamas), even though the cities are nominally under the control of Ramallah (PA). Beyond these areas, certain streets are under the control of the Popular Front for the Liberation of Palestine, while others are in hands of men that have vowed their allegiance to ISIS. The level of hostility among these factions is illustrated by the fact that all of them are more inclined to deal with Israel vis-a-vis.

The Palestinian Authority, as the central government, exerts clear and evident control over three large cities of the West Bank: Ramallah, Bethlehem and Jericho.

The loyalty can be noticed by comparing the graffiti in the squares of the villages. Another way is to verify who takes responsibility for terrorist acts. If, for example, there are two or more stabbings by Palestinians of Hamas, the village is theirs.

For now, Mahmoud Abbas maintains an apparent internal unity under the Palestinian authority. When he dies, there will be an internal struggle for the successor. It could even happen without bloodshed, areas A and B may rapidly lose their apparent cohesive administrative control.

8. Why do Mahmoud Abbas and other spokespeople of the Palestinian Authority complain about Israeli soldiers entering and acting on the territory that they dominate?

Indeed, their complaints are reasonable but "simulated". According to the Oslo B (1995), the Palestinian Authority should have the monopoly of the use of force, at least in Areas A. However, as was previously stated (question 7), alternative armed groups question the government of the Palestinian Authority. The most powerful of these forces is the Hamas, an Islamist group that was able to overthrow the PA in Gaza and intends to do the same in the West Bank.

The Palestinian Authority chases after the soldiers of Hamas and the Islamist Jihad, common enemies for both Abbas and Israel, by trying to destroy their local organizations. Often they ask for Israel's collaboration or witness how the Israeli forces enter their cities unilaterally to capture a suspect.

The 6,000 officers of the Palestinian Authority are sure to remain in their headquarters and in their stations when the Defense Forces of Israel persecute or make preventive arrests against those who plan terrorist attacks. The intelligence flows freely in the meetings between high-rank Israeli officials and their Palestinian equals under the command of Mahmoud Abbas.

Often, these meetings are photographed and appear in the Hamas media, which provokes a condemnation and mockery amongst the Palestinians that consider these actions as a form of collaboration.

The Israelis that mistakenly enter a controlled territory by the Palestinian Authority, or that intentionally challenge the prohibition of doing business in those areas and then are attacked, are often rescued by security forces of the Palestinian Authority.

The collaboration rises because of common interests: for Israel because it prevents the loss of innocent lives and for the Palestinian Authority because it could be a way to eradicate the threat of a coup. The event that might change this status-quo is the death of Mahmoud Abbas.

9. Why is the Palestinian Authority such an unstable government?

The usual propagandistic answer is that "Israeli occupation is so forceful" that Palestinians are not able to govern themselves effectively. Undoubtedly, confrontation with Israel has an influence on the instability, however, a more profound answer is necessary.

First and foremost, as in all the Middle East, the primary loyalty of Palestinian Arabs is to their clan or extended family (Jamula) and not to a western-style central government. An Arab living in Hebron feels more identified to his clan Qawasme that to his Palestinian belonging. The same can be said about the Al-Masri clan in Nablus or so many others. **The Palestinian national identity is undermined because the descendants of the different clans usually do not marry each other**.

Another factor that does not help stability is poor democratic culture. Although Mahmoud Abbas won the free presidential elections in 2005 (with no participation of Hamas), his government was supposed to last for 4 years but is still in force with no elections. As occurs with so many other non-democratic governments, the Palestinian Authority stands using three techniques: they pay for popular support with public funds (Soft State); they repress, harass and kill opposers... and blame their disgraces on their known enemy (the scapegoat, the State of Israel).

Another fundamental factor is the endemic corruption noticeably explained by the Palestinian Bassam Tawil in his article "The Secret World of the Palestinian Authority: the corruption silenced by western media". The PA has received billions of dollars in aid from the US, the European Union and other donor countries, however, the funds have not benefitted the Palestinian citizens. The Jerusalem Institute of Justice affirms that Yasser Arafat and Mahmoud Abbas, together, have robbed $31,000,000,000 from the Palestinian coffers.

10. Are there specific examples of alarming corruption cases from the Palestinian Authority?

The Coalition for Accountability and Integrity (AMAN), an alliance created in 2000 by a group of civic associations that work in the field of democracy and human rights, published a report in 2018. It states that, for example, the PA invested 17.5 million dollars in the construction of a "presidential palace" of 4,700 square meters for Mahmoud Abbas. To undermine the criticism, Abbas decided to turn the palace into an enormous library.

Another example of the misuse of funds is seen in the payment of the expenses and salaries of a non-existent airline called Palestine Airlines (it doesn't even have airplanes). "Hundreds of employees from this company continue to receive a salary and grants from the Palestinian Authority, even though the company is not registered according to the Palestinian law", AMAN affirms. They are not the only ones that do not work and collect. According to the quoted report, the members of the Palestinian Legislative Council (PLC) have been collecting monthly salaries even though the Parliament has been paralyzed for over a decade, as a consequence of the dispute between the Mahmoud Abbas's Fatah and Hamas. According to AMAN, the PA (2017) spent around 11 million dollars in a parliament that does not work. Half of the money was spent on salaries for these ghost deputies.

AMAN also detected an unjustified increase of high-rank officials among the Palestinians and the purchase of vehicles for them, their friends and family members. It is worth pointing out that the Palestinian law allows those terrorists that have spent more than twenty years in an Israeli prison to have a free car.

Palestinians urgently need more new schools and hospitals and not these types of expenses. **Palestinian corruption cannot be blamed on Israel and it has been worryingly ignored by the international media.**

11. Is it true that the Palestinian Authority pays those who murder civilian Israeli Jews from its national budget?

In its 2018 budget, the Palestinian Authority assigned about 360 million dollars, 7% of the national Palestinian budget, to two institutions that aid terrorists that are imprisoned in Israel, released prisoners and the families of the Shahids (martyrs) that perish during attacks against civilians or in confrontations against Israel.

The institutions that received the funds are the Commission for Detainees and Ex-detainees Affairs and the Martyrs Fund, both organizations dependent on the PLO that governs the Palestinian Authority. **The funds assigned to terrorists represent 46% of the donations received by the Palestinian Authority from abroad.**

Since 2014, the amount assigned to the Commission for Detainees and Ex-detainees Affairs had been hidden from the official budget to cover that the Palestinian Authority was, in fact, financing payments to imprisoned and liberated terrorists.

According to *Al-Hayat Al-Jadida*, an official news source of the Palestinian Authority, over 5,500 Palestinian prisoners receive money from this fund. Salaries range between 650 to 3,240 dollars, according to the sentence. **The more serious the crime, the longer the sentence, and therefore, the higher the payment assigned. So, if a Palestinian was not able to kill, but only to injure an Israeli citizen, he receives a much lower salary than the Palestinian who was able to kill one or more of them**. And the average salary is much higher than what a Palestinian public officer could dream of, therefore killing Israelis is more profitable than working.

In 2018, the government of Israel decided to deduct the exact amount paid by the Palestinian Authority to terrorists from the amount it must reimburse from the collection of their taxes.

	Salaries for Terrorists (annual) (U$)	Percentage of the Palestinian national budget	Percentage of foreign aid	Total of the PA budget (U$)	Total external aid (U$)
2013	271 million	7%	20%	3872 million	1.290 billion
2014	280 million	7%	24%	4000 million	1.150 billion
2015	290 million	7%	14.8%	4142 million	1.950 billion
2016	304 million	6.9%	29.6%	4406 million	1.020 billion
2017	345 million	7%	49.6%	4928 million	693 million
2018	360 million	7%	46%	5142 million	782 million

Data from official Palestinian documents published in the article "Palestinian Payments to Incarcerated Terrorists and Martyrs' Families Rise in 2017" by Brig. General (R.) Yossi Kuperwasser

12. Is it legal that the Palestinian Authority pays the salaries of terrorists from their budget?

The direct and indirect financing of international donors for the payment of salaries of incarcerated Palestinians for terrorist attacks is illegal. To avoid criticism, the Palestinian Authority gave the money to the PLO and from there to the families of the terrorists. **However, whether the PLO or the PA pays, both are illegal.**

According to the Oslo Accords (1993), PA-PLO must abstain and act to discourage terrorism. The countries, which are fund donors, help the Palestinian Authority to execute the Oslo Accords. **Therefore, the transfer of funds from donors to terrorists is incompatible with this requisite.**

The International Convention for the Suppression of the Financing of Terrorism of 1999 is one of many anti-terrorism international conventions. **It typifies as a crime the act of financing, directly or indirectly, any activity or use connected to terrorism.**

The Inter-American Convention against Terrorism of 2002 contains a specific article (the 4th) that describes how to prevent, fight and eradicate financing of terrorism; article 5 details the seizure and confiscation of funds or other actives; and article 6 relates it to money laundering.

The UN Security Council Resolution 1373 (2001) is a binding resolution adopted under the VII Chapter of the UN that forces the states to cooperate in fighting international terrorism and criminalizes every provision of funds for a terrorist purpose; it determines the freezing and prohibition of money transfers and goods to people who commit terrorist acts.

The Global Counter-TerrorismStrategy 2006 (UN) orders to prevent and fight terrorism, including to abstain from financing terrorism.

By paying salaries to terrorists, the Palestinian Authority is violating the international laws and also the Oslo Accords (1993) and Oslo B (1995).

13. How do Palestinians incite violence among their civilians?

Incitement to violence promoted by Hamas is different from the Palestinian Authority. "Martyrdom" for the cause, promoted by Islamist Hamas (Shahada), is broadcasted by the official media and social networks. The attackers receive all sorts of religious and economic promises.

During the Sixth Conference held in Bethlehem (Aug/8/2009), Fatah

(PLO) understood that the armed terrorism style of Hamas is not beneficial nor does it attain international sympathy. **They opted to substitute their armed fight model for one that could be presented as a popular fight, complemented with unilateral diplomacy, actions via UN and the promotion of boycotts (such as BDS). Palestinians call this "Popular *Habba*".**

Popular Habba Works this way: they use religious incitation by arguing that Jews (usually represented as military or orthodox) are acting to destroy the Al-Aqsa Mosque. When the specific actions are requested, the wording is modified by proclaiming:

"Will you not do anything to defend the Mosque?"

Such instigation provokes individuals to take knives or to throw their vehicles against Israelis. **The vast majority of these terrorists do not come out alive of these incidents. The next step of the Popular Habba is to develop a "martyr" cult that makes other individuals want to imitate them. If we add the payments that the Palestinian Authority offers terrorists, then the attacker will enjoy not only the money, but honor too**.

Possibly, Abbas, Fatah or the Palestinian Authority don't give direct orders for violence as Hamas does. However, there is no doubt that they agree, plan and create the infrastructure that facilitates and promotes violence.

14. Is the Israeli government (2019) interested in reaching a peaceful agreement with the Palestinians?

From 2009 to 2019 a national-religious alliance has governed Israel led by Binyamin Netanyahu, leader of the Likud party. Netanyahu considers that Hamas is a terrorist entity with whom it is impossible to dialogue, while the Palestinian Authority is incapable of making crucial decisions. It has attempted to reach their independence by internationalizing their conflict instead of negotiating directly with Israel.

The official position of Binyamin Netanyahu before the Palestinian-Israeli conflict was defined in the University of Bar-Ilan Speech (June 2009). Netanyahu accepts the principle of "two states for two people" (in other words, the creation of a Palestinian state as a neighbor to Israel) conditioning recognition to 1) Palestine will not have war weapons but only police weaponry; 2) Palestine will not sign pacts with countries that wish to destroy Israel; 3) Palestinian refugees will be integrated only in Palestine; 4) Jerusalem will remain indivisible and; 5) Palestine has to recognize that Israel is the national cradle of the Jewish people.

For the Binyamin Netanyahu defenders, the fifth condition was imposed to force the Palestinians to end the conflict by relinquishing their theological premises that reject the Jews as a people. For the opposition, Netanyahu does not really believe in two states and, therefore, provides a condition that is impossible to fulfill by the Palestinians.

Another pillar of the past governments in Israel was Naftali Bennet (previous leader of the Jewish Home party—Bait Ha-Yehudi). Bennet proposed to annex Territory C (60% of the West Bank) giving citizenship to 5%of the Palestinians. His proposal has not succeeded.

The left-wing and center parties in Israel propose to impulse the peace process, reaching some kind of regional agreement, maybe inspired by the proposals of the Saudi Initiative (see question 296). The parties that demand to annex all of the West Bank are poorly represented in the Knesset.

15. Are there radical Jewish forces that attack Palestinians?

The Hilltop Youth (Noar HaGbaot) are several youth subgroups with nationalist-religious ideology (known as Givonim). Mostly young people (second-generation Jewish settlers) that settle in illegal outposts in Judea and Samaria (West Bank). Many of them work in cattle ranching or agriculture, usually eat organic food and listen to Jewish New Age music

Settling throughout the Land of Israel, especially in the West Bank to establish faits accomplis, is an important component of their ideology. Many see this as the fulfillment of God's will and the acceleration of redemption.

Many members of Hilltop Youth defend radical right-wing positions. Some participate actively against the evacuation of outposts in Judea and Samaria and many others participated in protests against Gaza Disengagement (2005). The Israeli Security Forces believe that some of them participate in activities called Tag Mehir or Price Label

Price Label refers to illegal activities by radical right-wing activists. These actions, where the graffiti "Price Label" appears, began in 2008 and translated into acts of violence against Palestinians and their goods (such as throwing stones, damage to mosques, burning fields and crops and destruction of properties), as well as actions that damage goods belonging to Israeli police or the Israel Defense Forces. In some other cases, they threaten or attack Israeli or Arab Israeli left-wing activists

Image of a Hilltop Youth
(Source: Wikipedia)

These actions usually happen in response to the demolition of non-authorized structures in the outposts by the Police or the IDF or after administrative detention or restraining orders against their activists or after attacks against Jews.

16. Do the Intelligence Services of Israel act to control their radicals?

The security forces of Israel can issue administrative detentions and restraining warrants against suspects of "price tag" acts. They are controlled by the Police, the Jewish section of the Shin-Bet (Shabak) forces and the IDF. In 2011, a new group was established consisting of the Yasam and the Border police units.

According to legal Israeli sources, the perpetrators are between 12 and 23 years old and operate in small and independent groups without a leader.

The Israeli Police informed that since the beginning of 2012, 788 cases were opened, 276 suspects were detained and 154 accusations were presented. In April 2014, the State Department of the U.S.A., using reports from the UN and NGOs, estimated that in 2013 there were around 400 incidents, some of them within the Green Line.

In June 2013, the Political Security Cabinet authorized the Minister of Defense to declare the activists of "Price Tag" as an "illegal association". In March 2018, for example, two accused were sentenced to two and a half years and to five years in prison because of three counts of "pricing".

At the same time, the Palestinians exploit the subject as a defamatory weapon. On Nov/12/2014 a mosque was burned down in Al-Mu'ayyir, resulting in worldwide accusations against Israel. However, forensics proved that evidence was planted. On Oct/3/2015, the Palestinians informed that an Israeli colonist shot a 6-year-old Palestinian in Kalkilya. The investigation revealed that the child was injured while playing with his friends.

The "Price Tag" phenomenon, although smaller in comparison to the Palestinian terrorism, has been condemned by all Israeli authorities. In December 2011, an organization named Tag Meir (Light Tag) was established to fight the hate crimes committed by the Jewish Israelis against the "non-Jews".

17. What is the Gaza Strip?

The Gaza Strip is a small 360 km2 territory. It is 50 km long, and 6 to 12 km wide, bordering the Mediterranean Sea. It has the sea on one side and the State of Israel on the other side as well as to the north, and on the southern part is the border with Egypt. 1,800,000 Palestinians live there, the world's most densely inhabited place.

Products from Israel enter the Gaza Strip via the Keren Shalom crossing, and by foot through the Erez crossing.

The border between the British influence zone (Egypt) and the Ottoman Empire was established in 1906 and it is a line between Rafah and Eilat.

Until 1917, the Gaza Strip and all the surrounding land belonged to the Ottoman Empire. From 1917 to 1948, the area was dominated by the British. Egypt occupied it as a base to attack

The Gaza Strip
(Source: Wikipedia)

Jaffa-Tel Aviv and Jerusalem during the 1948 war, and later as an operations base for the attacks of the "Fedayeen". The cease-fire of 1950 determined that the small strip, with its current dimensions, would remain under Egyptian control (an illegal occupation). The Palestinians that were living there were not granted Egyptian citizenship.

After the signature of the Oslo Accords (1993), the Gaza Strip was turned

over to the Palestinian Authority and in 2005 Israel withdrew completely from this region, both civilians and military. The Gaza Strip was taken by force by Hamas (2007) and converted into a base for launching missiles and to construct tunnels to attack civilians in the State of Israel.

At present, the Gaza Strip is practically an independent state governed by Hamas.

18. What is the Gaza Strip Blockade?

Since 2001, the Hamas terrorists have fired 14,000 missiles and mortars intentionally against civil Israelis. Additionally, they excavated a hundred tunnels, one of which was used to kidnap the soldier Gilad Shalit (2006) within the Israeli territory. Then, Hamas used their budget for hate education and weaponry, monopolizing their ruling of the Gaza Strip since 2007.

While the Hamas leaders expose their population to missile and rocket launchers installed intentionally in mosques or in UNRWA schools, they hide in the basement of the Shifa Hospital in Gaza City.

During Operation Cast Lead (2008-2009), Israel declared a blockade against the Strip to avoid the entry of weapons. **The Blockade of the Gaza Strip is legal (according to the San Remo Convention of 1995 and according to the Palmer investigative Commission (UN) about the Fleet to Gaza- 2010).**

Palmer concluded that: 1) The naval blockade of Israel in Gaza was legal and Israel had the right to impose it; 2) The decision to break the naval blockade (by the fleet) was a dangerous and fearful act; 3) the conduct and the real objectives of the organizers of the fleet, particularly IHH, were violent. The report criticized Israel for boarding the ships in an "excessive and unreasonable" manner.

In order to be legal, the blockade must be general, known and public, and it must avoid a humanitarian crisis in the blocked zone. When a ship with humanitarian aid tries to reach Gaza, the Israeli navy detains it and takes it to Ashdod port. There, they search for hidden weapons and other products (they carry symbolic quantities), it is given to the Palestinians through the Keren Shalom.

19. Is it true that Israel does not allow Palestinian civilians from the Gaza Strip to enter its territory?

Until September 2000 (Second Intifada), the civilians of Gaza entered Israel to work or for health care. There were over one million entrances every year. Although Israel continues at war with Hamas-Gaza, only in May 2017 there were 2,282 entrance requests, of which 47.2% were approved, 2.1% rejected and the rest were published in Haaretz but were not answered. One of the people that was assisted in health in Israel is a direct family member of Ismail Hanye, leader of Hamas.

The entrance permits for the sick that come from the Gaza Strip must receive authorization from the Palestinian Authority, but due to the internal war between the PA and Hamas, for long periods the PA has rejected granting permits to Gazans.

In 1979, Israel dismantled the industrial area in the Erez crossing. Thousands of Palestinians worked in the region. Dozens of attacks and Palestinian rocket-launching happened there. On June/8/2003, three Palestinians shot grenades and bullets, killing 4 Israeli soldiers. On Aug/31/2004, the Israelis captured a suicide terrorist. On June/29/2005 a suicide terrorist was captured with a medical permit while she attempted an attack against the Soroka Hospital of Beer Sheeva. On May/22/2998 a bomb-car exploded in Erez with hundreds of kilograms of explosives.

The honest question should be: **why should Israel treat ill Palestinians from Gaza? In Gaza, the Hamas government acts to assassinate all Jews. If Israel assists Gazans, as it in fact does, it is only for humanitarian reasons.**

We could also ask why the Palestinians from Gaza do not cross to and from Egypt, a country they do not wish to destroy. The most illogical blockade is the one imposed by Egypt.

20. Is Israel guilty of the lack of development in the Gaza Strip?

In the book 100 Questions and Answers about the Palestinian-Israeli Conflict, Pedro Brieger (an Argentinian journalist) affirms that "The economy of the Strip is minimal and Israel has always obstructed its development, preventing the entry of raw material or capital goods and setting countless obstacles to the exportation of products – many of them perishable (like flowers)- that are not directly exported".

Facts contradict such affirmation. In the important Paris Accords (May/29/1994)- that is not mentioned in that text), the signatories agreed that Israel would receive the mutual import, collect the taxes and give the correct part to the Palestinian Authority... avoiding the entry of war material among the products. **Israel gives the corresponding money to the PA and, in 2018, it was Mahmoud Abbas who threatened Hamas with not giving them the**

right percentage for the purchases they make from Gaza.

In the 2007-2012 period, Israel gave Hamas 2,567 million dollars. Another 1,351 million was given to them up to 2011 through Israel's banking system. Journalist Orna Shimoni **(Ynet) affirmed that 80% of that money reached the hands of the leaders of the terrorist movement Hamas, who used it to build tunnels or produce rockets that were later fired at Israel.**

A second falsehood is that there is no entry of products to Gaza because of Israel. According to the military records of Israel 45,000 tons of products a week, around 400,000 tons of grains, around 60,000 tons of fruits and vegetables, 40,000 livestock heads, clothing, canned food and medicine went from Israel to Gaza in 2013 (and in the subsequent years). Before the coup d'état by Hamas (2007), the same trade reached 570 million while in 2018 it reached 325 million dollars.

21. Is it true that the Gaza Strip is currently (2019) undergoing a deep economic crisis?

Up to 2018, at least 50% of the products entering the Gaza Strip were coming from Israeli factories. Israeli trucks would arrive at the Kerem Shalom border crossing, unload the products; these were scanned and checked and then loaded to Palestinian trucks. In order to negotiate with Israel, a Palestinian must be registered in the Gaza Association of Palestinian Traders (controlled by Hamas).

Since Hamas has used and continues using construction materials to build bunkers and tunnels, the Hebrew state tries to deliver controllable amounts to Gaza. The same happens with double use materials, which can be used to make weapons or rockets (for example, fertilizers or iron). Most of the construction materials enter Gaza from the Egyptian side.

In January 2015, Hamas owed Israel 50 million dollars for energy purchased in the previous two years. This debt has increased. The Israeli newspaper Kalkalist informed: "Every day, two Israeli companies sell 200 thousand liters of fuel and benzene and a few thousand liters of cooking gas. Also, during the war (in 2014), companies continued to sell these products to the inhabitants of the Gaza Strip".

In 2018 a serious economic crisis came about because of the Palestinian Authority and the governing Hamas. The Palestinian Authority decided to punish Hamas economically by withholding payments. **As they don't have enough resources to buy products, the amount of trucks that pass the border of Israel towards Gaza has been drastically reduced.**

The economic crisis is such that Israel was forced to accept that Qatar delivers 15 million dollars in cash per month. This way, Hamas can pay for the salaries of the public employees.

22. When did Israel withdraw from the Gaza Strip?

In December 2003, Prime Minister Ariel Sharon presented the Disengagement Plan. Its goal was to unilaterally evacuate the 21 Israeli settlements in the Gaza Strip and 4 others isolated in the north of Samaria. There were 8,600 Israeli Jews living in these settlements.

Ariel Sharon stated that the Gaza Disengagement Plan would decrease international pressure on Israel; it was a show of Israel's will to achieve peace, and drastically decreased the military required to look after those civilians. Others affirmed that Sharon was distracting the media's attention because of the corruption cases against him that were being investigated at the time. His opponents argued that without the Israeli army, Palestinians would multiply their attacks with rockets from Gaza.

On May/16/2005, the Israeli Parliament (Knesset) approved the Disengagement Plan, with 50 votes in favor, 40 against and 5 abstentions. On Sep/9/2005 the evacuation was completed, with harsh criticism from those who were in favor (marked in blue) and those who were against (marked in orange).

Although Ariel Sharon voted against the Oslo Accords when he was part of the opposition when he was Prime Minister, he accepted the "Roadmap" (2003) that would lead to a Palestinian State; in this framework, with enormous resistance within his own party and among the settlers, the disengagement was produced.

Israel did not negotiate its withdrawal with the Palestinian Authority, because Sharon considered that they were not a partner for peace. It is important to remember that in 2005 they were living the epilogue of the wave of suicide attacks against Israelis (Second Intifada) that resulted in the assassination of 1,150 Israelis.

Thomas Friedman, a columnist from The New York Times, suggested to the Palestinians to make out of Gaza a new Dubai. Sound advice... not very simple.

23. Is Israel still occupying the Gaza Strip? When does the foreign occupation end?

Although the Law of Belligerent Occupation does not provide an explicit answer, the accepted approach is a "mirror image" of the conditions for its creation, that is, when the occupation army doesn't maintain effective control in the territory, but instead, there is a new regime that has control. Occupation may end with an agreement, or when the occupant is forced out, but also because of a unilateral act. Israel withdrew totally from Gaza in 2005.

Does Israel have an "effective control" over the Gaza Strip? If we review the ruling of the International Court of Justice in the case of Congo vs. Uganda, that is, when an occupation means to effectively exert authority over the territory, then Israel is not (not even remotely) an occupant of the Gaza Strip.

The basic formula to define an "occupation" is stated in Article 42 of the Convention of The Hague on the Laws and Customs of War on Land (1907) that states: "Territory is considered occupied when it is actually placed under the authority of the hostile army. The occupation extends only to the territory where such authority has been established and can be exercised".

The International Court of Justice (ICJ) states that there is a belligerent occupation when the occupying army actually exerts its authority over the territory, and in that way, supersedes the authority of the sovereign government in that area.

Some authors that are not very literate on legal topics argue that "if Israel withdrew unilaterally" it is guilty of not negotiating with the Palestinians of the Second Intifada, but if it "withdraws and there are no Israelis left in Gaza" then they'll say that they still "occupy" it. This way, they live with their materialistic prejudgments that it is all about "occupation".

PART TWO
- PAST EXPLANATORY -

24. What is the Zionist movement?

The Zionist movement claims the character of the nationhood of the Jewish people and its right to exist freely. Historically, the Jews have always seen themselves as a compound identity. The thinker Eliahu Kaplan claimed that Judaism was "a civilization".

This civilization had various pillars: 1) **The Jews are and have always been a people:** the descendants of the Judea Kingdom were the "Jews" while those from Israel are the "Israelites"; 2) **The Jews are also manifested as a religion**; 3) The Jews have a **culture similar or alike** to other communities in the world; 4) **The Jews possess a "collective memory"**. They consider themselves descendants of the slaves from Egypt, which suffered the Shoah or Inquisition; 5) they speak a particular language, Hebrew. In the Middle Ages, for example, a Jewish person that lived in Barcelona would not introduce himself as Catalonian, Spanish or as a "human being". He would simply be a Jew in Barcelona. What is Judaism then? It is a mixture of five variables.

Throughout the XIX Century, national identities began to join in Europe because of the French Revolution (every human being has rights), the Industrial Revolution (the appearance of a middle class) and the Spring of Nations.

The Jews suffered disappointing experiences in Europe. Many of them were promised emancipation, but anti-Semitism in the old continent was too deep-rooted.

Zionism is the Movement of National Liberation of the Jewish People. In other words, the philosophy that affirms that the Jews are "also" a people and that, just like many other people on the planet, they possess the right to self-determination. The Jews´ wish is to return to Zion, which is one of the names of Jerusalem, their national and religious center.

25. Are all Jews identified with Zionism?

The remarkable thinker Abraham Infeld affirms that the five pillars of the Jewish identity are: 1) Jewish history and memory; 2) The Halaha (the Jewish Law); 3) The family ties; 4) The Hebrew language; and 5) the bond with the land of Israel. Most of the Jews of the world feel they are part of the Jewish history and memories, they have family ties and they have a bond with the land of Israel.

It is important to consider that at the beginning of the XIX Century, Jews were invited to emancipate in several European countries. The answer of the

Jews was not consistent. A group of them did not feel identified with modernity and with this "lay" proposal, so they opted to reject the proposal (in fact, the orthodox Jews dress the same way they did when the offer came through as a way to emphasize their conservationism).

A second answer was one by many Jews, anxious to "be a part", detached from their Jewish identity. A third answer was one by Jews that separated their national identity (the Jewish people) from their religious identity. Many of them started to identify themselves as "French of Jewish religion".

A fourth group, disappointed by the failure of the emancipation, opted for the national emancipation that became Zionism.

At present, half of the Jews of the world live in Israel, and most of the Jews of the Diaspora feel identified and support the existence of a state for the Jewish people in the land of Israel.

So, do Jews have a double national identity? Yes, they do. There is a sentimental bond and also a national identification. Most Jews feel part of the Argentinean people and also of the Jewish people. The same happens with an Argentinean-Chinese, and Argentinean-Italian or an Argentinian-Spaniard.

26. When it emerged… were all the Jews supportive of Zionism?

Opposition to Zionism came mainly from three outbreaks: above all, among those who believed that Jews should accept the "Emancipation": to be Jews at "home" and "citizens" in the street. Within this group, we can include the reform movement.

The second opposition came from the orthodox Jews who considered the "European" secular nationalism as foreign to Judaism. Moreover, they felt threatened by those principles. Additionally, the Jewish rebirth would arrive with the Messiah and not before. With the formalization of the Zionist movement, part of the orthodox Jews formed political parties to prompt their interests within Zionism (Agudat Yisrael, for example) and, after the Holocaust, the opposition by orthodox to the State of Israel was practically irrelevant and minor.

The third opposition, by number and influence, came from the Russian-Polish Jews of the "BUND" movement. The BUND story is tragic. It was terminated by the Holocaust and rejected by the non-Jewish socialists. The gratitude of the socialist world towards the revolutionary labor of the Jews could be synthesized in that the BUND ran in the Polish elections after the Holocaust, they obtained a deputy and then were "invited" by the Communist party to dissolve. The first forbidden movement by the Communists was the BUND and even Stalin made them put a "J" in the Jews' documents because he considered them "suspicious Soviet citizens".

All the same, when Zionism rose, a small quantity of Jews immigrated to Israel. The most promising places were other fast-developing countries like the U.S.A., Canada or Argentina. Palestine, a remote province of the Ottoman Empire, was an inhospitable place.

The challenge was fit for few, it was faced mainly by young idealists who organized precarious socialist colonies (kibbutzim), drained the swamps and worked in lands desolate for centuries, with no experience in the task.

27. What is the relation between the rebirth of the Hebrew language and Zionism?

The concept of nation-state developed in Europe and influenced Jews as well. Zionism proposed the rebirth of the Hebrew language as an identity and a national manifestation. Until then, the Hebrew language was only used in prayers, with the Jews that lived in Eastern Europe (Baltic countries, Poland, Ukraine or Russia) using another common language called "Yiddish" (a Jewish language, mixing Hebrew and German), rich in literature, music and cultural traditions, and that many were not willing to give up.

According to Zionists, Yiddish was the language of the Diaspora Ghetto, while Hebrew meant "the rebirth of the homeland". On the other hand, Yiddish was the language of the Jews from Eastern and Central Europe (since the XI Century), but it was not a language that could be shared by all Jews. Sephardic and Middle Eastern Jews do not know Yiddish nor could they feel bonded to this language.

Eliezer Ben-Yehuda, born Eliezer Yitzhak Perelman (1858–1922), was a linguist and editor of Lithuanian-Jewish newspapers and was responsible for the rebirth and reinstatement of Hebrew as a spoken and written language in modern times. Throughout his life, his motto was "Hebrew, speak Hebrew!!" and he educated his children only with the national language.

During the first years, there was a tendency among Zionists to try to erase their past, names, language and culture from the countries where they had been born. It was said that in Israel a

Eliezer Ben-Yehuda
(Source: Wikipedia)

new people should arise, the product of this melting pot of cultures (Kur Hituch). In modern Israel, diversity, languages and international culture are valued and fostered. Probably this is the reaction for more social and personal security.

28. Is Zionism a consequence of European anti-Semitism?

Zionism is not a consequence of the anti-Semitism. However, it was strengthened by this hate. The factors that explained the emergence of the movement are varied: 1) the failure of emancipation. European Jews were guaranteed equality that was not fulfilled; 2) national and territorial sentiments that impregnated all of Europe; 3) a profound religious wish of "returning to Jerusalem", a desire that had not been translated in one effective and massive action; 4) European anti-Semitism. Therefore, Zionism did not emerge because of only one factor (anti-Semitism).

Not all the Jewish leaders considered anti-Semitism in the same way. Leon Pinsker considered that anti-Semitism was an incurable disease ("the Judeophobia is a psychosis, hereditary and incurable"). However, other Jewish thinkers considered that anti-Semitism could be abolished within the framework of the European liberalism, others thought that it would be in the framework of socialism and others (like Simon Dubnov) that the solution was "Autonomism". There were no unified criteria in this subject either.

For the founder of political Zionism, journalist Theodor Hertzl, anti-Semitism forced the Jews to seek "refuge". Ahad-Haam spoke less about a "refuge" and more about conforming a relevant "cultural center" for the Jews of the world. This situation did not require the translation of Jewish masses into "Palestine". Dov Ber-Borojov saw the Zionist movement as a Marxist Revolution while Aharon David Gordon saw it in Tolstoy language, as a reconnecting process with the land and the physical labor on the field. The national-religious movement reasoned it, in redemption terms...

Zionism was never an ideologically convergent movement. Whoever presents it as "uniform" is wrong. **However, in relation to anti-Semitism, Zionist leaders considered that the best way to fight against Judeophobia was by self-determination, by creating their own Jewish state.**

29. Who was Theodore Hertzl and what was the Dreyfuss case?

Continuing with the logic of the answers about emancipation (Question 25), we stated that journalist Theodore Herzl (1869-1904) was part of the group that wanted to assimilate to the national European identity.

Hertzl was raised in a Yiddish-speaking, bourgeois Jewish family from the Austrian-Hungarian Empire. He grew up in a comfortable environment, liberal and secular. During his youth he participated in the Burschenschaft association, which aimed for the German unification, so his first works were not focused on Jewish issues. His first important job was as a correspondent in Paris for the influential liberal newspaper from Vienna, Neue Freie Presse.

In 1894, as part of his job, he covered the "Dreyfuss Case". A Jewish captain serving the French Army, Alfred Dreyfuss, was unfairly accused of treason and charged of spying for Germany. Throughout the trial, and in an act of humiliation, the masses yelled "Death for Dreyfuss!" Death to the Jews!" The anti-Semitic agitation so impressed Hertzl that he was disappointed in assimilationism.

In February 1896 he published his new Zionist vision in the book "The Jewish State: proposal of a modern solution to the Jewish question", where he proposes to organize a political movement to seek a Jewish state, with worldwide support, as a means to solve the anti-Semitism suffered by the Jews.

His international diplomatic efforts had limited success. Moreover, he squandered a large amount of the fortune provided by his wife to bribe mediators that rendered him diplomatic interviews.

In 1897, he organized and presided over the First Zionist Congress in Basel, Switzerland. In 1920 he published his work Altneuland (The Old New Land), where he presented the future Jewish state as a utopia of a modern nation, democratic and prosperous.

Theodor Hertzl represents the idea of political Zionism. His great accomplishment was to convince the Jews of the world that the Zionist ideal was achievable.

30. Was Zionism an invention from the colonialism to occupy "Palestine"?

An important declaration: the European Jews used the term "Palestine" for years to imitate its European equals. While the Mameluk Empire ruled in Israel (1260-1517) or the Ottoman (1517-1917), the term "Palestine" was not used since it was a European term.

During the British Mandate in Palestine (1920-1948), the National Symphony of Palestine or the journal "Palestine Post", for example, were Jewish institutions. If anyone searched in the Larousse Encyclopedia (1938) for the Palestinian flag... Guess what you would find?

Zionism was not an invention of the English or of the powers to divide the Arab world like many still believe. However, it received the support of the English power, especially during World War I, for many reasons and not only because of "colonialist" motivations. The factors were: 1) **faithful Christians who considered that the coming of the Messiah was approaching and that it should be received in the reborn land of Israel**, with the Jewish people inhabiting it. These deep religious sentiments can be found among the German Templars or rulers like Prime Minister Lloyd George; 2) **Real Politik and anti-Semitic prejudices**: the British wished to maintain the Russians in war and entice the North-Americans. They assumed that the Jews had a disproportionate strength to lobby both countries in favor of the interests of the British. The British also promised things to the Arabs (for example, the MacMahon-Hussein correspondence of 1915). The Jews decided to translate these promises into actions to make their national wishes effective.

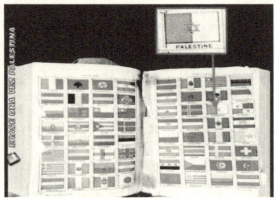

Flags of the world.
(Source: Larousse Encyclopedia, 1938)

The affirmation that Zionism is a synonym of colonialism intends to immediately erase the history of a people formed many centuries before those who accuse them of being an imperialist manifestation. **The demonizing intention is to transform the Jewish people into an artificial group".**

31. What is anti-Zionism?

It is the non-acceptance that Jews are (also) a people and that their national aspirations in the land of Israel (not necessarily all of it) are legitimate.
Until the creation of Israel (1948), anti-Zionism was almost exclusively Jewish. There were three anti-Zionist positions (orthodox, socialist and liberal) that had their Zionist counterparts: the national religious (national recovery as the beginning of redemption), socialist Zionism (the contribution to world socialism would be done via a self-experience of cooperative construction) and the liberal and free-thinking Zionists, who understood that for Jews to

genuinely assimilate to others, they should do it as a people and not by diluting their identity.

The first and bluntest opposition to Zionism came from the Arab and Islamic world since the 1920s and not from the world's left-wing. During the 1950s and 60s, Israel was a symbol for the world's socialists. The Arab Palestine leadership, under the disastrous Mufti Hajj Amin Al-Husseini and others, rejected the right of the Jews to self-determination.

The left had increased its criticism towards Israel because of the structures of the global alliances (with the U.S. supporting Israel and the left-wing movements of the world aligning with the Soviet Union and with Cuba in our continent). With the Berkeley Revolt (1964) and the French May (1968), the New Left began to attack Israel, accusing it of being a "colonialist manifestation", despising its national identity, beyond whatever the Israeli government did or did not (at the time and until 1977 in hands of the Socialists).

At present, those who used to hate the Jews, find that demonizing the State of Israel and Zionism is more "politically correct".

32. Why have the extreme left, and part of the moderated left, raised quite firmly an anti-Zionist flag?

It is possible to explain a part, or most of, the criticism from the left around the world towards Israel by the principle of "intersectionality". Intersectionality is a term coined in 1989 by Kimberly Williams Crenshaw, activist and academic. Crenshaw believes that we should think about every element or trait of a person as inextricably united with every other element. That way we can understand how systematic injustice and social inequality happens from a multidimensional base. **Therefore, there are groups, which feel affected or under unjust situations, that have united and created alliances (even though some are incomprehensible, for example, the extreme left and the Islamic radicalism).**

Most organizations from the European left and some from Latin America are indifferent, they unite and many times promote Judeophobia. Examples? During the annual convention of the Labor Party of Great Britain (2017), its leader Jeremy Corbyn was urged to act because they distributed pamphlets from the Marxist Labor Party that argued the "communion between Zionists and Nazis" and cited Reinhard Heydrich, the architect of the Final Solution, stating that the "nationalists did not have any intention of attacking the Jewish people". Another one: Pablo Iglesias from the Podemos party in

Spain, who receives Iranian donations, via contracts, to make a TV program in "Hispan TV". In Latin America, there are manifestations such as in Venezuela, Cuba, Bolivia or the clear anti-Semitism from the Quebracho left in Argentina.

Anti-Zionism from the left uses many Satanist mechanisms from the classic European anti-Semitism. It is hard for them to hate the Jews but they demonize the "Jew among nations" (Israel). **Jean-Paul Sartre would feel ashamed of the current behavior of the left towards the Hebrew state… "Israel is imperialist with its kibbutzim, and the Arabs are socialists with their feudal states",** he mocked those who presented Zionism as "colonialism".

33.   Are there other anti-Zionists in modern times?

In the Middle East, the most extreme anti-Zionism lies within the Islamic radicalism. Muslim anti-Zionism considers that Israel occupies Dar al-Islam (the Islamic holy land). Islamic groups or the government of Iran insist that Israel is legitimate and call it the "Zionist entity".

The opposition also arose from the Catholic Church, which considered that the "old pact" (Judaism) exists to witness the superiority of "the (Christian) truth". Certain Christians believe that the State of Israel has no right to exist because it contradicts the destiny of the Jewish subjugation. **Currently, the Vatican acknowledges Israel but not as an expression of Jewish redemption.**

After the Basel Congress (1897), the journal Civilita Cattolica published on Zionism: "1,827 years have passed since the fulfillment of the predictions of Jesus of Nazareth… [after the destruction of Jerusalem] Jews would be taken far away to become slaves among the nations and remain dispersed [Diaspora] until the end of the world." The World Council of Churches is an example of this obsession to delegitimize Israel. **In contrast, at present, Catholic groups such as Opus Dei feel quite related to Israel.**

Anti-Zionist feelings also come up in different forums such as the Organization of African Unity and the Non-aligned Movement, which approved resolutions that condemned Zionism and equaled it to racism and Apartheid during the 70s' decade.

Opposition to Zionism also influences Afro-American identities. Afro-American support to Palestinians is usually moved by "color" considerations. Political scientist Andrew Hacker writes: "The presence of Israel in the Middle East is perceived as an attempt to frustrate the legitimate status of colored people. Some blacks see Israel essentially as a white and European power, with external support".

34. Can you be anti-Zionist without being anti-Semitic?

In theory, it is possible. From a practical point of view, it never occurs. If someone considers that no people on the face of the earth deserves to be called a people or thinks that very few peoples have the right to have such title and acts and promotes the destruction of every state in the world, then we can suppose that within such maelstrom there is a wish to destroy the Jewish people's state. **Anti-Zionists fight in the field only for the destruction of one state: the Jewish one.**

To affirm that the Jews are not a people when the mass majority of the Jewish people in the world do believe it is to "discriminate the Jews". Most of the Jewish people consider that Judaism is as much as a religion as a national identity. The philosopher Eliahu Kaplan defined Judaism as a "civilization".

To deny that the essence of the Jewish people awakens a warning about the "denier", especially when there is so much archeological evidence that demonstrates the existence of the Jewish people before the emergence of states and European or Latin American people. **To consider that all peoples should have the right to declare themselves as a "people" except for the Jews is to discriminate against the Jews. To believe that all peoples have the right to self-determination "except for the Jews" is to discriminate against the Jews. To hate the Jews that declare themselves Zionists when almost all the Jews in the world identify themselves with the principles of Zionism and love or sympathize with the State of Israel is to hate almost every Jew. To accept the existence of 193 countries but demand the extinction of one is anti-Semitism, or more precisely: Judeophobia.**

After World War II, it was politically incorrect to be "anti-Semite". Currently, it is seen as "legitimate" (among people with a low moral level) to be "anti-Zionist".

35. How can we recognize a modern Judeophobe?

We can highlight two ways to recognize a modern Judeophobe trying to camouflage as anti-Zionist. Thinker Gustavo Perednik considers that an anti-Semite can be recognized with three criteria: his obsession with Israel or Jews, coprolalia (insults – "Israel is a Nazi state", for example) and Manichaeism (everything Jewish and Israel is negative). It is important to repeat that direct and crude hate against Jews is usually condemned by national laws because the world still remembers what such Judeophobia did to it. However, for anyone with an uncalibrated moral compass, hating Jews as a state is a conduct with which they can coexist at peace.

Another method is the "3D Anti-Semitism Test": Delegitimize Israel, Demonize Israel, and submit Israel to Double standards. This well-acknowledged parameter was developed by Nathan Sharansky, former Minister of Israel and ex-president of the Jewish Agency for Israel.

Criticizing Israel doesn't mean being anti-Semitic; criticizing Israel obsessively, especially in a Manichaean way, qualifying the country with insults, using double standards, demonization and promoting delegitimation IS being a Judeophobe.

Almost all countries present themselves as "nation-states of a determined people": Spain is the national cradle of the Spaniards, Argentina of the Argentineans and Russia of the Russians. All these countries host national minorities. No one says or dares to express that they are "in favor" of destroying Argentina because, for example, the country doesn't dissolve to conform a new state to include Bolivians, Peruvians and Venezuelans. However, when it is about Israel, it is demanded that it renounces to be the national state of the Jewish people (80% of its population). This is discrimination.

36. Is every person who criticizes Israel an anti-Semite?

Evidently, every person who criticizes Israel is not a Judeophobe. **To criticize Israel is legitimate and those who do it the most are the Israelis themselves.** Fortunately, the attacks against Israel from the Jews do not have the same destination as the critics from Muslims against Islamism. **Those who obsessively criticize in a Manichaean manner and insult Israel are Judeophobes (anti-Semites).**

Jews tend to be especially sensitive when they hear obsessive criticism against them or Israel. In fact, they've had twenty-one centuries of "experience" with hate manifestations against them promoted by Christian authorities and, currently, by Islamic representatives, or from the extreme left or right. They have proof of blood libels from ancient and modern times, assassinations and pogroms or forced conversions. Since the Inquisition, through Jewish massacres in Bogdan Jmelnicki's Ukraine, to the last big massacre of Jewish people in World War II and ending with the modern Islamists or their allies who want to destroy Israel "because it is not a binational state". **It is worth revising the comments by readers when they discuss news related to Israel to verify that twenty-three centuries of hate have not disappeared after the Holocaust (Shoa).** To affirm that the suspicions of the Jews are a close reaction to "intellectual extortion" would detract from those who affirm it.

Now, the exaggerated and deficient over-use by some Israeli leaders before and now about Nazism and the Holocaust is not beneficial. **First and foremost, because of the anti-Semitic hides in the argument that "everything is an exaggeration". On the other hand, those guilty of genocides like the Holocaust (Europeans and their allies) try to erase their murderous past by blaming Israel of doing the same thing they did (or allowed) pretending to be cleared or cleansing their past sins.**

37. Can a person be Jewish and at the same time an anti-Semite (Judeophobe)?

This is a well-studied phenomenon. The most important work addressing this issue is the book by Theodor Lessing (1930), Jüdischer Selbsthaß, (The Self-Contempt of the Jews).

The self-hate phenomenon appears not only among Jews. We also see it among colored people that do impossible tasks to detach from their physical qualities (for example, those who straighten their hair obsessively to eliminate their "afro" or undergo operations to change the color of their skin)

Not too many Jews suffer from self-hate, although there are some extreme cases. In 1935, a German Jew, Max Neumann, founded the Verband Nationaldeutscher Juden (the German Nationalist Jewish League), identified with the Nazi ideology.

Reasons that lead to self-hate differ among Jews. Some think that by exaggerating their declarations they free themselves from the "weight" of being a Jew, others because they feel embarrassed of being Jewish, others because they long to be accepted by the majority (they are usually used as "good Jews" by those that hate Jews).

Self-hate Jews consider that Judaism is not a people but a religion or a culture, and their formation in Jewish historic and religious topics is quite weak.

A great man of Israeli socialism, Berl Katzenelson, said (1936): "is there by any chance another people on the face of the Earth whose children are so twisted, emotionally and mentally, that they consider as despicable and hateful everything their country does, while every murder, violation and assault committed by their enemies fill their hearts with admiration and reverence?".

The fact that those who criticize Israel obsessively are Jews or of Jewish descent is totally irrelevant. The fact that such a person criticizes Israel in an obsessive, Manichaean and insulting way, transforms such a person into an anti-Semite, no matter if he is a Jew or not.

38.   But... is the term "anti-Semitic" properly used?

The correct term is Judeophobia. Leon Pinsker used it correctly in 1883, clarifying that the phenomenon described the "irrational hatred" towards Jews, specifically.
The Semitic adjective was coined by the German orientalist August Ludwig von Schlözer in 1781. Schlözer did not refer to one race – a concept that appeared fifty years before in the work of the French Henri de Boulainvilliers – but a group of languages called Semites, which would be those spoken by the descendants of the son of Noah, Sem.

The term "anti-Semitism" appeared later, in 1873, in the German journalist's work Wilhelm Marr (a Judeophobe). **Marr confused many people because he led them to believe that the hatred was and is towards the "Semites" when there was never a Semite race or people (Semites are languages, four of them).** One cannot hate an Ethiopian who speaks Amharic nor hate the Arabs and Aramaic because they speak Semitic languages. They only hate the Jews.

Wilhelm Marr, creator of the term "anti-Semitism"
(Source: Wikipedia)

This dialectical trick by Marr allows Arab Judeophobes (or their descendants) to falsely argue "How can I be anti-Semitic if I am a Semite?" An argument that can be rebutted by pointing out their specific and irrational hate towards Jews and not towards those who speak Amharic, Arab or Aramaic. Furthermore, one can have Jewish origins and hate the Jews (there are few cases but they exist).

As a Universalist thinker with an acute moral compass once said: "I refuse to call an opinion to a doctrine that points towards specific people and that tends to suppress or extinguish their rights. Anti-Semitism does not fall into the protected thoughts category because of the right of freedom of opinion". "The anti-Semite is, in the deepest part of his heart, a criminal. What he desires, what he prepares for, is the death of the Jews" (Jean-Paul Sartre).

39. Why did Jews choose Palestine to develop their State?

The answer can be found in the Declaration of Independence of Israel: Eretz Israel has been the cradle of the Jewish people. This is the place of the development of its spiritual, religious and national personality. This is the place where it has lived as a free and sovereign people; this is the place where it has created a culture with national and universal values". The land of Israel is full of historical and archaeological proof of the presence of the Jewish people. Among others, this is where the ministry of Joshua (Jesus) was developed. He was from Nazareth, though he was born in Beit-Lechem (Bethlehem).

Zionist ideologists were mostly secular Jews, though the territorial reference for their identity as a people and a nation was, no doubt, the land of Jerusalem, or its alternate name, Zion (the origin of the name of the movement).

Zionism sought the national reconstruction in Israel, because it always was the center of their prayers, their collective memories and because it was the place associated with the past Jewish political sovereignty. Biblical references reinforce this link. The territory had been subject to the Ottoman Empire, and their "property deed" was having conquered it by force (the same as Arabs did previously). The Jews wanted to recover the sovereignty by purchasing the land, with their work and with massive immigration. In his book, Hertzl asked himself if Palestine was a better place than Argentina. Certainly, Argentina was mentioned, but it was never a solid proposal.

The Argentina Project was led by philanthropist Baron von Hirsch, and it was meant to "save" the European Jews in agricultural colonies, with no national pretense or linkage to Zionism (with the consent of the Argentinean authorities). The territorial alternative to Palestine that was presented to Zionism was Uganda, a British colony, more affordable than Ottoman Palestine. However, the proposal was rejected by Zionists: they wanted only Zion.

40. When Zionism began, did the Palestinian people exist?

The nationalist ideas came to the Middle East during the mid-XIX Century together with European expansionism and the influence of national ideologies. However, the ideas from the French Revolution, which assigned the individual inalienable rights, did not penetrate the region and are not considered indigenous. The Middle East did not experiment with the Industrial Revolution either, which generated a middle class that demanded political rights. Evidently, the format of European state-nation was foreign to the tribal societies. The primary and natural identity of the individuals of the Middle East belongs to "Jamula" (a clan or an extended family). The European powers knew how to make alliances, by interests, with certain clans. For example, they made a pact with the Saud clan in Saudi Arabia (at the expense of the Hashemi-Hussein clan from Mecca).

The early emergence of Palestinian nationalist signs is a minor subject in academic discussions. **Few renowned academics "detect" a European-style national sentiment among the Arabs who then, under the British, would be known as "Palestinians".**

The precedent of this Palestinian identity was noted by Israeli historians Baruch Kimmerling and Joel Migdal in 1834. **While the Arab historian Rashid Khalidi underlines that the Palestinian identity was never exclusive and that Arabism, the religion and the local loyalties have always played a highlighting role. The historian Khalidi's line is much more accepted and realistic.**

Most historians consider that Palestinian nationalism is part of a more extended Pan-Arabic movement during the XX Century that was spurred by the Young Turk Revolution (1908). For the times of the Zionist migration (from 1881-1882), it seems artificial to speak seriously about a national Arabic-Palestinian conscience, which does not mean that this identity does not exist at present.

41. What happened in 1834 and when did the Palestine national identity develop?

In 1834 the Falachim, rural farmers, rebelled against the modernizing government of the Egyptian Muhammad Ali. The reason was their opposition to mandatory military enrollment. The leaders of the revolts were the chiefs of the clans (Jamula) of Nablus, Hebron, Jerusalem and Jaffa. In the process, as on other occasions, they also assassinated Jews. To argue that this revolt is a sample of "Palestinian nationalist" is not very serious.

National models in the Palestinian arena came about especially thanks to the contact with the organized West, according to the national principle, and especially as a reflection of the Zionist nationalist that was being developed in their own community.

For example, when the local Arab newspapers began (they expressed certain national identity such as Al-Quds (Jerusalem) 1908; Al-Karmil (Carmel) 1909 or Falastin (or Palestine) 1911) the clans had been already in contact for 30 years, with Jewish Zionism imported from Europe.

Throughout World War I, Arab-Palestinian clans were more interested in forming a regional pan-Arab kingdom centralized in Damascus. Later, when the Syria-Lebanon region was left in the hands of France and Israel-Jordan governed by the British, this proposal became irrelevant. Besides, when the British declared their intention of creating a Jewish State or National Homeland, the main reaction of the dominating clan (Husseinii) was to promote a religious-national rejection, much more religious than national.

The first step in creating the Palestinian identity happened during the 20s decade of the twentieth century; the intermediate steps happened after the Arab defeat in the 1948 War (Palestinian Arabs were left under the control of Jordan in the West Bank and others under Egypt in Gaza). **The final realization of the identity happened after the 1967 War, when both sides fell under the control of the Israeli government.**

42. Is it correct to say that the Jews stole the land from the Palestinians before 1948?

Argentinean journalist Pedro Brieger wrote (100 Questions and Answers): "Nationalist leaders had already realized that some Arabic peasants - whose lands had been sold by the landowners to the Zionist movement – competed to return and crashed with the new immigrants". This "anger" began during the British mandate while in the Ottoman days (until 1917) it was a minor subject.

These lands were not the property of the Arabic-Palestinians (regarding Brieger's incorrect affirmation "whose lands"). Arabs lived in those lands, bought by the Jews, following the model of Buztan (leases).

In 1858, the Ottoman Turks drew a first register of the lands. The register was doubly compromising: they had to pay taxes and they could be drafted to the army since they knew where they lived.

Rich landowners, many of them Christians from Lebanon, acquired the properties. The landowner rented the land for its development or a small production. Zionists bought the properties "from their legal owners" and, after paying exorbitant prices, decided to work and protect the lands by themselves. **Motivated by socialist principles, they believed in working and producing directly without exploiting others.**

The contact between the Occidental Jew and the Arabic customs produced tensions. For example, picture a group of Jews working in a plot of land. The Arabs had the custom of granting public access to the remains of the harvest. Now, let's imagine a guard who scares the invaders away from the private property at gunpoint. The person who runs away will call his clan to ask for help and then we have a conflict.

To acquire lands and redeem them, the Zionists founded the K.K.L. (Keren Kayemet Le-Israel or Jewish National Fund), created in 1901 in Basel (Switzerland). Since its creation, KKL has planted over 240 million trees in Israel, built 180 dams and developed 250.000 hectares.

43. Was the phrase "a land without a people for a people without a land" true?

Two questions can be distinguished: How many people lived there? and, Was there a Palestinian national consciousness when the Zionists began to arrive?

The demographics are very weak because of the lack of census (read "The Arab and Jewish Population in Palestine – During the Ottoman Empire and the British Rule" in MidEast Web). The land we know today as Israel-Palestine was scarcely inhabited (during the 1800s), by 250,000 people (20,000 to 25,000 Jews). The territory had a migratory wave during the nineteenth century for several reasons: the construction of the Suez Canal caused the emigration of Egyptian clans that didn't want to be forced to work. Also, the moderate modernization after the government of Muhammad Ali fostered the settlements. The increase in Arab immigration multiplied with the arrival of Zionists and the British Mandate. A massive immigration occurred, increasing the Arab population from 250,000 (in 1800) to 1,300,000 people in 1947.

Moreover, if in 1881 someone would have asked a local Arab if he was "Palestinian", it would have scared him. Palestine is a European word (European Jews used the term), and not even the Ottoman or the Mamluks used it to name the land and its inhabitants. It seems incredible, right? Not so much: try asking an Arab-speaking person to say "Palestine" with a P, and you'll see how he will only be able to say "Balestine". This is another proof that the name of the people is not autochthonous.

The expression "a land with without a people" is an exaggeration of the situation of those years. There were local Arab-speaking inhabitants that did not form a people. This statement can be verified by thousands of testimonials from that time: "There is no such thing called Palestine in history, absolutely not", stated Professor Philip Hittu (an Arab historian in 1946). Such a statement does not determine that there is not a Palestinian people at present.

44. Why are there so many testimonies that affirm that Israel was abandoned before the arrival of the Zionists and the British?

At the beginning of the Zionist movement, Jewish people did not feel that there was a Palestinian people in front of them: "There is no country called Palestine. 'Palestine' is a term invented by Zionists... Our country has been a part of Syria for centuries. 'Palestine' is foreign to us", confirmed Auni Bey Abdul-Hadi (Syrian Arab leader in the British Peel Commission of 1937).

The perception of Palestine as a semi-abandoned territory was not born from the Jews but from European travelers from the XIX Century, maybe imbued by the colonialist spirit although it was also a reflection of reality. The land had been deserted after a long history of wars and conquests and it was a forgotten and poor province of the Ottoman Empire. Mark Twain, who visited the site (1867), wrote: "... [a] desolate country whose soil is rich enough, but is given over wholly to weeds-a silent mournful expanse... A desolation is here that not even imagination can grace with the pomp of life and action... We never saw a human being on the whole route... There was hardly a tree or a shrub anywhere. Even the olive and the cactus, those fast friends of the worthless soil, had almost deserted the country".

The report from the Royal Commission about Palestine describes the coast plateau in 1913: "The road that goes from Northern Gaza was just a summer road suitable for transporting camels and carts... there were no orange groves, you couldn't see orchards nor vineyards until you arrived at [the Jewish village of] Yavne... the occidental part, facing the sea, was almost a desert... There were few villages in that area and they were barely populated. Many ruins from the villages splashed the region and because of malaria, many of them had been abandoned".

45. Did the Zionist ideologists consider the possibility of a confrontation with the local Arabs?

The first ideologists did not consider in depth the presence of the 250,000 non-Jews (Arabs) that inhabited the region. In The Old New Land Theodor

Hertzl even describes an ideal coexistence where Arabs would "thank and enjoy" the progress brought by the Jews. The pioneering Zionists did not take into account a national Palestinian identity that developed later (1920s-1930s). The local inhabitants were Arabs and Bedouins and some powerful families such as the Nashabibi or the Husseini

The Socialist ideologists considered that a just society had to be constructed based on the proletariat. **National conflicts were subject to class conflicts, being that class conflicts were not to arise in a just and inclusive society.** Socialist Zionism patriarch, Dov Ber Borhov, wrote: "When unproductive lands become prepared for colonization, when the new production techniques are introduced, and when other obstacles are removed, there will be enough land for Jews and Arabs. The normal relations between Jews and Arabs will prevail".

In 1907, Zionist leader Isaac Epstein, presented the problem clearly: "There's one thing we forgot: our dear land holds an entire people that has held on to it for hundreds of years and never thought of abandoning it". Epstein's words don't imply that there was a Palestinian nation, but in a certain way, the leader had some sensation of not considering the local inhabitants.

Only two Zionist ideologists foresaw the conflict: Ahad HaAm and Zeev Jabotinsky. In 1923, after gaining some experience, Jabotinsky constructed a wide vision on the topic in his essay "Iron Wall" that acknowledges the existence of local identity and respects (and understands) the opposition to the Zionist arrival.

46. So, does a Palestinian people exist (2019)?

As previously explained, the primary identity in the Middle East is tribal (clans – Jamula). When an Arab country is led by only one Jamula, without any competition, it goes through "stability". The Al- Thani dominate preponderantly in Qatar and the Al-Sabah clan in Kuwait. The other face is Iraq with 10 religions, many divisions: Kurds, Arabs, Turkmen and Persian people; and at least 70 tribes.

Could a country with multiple clans conform into one homogeneous people? Surely, if the clans begin marrying each other. Between the Jews in Israel, there are multiple and varied marriages between people from different origins. However, few marriages are produced between Jews (80%) and Arabs from Israel (20%). Thus, is it possible to talk about one people in Israel?

What happens among the Palestinians? There are many clans that do not usually marry each other. If the clan has the name Al-Masri, "Egyptian immigrants"; Al-Lubnani - "Lebanon"; Al-Dimashqi - "Damascus Syria"; Al-Hijazi - "Hejaz Saudi Arabia"; Al-Bagdadi - "Bagdad Iraq"; Al-Trablusi - "Tripoli Lebanon"; Al-Mugrabi - "Magrebies"; Al-Otman - "Ottomans"; Al-Tikriti - "Tikrit Iraq"; Al-Masrawa – a variable of Egypt; Al-Jumblatt - "from the Jumblatt valley in Kurdistan"; Al-Jzayer - "Algeria"; the Nashashibi – Syrian descendants; Al-Khaurani - "Hauran Syria"; Zouabi - "Jordan and Iraq".

Since there is no dominant clan, peace proposals arise such as the one by the eminence in Islam, Dr. Mordechai Keidar (Bar-Ilan University) titled "The Eight-State Solution: a Viable Alternative for Israel's Future".

Currently (2019), the Gaza Strip is a state that is practically independent and dominated by Hamas. There is a different authority in the West Bank, led by Fatah. **However, and in the same way that it is unacceptable for the Palestinians to reject the right of the Jewish people to be identified as well, it would be disrespectful to deny the current Palestinian identity.**

47. Is it true that Zionism planned for a State "only for Jews" and that this created the conflict?

Theodor Hertzl, promoter of the first Zionist Congresses and ideologist of the creation of a Jewish State, describes in his novel The Old New Land (1902) an imaginary future (1923) during national elections. There is a debate about the right to universal vote, including women and Arabs. One of the heroes is Rashid Bey, an Arab engineer from Haifa. The book describes how the discriminatory practices of Europe would not have a stand in the new society. Moreover, at present, the majority of the Israeli Arabs (73%) feel part of the Jewish state and 60% is proud to be Israeli, according to a survey by the **New Wave Research Institute (2017).**

What did the dominant socialist Zionists have to say? They advocated for a just society based on a proletarian class, of which the Arabs would be an inseparable part. Indeed, the great men of Zionism were more interested in finding a refuge for the persecuted Jews that thinking about what could happen in a second instance (for example, Theodor Hertzl or Leon Pinsker)

The dominant ideologists of Jewish nationalism (right-wing), such as Zeev Jabotinsky, wrote that in all societies there are national minorities that coexist, and his ideal was "a state with a Jewish president and an Arab Vice-president" (Jabotinsky was one of the writers of the Program for the Defense of National Minorities, 1901).

The Declaration of Independence of Israel (1948) clearly states: WE APPEAL – in the very midst of the onslaught launched against us now for months – to the Arab inhabitants of the State of Israel to preserve peace and participate in the upbuilding of the State on the basis of full and equal citizenship and due representation in all its provisional and permanent institutions". Those were not just words, it is the foundational document of the State of Israel.

48. Why did the British and French divide up the Middle East in 1916?

Most of the Middle East was occupied for 400 years by the Ottoman Empire. It was a weak empire that did not previously dissolve so as to prevent the expansion of the emergent German power. The dominant imperial ideas sought to increase the countries' prestige, create markets to sell products, dominate raw materials and sometimes it happened because of their own particular dynamics (dominate a territory so that the competition would not). The economy was not the only explanation for colonialism, even though the powers wished to occupy geostrategic places that were fundamental for world commerce when it was clear that the region was a source of oil. For example, the French colonies in Algeria (since 1830) or the inauguration of the Suez Canal in 1869 in Egyptian lands were not "oil powers".

After the fall of the Ottoman Empire during World War I, three powers divided their territory. The main ones were distributed between England and France. The third part, according to the agreement, was for Czarist Russia that, after the coup of the communist state, revealed to the world the secret pact (Sykes-Picot 1916). The Austro-Hungarian Empire also dissolved and formed Czechoslovakia, Hungary, Poland, the Kingdom of Serbia, Croatia and Slovenia, etc., according to the borders set by the winning powers. Likewise, they occupied what is currently Egypt, Jordan, Iraq, etc.

In the case of Israel and the Middle East, the British had two commitments: **one was to favor a national home for Jews in Palestine and to award the Arabs who supported them in the war against the Ottomans.** For the latter, they gave Iraq and what today is Jordan to a specific clan: the Hashemite (originally from the Arab Peninsula). The official name of Jordan is the Hashemite Kingdom of Jordan.

49. What is the secret Sykes-Picot Agreement of 1916?

The Agreement is officially known as the Asia Minor Agreement. Diplomats Mark Sikes (Great Britain) and François Georges Picot (France) negotiated the terms; a secret pact signed between Great Britain, France and Russia to distribute the influence and control of the three countries after the fall of the Ottoman Empire in World War I. It is generally considered that the Agreement shaped the region.

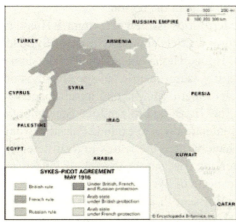

Sykes-Picot Agreement, 1916
(Source: Encyclopaedia Britannica)

The British controlled the areas from the Mediterranean Sea coastline up to the Jordan River, what today is Jordan, the south of Iraq and a small area that included the ports of Haifa and Acre, to maintain access to the Mediterranean. The French kept control of southeast Turkey, the north of Iraq, Syria and Lebanon. The Russian Empire would receive Istanbul, the Turkish Straights and Armenia. Each power would decide the borders within their areas.

In fact, there were five areas: one under British control, one under French control, one under British influence or protectorate, one under French influence or protectorate, and one under international administration (including the cities of Jerusalem and Nazareth). These agreements were endorsed during the San Remo Conference and were backed by the League of Nations (predecessor of the UN).

The British constituted the British Mandate for Palestine between 1920 and 1948 and the British Mandate for Iraq (1920-1932); the French Mandate of Syria and Lebanon lasted from 1923 until 1946. The Government of the Czars in Russia was a minor part of the Agreement, and when the Russian Revolution came about, it was the Bolsheviks that divulged the Agreement on Nov/3/1917 to show the disgraces of imperialism. The British and the French were embarrassed and the Arabs were dismayed.

50. What do the promises to the Arabs or the letters of McMahon-Hussein from 1915 mean?

It is a series of 10 letters exchanged between the governor of Mecca (Hashemi clan), Hussein Iben Ali, and the British commissioner for Cairo, Henry McMahon (July/14/1915-January/30/1916). The British proposed an Arab uprising against the Ottoman Empire during World War I in exchange for the recognition of the alliance of an Arab state in the region.

In the letter dated Oct/24/1915 the territories assured to recognize Hussein are all "less": "the Mersin and Alexandria districts and the regions of Syria to the west of the districts of Damascus, Homs, Hama and Aleppo". The status given to Israel-Palestine was not clear, it was not mentioned specifically, nor the administrative entity or Sanjak of Jerusalem. McMahon himself, once retired (1922), clarified these letters to The Times and to Sir John Shuckburgh from the British Colonial Offices: "My intention was to exclude Palestine from an independent Arabia and I hope to have written the letters in a sufficiently clear manner in every way [...] My intention was, surely, to exclude Palestine, the same way as the coastal parts of the north of Syria".

To promote the uprising, the English sent "Lawrence of Arabia" in an operation that would last two years and that did not count with the Palestine leader Hajj Amin Al-Husseini, who participated in favor of the Ottomans. After the letters, the empires distributed the lands in the Sykes-Picot Agreement (1916) and also promised Israel to the Jews in the Balfour Declaration (1917).

Regarding the Hiyaz Kingdom, the Arab State created justly by Hussein Iben Ali from Mecca at the beginning of the riot, which was out of the distribution and mandate politics, was conquered and annexed by its neighbors when Saudi Arabia was constituted.

51. What is the importance of the Balfour Declaration?

While the Sheik of Mecca, Hussein Ben Ali, was encouraged to combat by the British in exchange for promises of a kingdom, the Zionist movement was also being seduced diplomatically. Promises to the Jews were made to an organized Zionist movement, with European-style national aspirations with effective actions in the field, with farms and cities established in Israel. **Promises to Arabs were made to tribal chiefs and non-constituted elements from a national perspective, leaders that did not live in what today is Israel- Palestine.**

On Nov/2/1917, British Chancellor Arthur James Balfour wrote a letter to the banker and ex-congressman Baron Lionel W. Rothschild, to be delivered to the Zionist movement and with whom he had close links. The text said: "The government of His Majesty sees favorably the establishment in Palestine of a national homeland for the Jewish people, and will employ its best efforts to facilitate the realization of this objective". It added, "it is understood that nothing will be done to damage the civil and religious rights of the non-Jewish communities that exist in Palestine".

The Balfour Declaration was "a declaration" by the main power of the time. **In 1920, in the San Remo Resolution, the League of Nations (the UN today) granted the Mandate to the British over Palestine, to establish a state for the Jewish people according to the Balfour Declaration. The international legality derives from the San Remo Resolution and the predecessor of the UN, and not from the Balfour Declaration.**

Zionists were excited with the Balfour Declaration, and even more so when the League of Nations ordered Great Britain to administer the land in order to fulfill the declaration.

52. Why did the British issue the Balfour Declaration?

Avi Shlaim in The Balfour Declaration and its Consequences (2005) affirms that there were two reasons to justify the declaration. One was because it resulted from good Zionist lobbying and the other because it was of imperial interest for the British.

Some historians say that the decision of the British government reflects what James Gelvin calls "patrician anti-Semitism", the overestimation of the Jewish power in the U.S. and in Russia. This logic indicated that the Russian Jews could pressure their own to keep them in the war while the North Americans were urged to fight in World War I (two advisors to Woodrow Wilson were advocates of Zionism). Furthermore, the British intended to avoid the foreseeable French pressure for an international administration, especially for the sacred places.

Lloyd George, in his Memoirs (1939), presented a list of nine factors that motivated his decision as Prime Minister to issue the declaration, including his opinion that a Jewish presence in Palestine would strengthen Great Britain's position over the Suez Canal and their imperial dominance in India. Lloyd George said to the Royal Commission of Palestine in 1937 that the Declaration was issued "due to propagandistic reasons [...]" and that it "would be harder for Germany to reduce their military commitments and improve their economic position in the Oriental front".

Another reason was the profound conviction of the British Christian authorities to accelerate the Jewish redemption to promote their Messianic return. In the meantime, others presented it as an appreciation for the invaluable contribution by Chaim Weizmann (President of the World Zionist Organization) to the British military power through his scientific developments. Certainly, the British felt closer to the European Zionists than to the Middle East Arabs.

53. What was the British Mandate of Palestine?

The Conference of San Remo (April 1920) ratified and legalized the territorial distribution of the declining Ottoman Empire, previously agreed between France and the United Kingdom in the Versailles Treaty (1919). Syria and Lebanon (separate lands) were now under French mandate; Iraq was conceded to the new king Feisal (the son of Hussein of Mecca) as part of the British mandate of Mesopotamia. Palestine, now detached from Syria, was under British mandate (the territory included what is now Israel-Palestine-Jordan).

The League of Nations confirmed (Jul/24/1922) that the results of San Remo were a form of a mandate, meaning that the mission was to help the locals build their self-determination. **The introduction to the text explained clearly: "Considering that the principal allied powers also agreed that trustees shall be responsible to implement the original declaration on Nov/2/1917 by the government of His Majesty and adopted by said powers in favor of establishing in Palestine a national homeland for the Jewish people, it is clearly understood that nothing shall be done to adverse the civil and religious rights of the non-Jewish communities living in Palestine, or the rights and political status of the Jews in any other country".**

Some say that the whole issue was about the betrayal of the Arabs for the benefit of the Jews. Let's see: the colonial empires received in the Middle East about 7,000,000 km2; 120,000 km2 were promised to the Jews, but in 1922 a good part was taken from them, leaving only about 25,000 km2. **In other** words, the Arab tribe chiefs received 99.65% of the land and the Jews 0.35%, and this is why... exactly for this reason, that the conflict began. It doesn't sound too serious.

54. Is it true that the British created an artificial state called Jordan?

The British were in trouble. They had physically conquered Damascus-Syria but, because of the Sykes-Picot Agreement (1916) and after the San Remo Conference (1920), Syria had to be turned over to France. The British had elected the son of their ally Hussein Iben Ali from the Mecca (Faisal) as king of Syria. After Sep/30/1918, they declared Hussein a loyal government and named him "King of the Arabs". In light of this, the French argued that they had the right to decide who was going to govern in Syria. In fact, Foreign Minister Stephen Pichon said that France had no agreement with King Hussein.

If the British government had accepted then that Damascus, Homs, Hama and Aleppo were included in the direct scope of influence of France, the British would have had to break their promise to the Arabs and they were not willing to do so.

With the Versailles Treaty (1919), Great Britain not only obtained the mandate in Palestine (confirmed in San Remo) but also Mosul, adding Basra and Bagdad and creating the kingdom of Iraq. It took the Upper Galilee region from Syria to build the pipeline from Mosul to Haifa.

In the face of the French pressure, the British proposed to compensate Hussein with a kingdom, governed by his son Feisal I, in the rich lands of Iraq. Feisal's younger brother, Abed Allah (Abdallah) also wanted to have "his part" harassing French and Jews on the Upper Galilee, in the border with Syria. The British wished to eradicate the Islamic influence of the Turks, putting "their people" in their vast territories. **They gave Abdallah 76.5% of the 120,000 km2 of the British Mandate creating the Hashemite Empire of Transjordan (the Hashemite Kingdom of Jordan). The territory was divided in 1922, contradicting the international commitments set forth in the San Remo Conference.**

55. Is it true that the Zionist leaders met with the Arabs in order to achieve a coexistence agreement in the Middle East in 1919?

The Agreement between the Zionist leader Chaim Weitzman and Faisal, son of Hussein of Mecca, of the kingdom of Hijaz (destroyed and joined to Saudi Arabia for the benefit of the Saud clan) was signed in London on Jan/1/1919 as an attempt to fix the relations between Zionists and Arabs that were eager to create their kingdom (as was mentioned in the McMahon-Hussein correspondence). This idea disappeared between the spring and the summer of 1920

The relations between Zionists and Arabs guided by Hussein were not necessarily bad at the beginning of the twentieth century. **In March 1918, "Al Kibla", a newspaper faithful to Hussein of Mecca, published a "declaration of the Arab desire to bless their Jewish brothers that were returning to the land of Israel".** Weitzman and Faisal met for the first time in Akaba-Jordan on June/6/1918 and continued meeting during a year. In November of 1919, they reached an agreement that stated the following: 1) relations between Arabs and Jews in British Palestine would be collaborative and would be based on the Balfour Declaration; 2) A wide and massive Jewish immigration to Palestine was requested to create a strong community; 3) the promise of freedom of worship as the Muslims would take over their holy sites; 4) a committee organized by the Jews would be sent over to present projects for economic opportunities, led by Arabs and Zionists.

Why wasn't this agreement implemented? **Faisal conditioned the agreement to the British fulfilling the Arab desire for independence, and if there was any small change (such as removing Faisal from his government in Syria after only four months in office to send him to Iraq), then the agreement would be canceled.** The Jews weren't 100% excited about the agreement because it didn't recognize a future independent Jewish State.

56. At what point did the physical confrontations occur between Jews and Arabs?

"As the Arabs realized that the Jews that arrived in Palestine were thinking openly and clearly about creating a State for them alone, they opposed and confrontations began", Pedro Brieger writes in his book *100 Questions and Answers*. **However, the Jews had already stated their desire to constitute a State 30 years before the violence began. Furthermore, it is incorrect to state that the Jews wanted to create a state for them alone.**

The first incited acts of armed violence occurred in 1920-1921 and were more a religious conflict than a national one. The failure of the Great Syria plan, the development of nationalist ideas after the Young Turk Revolution (1908) and the traumatic contact with European nationalism from British and Zionists created the environment for the appearance of the instigator.

A local leader, the Mufti Hajj Amin Al-Husseini (from the Hussein clan), who competed with the Nashashibi clan, provided military help to the Ottomans against the British. He did not receive a promise from the British and, since the beginning, he supported the idea of a Great Syria (not an Arab-Palestinian State). Amin Al-Husseini opposed the British Christian intervention in the region and, of course, he was against Zionism.

The pattern of religious incitement and violence was revealed with total forcefulness in the Jewish killings by the Arabs (in the best pogrom style) in 1929. The most important armed movement was the big riot in 1936-1939, lead again by the Mufti of Jerusalem, together with his ally Hitler, who focused especially against the British. The situation at the beginning of the XXI Century shows that religion is still considered a trigger to incite violence, even after 100 years.

57. Is it true that Zionist Jews wanted to create a state "only for them", based on what Yosef Weitz said?

One of the recurrent references to discredit Zionism states that: "In 1940, Yosef Weitz, head of the Jewish Agency, stated clearly: It must be clear among us that there is no place for both peoples in the country (…). With the Arabs in the country, we cannot achieve our goal to become an independent people in this small territory; the only solution is an Eretz Israel (the land of Israel) without Arabs (…) And there is no other resource than to move the Arabs to the neighboring countries, all of them must be transferred, not a village or tribe can remain, and this transfer must be done towards Iraq, Syria and even Trans-Jordan" (same book by Brieger)". With this quotation, some try to sustain two falsehoods: 1) that violence began because of this "Jewish exclusivism"; 2) that "this is proof" for the expulsion of the Palestinians in 1948.

Let's set this straight: Yosef Weitz was not the head of the Jewish Agency (the political arm), but of the KKL (Keren Kayemet LeIsrael, in charge of the purchase and forestation of the lands), a position quite inferior in the Zionist hierarchy. In other words, this person did not have the power stated in the quotation.

Yosef Weitz formed part of the Commission for Population Exchange organized by the Jewish Agency after the Peel Commission. It was the British who proposed in the midst of the commission a "transfer" of peoples. **Yosef Weitz supported this transfer, but only if it was approved by those involved. He believed that a forced transfer was not real or implementable.**

Yosef Weitz tried to convince the Zionist leadership to prepare a "Transfer" plan and in 1943 the accountant of the Jewish Agency, Eliezer Kaplan, decided to assign some funds to study the issue, with no concrete results. The Zionist leadership did not approve or act according to what Weitz said.

58. What did Yosef Weitz really say?

The complete citation of the Transfer Proposal from the director of the KKL Yosef Weitz states: "After the war, the question about Eretz Israel and the Jewish matter will stop being an issue only about the 'development' (of the land). It must be clear, among us, that there is no place for both peoples in the country. There is no sense of 'development' that will take us to our objective of being independent in this small land. If the Arabs leave the land, its extent and luxuriance will be left for us, and if the Arabs stay, the land will be small and narrow…" The transference should not be forced but agreed on.

"And when the war ends with the triumph of the English, and when the people sit down to judge, our people must present our arguments and the only solution is that one of the territories of Israel, at least the west side, must remain without Arabs. There is no place for consensus here! The Zionist labor we have done until today was like a training and preparation test for the creation of a Hebrew State in Eretz Israel, something well and appropriate at the moment and we could be satisfied with ¬"the purchase of the land"; but the only way is to transfer the Arabs to neighboring countries, transfer them all, except maybe those in Bethlehem, Nazareth and the old Jerusalem. Not one village nor tribe should be left. And the transfer should be to Iraq, Syria and even to Transjordan. For this, we will find funds and money. Only with this transfer will the country be able to absorb millions of our brothers and the Jewish matter will conclude and will have a solution. There is no other way."

Weitz did not manage to convince the Zionist leadership. Currently, there are 20% of Arabs living in Israel.

59. Is it true that throughout history Jews and Muslims coexisted in harmony and that only "Zionism" ruptured such an idyll?

For Islam, the Jews are not a people, and even if they are a "religion" it is false and it must be subdued. Currently, many Muslims do not wish to carry out such a premise, but others do. In the theological basis of Islam, two other previous religions are accused (Judeo-Christians) of "deforming" the teachings of the Furkan, before the arrival of the only truth (Islam).

In theological terms, Jews and Christians can opt for three pathways: conversion, death or subduing to Islam under clear rules (the rules of Omar) that include the payment of a head tax (Jizya). If the theological relation of Islam to Judaism is clear and the religion is fundamental, then the origin of the conflict is deeper than what is presented by materialists. **How is it possible that a subdued and false religion (Judaism) dares to demand an independent state?**

For centuries, from the IX Century to the XI Century, 90% of the Jews lived under Islam as a "subdued people" (Dhimmi). It is true that the European Christian aggressiveness towards Jews was more frequent than the Muslim. This doesn't mean that Jews in Islamic societies lived in paradise. During the last century, for example, Jews were expelled and murdered in Iraq, Syria or the north of Africa.

Since just before World War II, the Muslim world adopted several premises of the Nazi ideology, as can be seen in modern Arab and Islamic media. Since the 30s decade, the Palestinian Mufti Hajj Amin Al-Husseini became an ally of Hitler, and proposed to murder the Jews in crematoria to be built in Emek Dotan (Israel), he implemented a failed plan to contaminate the waters of Tel Aviv and directed a Nazi radio station in Arabic and Persian (Radio Zessen).

60. Did the Arabs and the Jews agree on the British occupying Palestine?

The British Mandate over Palestine, given by the League of Nations, was not a "classic" model of colonialism. The precursor of the UN clearly stated that the British should help the local people to develop until they reached their independence, according to the "Balfour Declaration". **In other words, the British began their mandate favoring the Jews because they were ordered to by the authorities that gave them the power to govern these lands.**

The original policy of the British Mandate was, in fact, to open Jewish immigration, but it did not produce a massive arrival. **When the migratory wave increased, so did the Arab discontentment manifestations, and the English began a restrictive policy that would become harder just when the entry of the immigrants was needed the most because of the deterioration of the European situation.** The Arab violence provoked the British authorities to gradually retrieve from their commitment to the League of Nations.

The demographic relation indicates that the Jewish population reached 11.14% of the population in 1922, to 16.90% in 1931, 27.91% in 1939 and

32.96% in 1945. **If there were no more Jews it was because the British did not issue the immigration certificates, limiting the arrival of Jews.**

In 1922, the Arabs who lived in the region received 76.5% of the British Mandate territory in Palestine (120,000 km2) to form another Arab kingdom, Jordan. In other words, Palestine had already been divided by the British for the benefit of the Arabs. The Palestinian-Israeli conflict occurs in that remaining 23.5%, where the United Nations decided to give the Jews a little over 10% of the 120,000 km2. The Arab-Palestinians did not accept any concession and began a war against Great Britain in 1936.

61. What happened during the Arab massacres of 1920?

The first important pogrom of Arabs against Jews in Palestine happened during the revolts of 1920. On one side, they attacked from the north, resulting in 8 dead Jews in an Arab attack against the population of Tel-Hai. In the high Galilee, the Arabs were fighting against the French for separating the pro-British King Faisal (who ended up in Iraq). Meanwhile, the Arabs attacked the Jews in Metula, Ayelet Ha Shachar, Degania and Tel Hai.

One month later the massacres began in Jerusalem and its surroundings. On April/4/1920, during the festivities of Nabi Mussa, Hajj Amin Al-Husseini and Aref El-Aref delivered a sermon that made the Arab masses run towards the Old City of Jerusalem yelling "Itbah Al-Yehud!" (Massacre the Jews) and "A-Daula Maana" (the British are with us)

So the Jews of the neighborhood of the Old City were attacked resulting in 7 Jews and 4 Arabs, and 250 Jews injured. According to reports before the Arab massacres against the Jews in 1920, the Arab public yelled in the streets of Jerusalem "Palestine is our land, the Jews are our dogs!" The Arab police joined the applause and the violence began, the *Chaim Yeshivat Torah* was attacked and the rolls of the Torah were damaged and thrown to the floor while the building was burnt down. In just three hours there were 160 Jews injured.

At the same time, the British military responded irregularly and late in containing and preventing this unrest, that lasted four days. Ironically, the British authorities detained Jewish members of the *Hagana* (Defense) and Zeev Jabotinsky, the organizer, who were trying to defend those under attack, and sentenced them to 15 years in prison (they were pardoned a few months later).

62. How did the Jews and Arabs react to the massacre of 1920?

In 1920, the Jewish leaders asked the British to arm and prepare Jewish defenders to compensate for the lack of adequate British troops. Dozens of reports ensure that the British military governor, Ronald Storrs, encouraged the Arabs and stopped the Jews from defending themselves. The voluntary petition was rejected and Zeev Jabotinsky together with Pinchas Rutenberg trained Jewish volunteers for their own community defense. The Jews informed the British of these efforts. Many of the volunteers were members of the Maccabi sports club and some of them were veterans from the Jewish Legion that fought with Great Britain in the First World War. By the end of March, around 600 people had done military training in Jerusalem.

After the massacre, the Jews came to the conclusion that the British were not willing to defend the Jewish settlements from the Arab attacks, which is why they established entities of self-defense called *Hagana* (Defense).

At the same time, Arab sheiks from 82 villages around Jerusalem and Jaffa (who affirmed to represent 70% of the population) protested in a document because of the manifestations against the Jews. However, other Arabic spokespeople affirmed that this sentence had been obtained through bribery. There may have effectively been a majority of Arabs that were against the killing of their fellow Jewish citizens, but, also, the radicals were the ones who ruled and established the agenda.

From the Palestinian side, the revolts provoked the Arab leadership in Palestine to be seen less as part of the south of Syria and more as an Arabic community unique and separated. There was no concept of the Palestinian people. In the frame of this change, where the Arabs were left under the direct control of the British Mandate, the radicalized role of the born leadership became fundamental.

63. How did the British react to the Massacre of 1920?

The new British civilian government, led by the Jew Herbert Samuel, pardoned the main instigator of the massacre, Hajj Amin Al-Husseini (March 1921) and later named him the "Mufti of Jerusalem". The Muslim Supreme Council was formed a year later, and Husseini demanded the title of "Great Mufti", and it was granted to him. **If the British would have ended the Arab violence instead of believing that they could calm them by flattering them, there might not be a conflict today.**

During these excesses, the British military administration of Palestine was severely criticized for withdrawing their troops from Jerusalem and for responding so slowly to recover control. The British soldiers found most of the weapons hidden in the clothes of the Arab women.

As a result of the unrest, the trust between the British (who protected the instigator Mufti of Jerusalem), Jews and Arabs was eroded.

The Palin Commission, a group of British investigators that arrived in May 1920 to examine the reasons that caused the events, affirmed that the violence was provoked, according to Palin, by (a) the Arab deception because of the failure of the promise of independence they had received, they said, during World War I, (b) the Balfour Declaration (1917) that according to the Arabs denied them the right to the Arab free determination, (c) the Pan-Arab propaganda of the Emir Faisal, as king of reunified Syria, and the impatience of the Jews to achieve their goals...

As a result of the attacks of the Arabs against the Jews in 1920, Jewish immigration was stopped temporarily by the British.

The unrest preceded the San Remo Conference, to be held April 19 to 26 of 1920, where the British Mandate of Palestine was established, following the Balfour Declaration (1917).

64. What happened in the Arab massacre from 1921?

The outrages from 1921 were a series of attacks against the Jews between the 1st to the 7th of May 1921. During the 1st of May, the "Jewish Communist Party" celebrated a parade in Jaffa to commemorate Labor Day. The night before, flyers were given out written in Arabic and in Yiddish that asked to overthrow the British administration. That morning, a leader from the Jaffa police, the Arab Toufiq Bey Al-Said, visited the headquarters of the party to inform the 60 present members not to go to the parade. Another parade was organized in parallel in Tel Aviv by the socialist rival, "Working Unit", with official authorization. When both parades met, a fight exploded and the police force from the British Mandate chased the communists from Jaffa. When they heard about the conflict, the Arabs from Jaffa took the advantage to murder Jews.

The attacks were extended to Rejovot, Kfar Saba, Petah Tikva and Hedera. Dozens of British, Arab and Jewish witnesses informed that many Arabs armed with knives, swords and pistols burst into Jewish buildings and killed the inhabitants. They destroyed Jewish houses and stores, hurting Jews in their homes and, in some cases, the victims´ skulls were opened.

Tombs and monument dedicated to those murdered in 1921, Trumpledor Cemetery, Tel Aviv *(Source: Wikipedia)*

The Arab violence against the Jews in 1921 extended to Abu Kabir. The Jewish family Itzker, owners of a dairy product farm in the outskirts of the neighborhood, rented rooms. At the moment of the revolts, Yosef Chaim Brenner, one of the pioneers in Modern Hebrew literature, was living in the place. On May/2/1921, in spite of the warnings, the Itzkers and Brenner refused to leave the farm and were murdered.

The revolt resulted in the death of 45 Jews (and 5 more murdered in Jerusalem) and 48 Arabs (who confronted the British troops). 146 Jews and 73 Arabs were injured.

65. How did the British react to the massacre of 1921?

In order to calm the Arab instigators, the British High Commissioner for Palestine, Herbert Samuel, declared a state of emergency, censored the press and called in reinforcements from Egypt. Samuel met with Musa Al-Husseini, who had been removed as mayor of Jerusalem due to his participation in the massacres of 1920, and who was requesting the end of the Jewish immigration. Samuel accepted, and two or three small vessels were denied permission to disembark and returned to Istanbul. At the same time, Hajj Amin Al-Husseini, the other Al-Husseini's nephew, was named Great Mufti of Jerusalem.

In his speech for the occasion of the royal birthday in June 1921, the British Commissioner Herbert Samuel emphasized the commitment of Great Britain to the second part of the Balfour Declaration of 1917 (avoid harming the rights of the other local inhabitants) and declares that Jewish immigration would only be allowed if the economy could absorb new citizens. Later, Jewish immigration was suspended for some time. Those who heard Samuel's speech were left with the impression that he was trying to calm the Arabs after the massacres of 1921, and some Jewish leaders boycotted him for some time.

The investigating commission established by Commissioner Samuel was headed by the President of the Supreme Court of Justice of Palestine, Sir

Thomas Haycraft. His report confirmed the participation of policemen in the Arab revolts and found as adequate the measures adopted by the authorities. The report upset Jews and Arabs, but to balance the statements he said that "the fundamental cause of violence is that Zionists were not doing enough to mitigate the fears of the Arabs". Also, he blamed the increase in Jewish immigration.

66. What are the British White Papers of 1922?

Churchill's White Paper (June/3/1922) is the first of three documents to limit the purchase of lands and Jewish immigration. It was meant to be a "conciliatory" answer to the massacre of 1921 (the British believed that by giving in to the Arab violence they would defuse such anger).

The British White Paper concluded that the violence was provoked by the resentment towards the Zionist Jews and the perceived favoritism towards them from the British, as well as Arabs that feared subjugation. While maintaining their commitment to Great Britain through the Balfour Declaration and their promise of a National Jewish Home in Palestine, which was "internationally guaranteed" and "recognized as an ancient historic connection", the document emphasized that the establishment of a National Jewish Home would not impose the nationality of the Arab inhabitants and "in front of the eyes of the law the state of all the citizens of Palestine will be Palestinian".

To reduce the tension between Arabs and Jews in Palestine, the Papers limited Jewish immigration to "the economic capacity of the country to absorb the newcomers".

During the same process, the British decided to separate the territories east of the river to give to Abdallah, son of Hussein from Mecca, the Arab Emirate of Transjordan (current Hashemite Kingdom of Jordan) (article 25 reviewed from the Mandate). This, an obvious violation or contravention to the letter of assignment of the British Mandate written by the League of Nations, only two years after the agreed commitments in the San Remo Conference (1920)

The authorities from the World Zionist Organization, led by their president Chaim Weizmann, decided to approve the document. The Arabs rejected it and ordered the return of the commission once it got to London.

67. What happened during the Arab massacres of 1929?

In 1928 the Muslims tried to gain from the British the sole rights over the Wailing Wall, including a small space used by the Jews since the days of the Mamluks. Meanwhile, bricks from the "reconstruction of the Al-Aqsa Mosque" fell "accidentally" on Jewish worshipers. The muezzins increased the volume of their call to prayer to disturb the Jewish payers. The Mufti of Jerusalem, Amin Al-Husseini, ordered (August 1929) opening the southern side of the alley that crosses the Wall. Mules passed through the alley, usually throwing their wastes and bothering the Jews that were praying in this holy site. This resulted in protests of the Jews to the British, who remained indifferent.

The Jewish community was requesting that the Wall remain in Jewish hands (the Temple Mount, the most sacred site of Judaism, remained under Muslim domain). On August/14/2019, after the attacks against the Jews who were praying in the Wall, 6,000 Jews protested in Tel-Aviv: "The Wall is ours". The next day, on the fasting day for the Jews (Yom Kippur), 300 Jewish youth raised the flag and sang Hatikva (the hymn of the Zionist movement) facing the Wall. A day later, on Aug/16/1929, an organized mob of 2000 Muslims descended to the Wailing Wall and Destroyed liturgical objects, burned prayer books and plea notes.

During the week of the unrest, at least 133 Jews were murdered, 116 Arabs lost their lives, and 339 were injured. As still happens currently, Muslims instigated the crowds accusing Jews of robbing holy Muslim sited. The instigators assured that the Jews had burnt the Mosque.

The main instigators were the Mufti of Jerusalem, Hajj Amin Al-Husseini (later a noticeable Nazi ally) and Aref Al-Aref.

68. Are there testimonies of the Arab massacre in 1929?

Baruch Katinka, a member of the *Hagana*, said about the massacre: "We arrived at Hebron after midnight and went to Eliezer Dan Slonim's house, the manager of the regional bank and chief of the Jewish Community. We woke him up and told him they had brought weapons and people to protect them. He started screaming and said that if he wanted weapons then he would ask for them because he had an agreement with the Arabs, who needed the credit, that they were under his influence and that he would not hurt them. The massacre occurred the next day."

After the 1929 massacre, British Lieutenant Raymon Cafferata, chief of the Hebron police testified: "After hearing screams I went in and saw an Arab about to cut a child's head off with a dagger. He had already beaten him up and as soon as he saw me he ran towards me, but he was wrong: he practically went into the barrel of my gun. I shot him low, in the groin. Behind him, there was a Jewish woman covered in blood with a man who admitted to being an agent from the police called Issa, police superintendent from Jaffa. He was standing behind the woman with a knife in his hand. I shot him."

In Tzfat (or Safed), just like in Hebron, around twenty Jewish people were murdered, including women, children and elderly people. The massacre occurred throughout August/29/1929 until de British Mandate authority was able to control the Arab murderers. Additionally, the Arabs burned and robbed the Jewish neighborhood. These killings were part of the 1929 protests. The disappearance of ancient Jewish communities had deep historical consequences (Hebron was recently repopulated in 1968). During that week, at least 133 Jews were murdered by Arabs.

69. Is it true that in 1929 the Jewish community of Hebron was massacred?

Hebron, a city located 30 kilometers south of Jerusalem, is the second most sacred place and one of the four holy cities of Judaism. The three patriarchs of Israel are buried there and three of the four matriarchs. The Sephardic Jewish community lived continuously in Hebron for over 800 years under different occupations, while the Ashkenazi had returned a century before

Throughout the 20s decade, Arabs constantly harassed the Jews in Hebron: insults in the streets, beating, breaking windows of their homes with stones, and occasionally, unrest in the Cave of the Patriarchs. During this period, the Jewish community denounced these events several times to the British police, claiming that not enough was being done to protect them. The Jews blamed most of the problems to the activities of the Arab nationalists of the Muslim-Christian Association, who distributed racist propaganda and even songs that incited against the Jews.

After a first murder in Hebron (1929), 40 Jews met at Eliezer Dan Slonim's house (the head of the community) thinking that his influence could help to save them. That Saturday, the Arab protesters came up to the rabbi and offered a deal: "turn in the Ashkenazi Jews and you, Sephardim, will be saved. Rabbi Slonim refused, and he was murdered instantly, together with his wife and 4-year-old child. Finally, 12 Sephardic and 55 Ashkenazi Jews were murdered.

The massacre of 1929 wiped out the Jewish community of Hebron. The survivors were forced to flee and their properties were taken by the Arabs until the Six-Day War (1967). After the war, some of the Jews returned to the city to resettle.

70. What was the Jewish people's reaction to the 1929 massacre?

Attacks against the Jews not only happened in Jerusalem and Hebron. On Friday Aug/23/1929, angered by the fake rumors that the Jews were about to attack the Al-Aqsa Mosque, the Arabs started attacking Jews in the Old City of Jerusalem. Other killings occurred in Safed, Motza, Kfar Uriah and Tel-Aviv.

On Aug/20/1929, after a first Arab attack on the Jews in Jerusalem, the leaders of the *Hagana* proposed to send defense forces for the approximately 800 Jews of Hebron. The leaders of the Jewish community underestimated this offer, insisting that they trusted the A'yan (notables) to protect them from the violent sectors of the Palestinian-Arabs.

Amongst the defenders of Jerusalem, prominent Officer Abraham Tehomi (alias "Gideon"), rumors began to be spread that the British did not protect the Jews properly and that the *Hagana* policy, the Havlaga (contention) was not the adequate response to these aggressions. At the same time, critics complained about the lack of weapons.

On Apr/4/1931 commanders and directors of a Jewish paramilitary entity announced their refusal to return the weapons that the Hagana had requested before the holiday Nabi Mussa. Tehomi, together with other founding members and commanders of the *Hagana* and members of the Juvenile Labor Party, conformed the *Hagana* B, which throughout the years co-opted many volunteers from the nationalist young movement Betar and began to be known as Irgun Tzvai Leumi or Etzel (National Military Organization) with the purpose of highlighting its activist character, in contrast with the *Hagana*.

The 1929 massacre provoked a new disappointment over the possibility of coexisting with the Arab-Palestinian political leadership. In the field, this was translated into the formation of a clandestine entity that would prevent and break any future attacks.

71. What did the British decide after this new wave of Arab violence of 1929?

As in the previous massacres (1920-1921), the British called for an investigating commission that concluded that the best way to calm aggressions was to disengage a bit more from the Balfour Declaration.

50,000 Jews of Warsaw protesting against the White Letter of 1930
(Source: Wikipedia)

The Passfield White Paper (Oct/20/1930) was issued by the colonial Secretary, Lord Sydney Webb Passfield, a formal declaration of the British policy on Palestine, previously established by the Churchill White Paper (1922). The new declaration resulted from the investigation by the Hope-Simpson Commission on the causes of the massacres of 1929.

The paper stated that "with no available lands", the lands could be sold to the Jews only if it didn't harm the Arabs. It limited the capacity to absorb Jewish immigrants and to provide employment as long as there would be an improvement in the unemployment within the Arab sector. The British accepted that they had made contradictory promises to the Arabs, and therefore advised organizing a Legislative Council representing both sides.

In response to the British document, the main supporter of the Zionist-British Alliance, the President of the World Zionist Organization, Chaim Weizmann, resigned his post.

Zionist organizations worldwide set up a vigorous campaign against the document. In Great Britain, Prime Minister Ramsay McDonald was consequently forced to clarify the White Paper to the British House of Commons. In a letter to Chaim Weizmann in 1931 (the MacDonald Letter) he tried to calm the Zionists, though, at the same time, the Arabs were labeling the document "the Black Letter". However, the British Prime Minister addressed the Parliament on Feb/11/1931 stating he was "quite unwilling to give the letter the same status as the dominating document". In other words, he was confirming that the Passfield White Paper was more important than his own clarification letter.

72. What role did Hajj Amin Al-Husseini play in the conflict?

He was one of the main instigators of the Palestinian-Israeli conflict. If we had to reference it politically in today's world, with his ardent anti-Semitism, his religious instigation that began the pogrom (1920, 1921, 1929 and from 1936-1939) we would reference him as an exponent of the Palestinian Islamist terrorism. In that sense, Jerusalem's Mufti was a pioneer.

His name was Muhammad Amin Al-Husseini and he formed part of the acknowledged Husseini clan. He was born in Jerusalem in 1895 or 1893 and peregrinated to Mecca in 1913, earning the honorary treatment of Hajj. Amin al-Husseini studied the Muslim religious law at Cairo University and later went to the Administration school in Istanbul.

During World War I, he was a soldier and an Imam, in charge of the spiritual necessities of the Ottoman army fighting against British forces. However, in 1917 he returned to Jerusalem and switched sides joining the British army when it was clear that they were victorious in the war.

Amin Al-Husseini was one of the instigators of the Jewish massacre in 1920. However, the British civil government, led by the weak Herbert Samuel, and advised by officers of the king who opposed the Jews, pardoned him in March 1921 and named him "Mufti of Jerusalem". In other words, he fought against the British in World War I and then encouraged the killings of Jews but the British pardoned him and named him a legitimate spokesperson. Madness!

Amin Al-Husseini's goal was to eradicate every Jew from Palestine. For that, he used ruthless religious rhetoric, arguments that were useful for funding to rebuild the Al-Aqsa Mosque (Jerusalem) in 1928, and of course, to instigate violence against the Jews.

73. Is it true that the Palestinian Mufti of Jerusalem, Hajj Amin Al-Husseini, was Hitler's ally?

When the British had enough of the Mufti (1936-1939), they went looking for him at the Temple Mount, but he had already fled to Iraq, dressed as a woman. In Iraq, he supported the pro-Nazi coup led by Rashid Ali Al-Gailani. When the coup failed, he fled again with an Italian passport to Mussolini's Rome

During World War II Al-Husseini was already settled in Belin, as an ally of the Third Reich. In 1941, after the successful invasion of Yugoslavia, Al-Husseini fostered the recruitment of Bosnian and Albanese Muslims for the SS Waffen, contributing to the formation of the SS Handschar 13th Waffen

Mountain Division. This division became famous because of the particularly atrocious massacres they committed against the Yugoslav partisans.

Al-Husseini was able to meet with Adolf Hitler (November 1941) and according to Professor Bernard Lewis, he tried to convince him to increase the extermination of Jews to the territories of France-Vichy and Fascist Italy, and also proposed that the Luftwaffe bombard Tel Aviv. Once the Nazis would conquer British Palestine, Amin Al-Husseini would build gas chambers in Emek Dotan to eliminate the remaining Jews from the British Mandate.

During those years, he founded the Nazi radio station Radio Zezzen, in Arabic and Persian, an important influence for the Nazi-style anti-Semitism of today's Islamists.

In 1944 he activated a special force of the SS-Waffen (Operation ATLAS), with German intelligence and the Mufti himself, and on the night of Nov/5/1944, he sent a paratrooper commando integrated by the Palestinians Hassan Salameh and Abdul Latif and three German Templars that knew Israel. Their mission was to poison the water reservoirs and murder 250,000 Jews in Tel Aviv. The plan was uncovered by an astute Arab policeman of the Jericho area.

74. What happened to the Mufti Al-Husseini after World War II and his Alliance to the Nazis?

Amin Al-Husseini has been considered by some Jewish historiography, at least from an ideological point of view, one of the "architects of the Holocaust". According to the writer Pamela Geller, during his time in Europe, he may have advocated for the Nazi regimen to proceed with the Jewish genocide to its fullest and he may have even asked the Nazi leaders to assassinate 400,000 Jews that the Germans wanted to deport to Palestine.

After World War II, he tried to flee to Switzerland but was rejected in the border and forced to return to France, where he was placed in house arrest for a year. Hajj Amin Al-Husseini mocked

Mufti Hajj Amin Al-Husseini
(Source: Wikipedia)

the French security in 1946 and arrived in Cairo, where he requested political asylum and took on the leadership of the recently formed Arab Higher Committee. The Zionist Movement requested the United Kingdom (in that time Egypt was a British protectorate) his extradition to judge him as a war criminal. Nevertheless, the British did not accept the request since Al-Husseini enjoyed great prestige in the Arab world. Yugoslavia, which suffered from the killings, also tried but the Arab League and the Egyptian government denied once more the extradition request.

Once in Egypt, Al-Husseini fought for the Arab countries to launch massive attacks against the recently created State of Israel in 1948 and he was tenaciously opposed to every armistice or negotiation. His popularity decreased in importance, making him move to Lebanon, where he died.

He died in Beirut in 1974. He was not allowed to be buried in Jerusalem, as was his wish, because of the denial of the Israeli government, which ruled in all of the city after its triumph in the Six-Day War of 1967.

The Palestinian terrorism continued and was a part of the Mufti Hajj Amin Al-Husseini family tree, who was great-uncle to... Yasser Arafat.

75. Why is it possible to affirm that the conflict exploded in 1929?

Some state that the Palestinian-Israeli conflict began after the war of 1967 because of Israel's conquest of the West Bank. During the Six-Day War, the Palestinians of Gaza (who were under Egyptian control) and those of the West Bank (under Jordan control) were left in the hands of an Israeli military government. For those who consider that "it's all about the occupation", the conflict began in 1967. But as has been stated in the previous pages, violent actions had registered almost 50 years before the Six-Day War, therefore the argument "it's all about the occupation" has little factual foundation.

Others affirm that the Palestinian-Israeli conflict began in 1948 with the creation of the State of Israel and the beginning of the problem of Palestinian refugees. A not very convincing argument if we consider that from 1920 to 1948 at least 808 Jews and 613 Arabs lost their lives to national-religious violence.

Some affirm that the unfortunate events of 1936 to 1939 triggered the conflict. It was an Arab revolt against the British although in the process Jews were murdered.

Historians that study the Palestinian-Israeli conflict discuss two probable dates as the beginning of the conflict: 1929/1921 or 1929. Those who affirm that the massacres of 1920/1921 are the starting point base their theories on the proof of violence and the fact that Palestinians were showing a national identity that was unknown until then. Those who state that the right date is 1929 show the clear Islamic religious arguments used to instigate the Arab-Palestinian violence (Mufti Al-Husseini affirmed that the Jews wanted to destroy the Al-Aqsa Mosque and that they had even set fire to it). The 1929 arguments are similar to the current ones.

76. What does it mean when the Palestinian narrative transforms the order of the facts?

If we pay attention, the way that the Palestinian spokespeople argue follows a repetitive pattern: **The consequence of their last aggression is the motive for the next one.**

Currently, when interviewing a Palestinian spokesperson, the most repeated argument is: "they live under the Israeli occupation" and, therefore, the conflict remains. When you ask them to give solutions to the Gaza Strip problem, where there are no Israeli military nor civilians, the previous argument is undermined. Sometimes, they blame everything on said occupation, including their endemic corruption.

What happened was that the Palestinian violence against the Jews began prior to 1967. For example, the PLO was founded in 1964 declaring their desire to forcefully destroy Israel. **In addition, the "occupation" would not have existed if Jordan, Egypt and Syria had not declared the 1967 war since the Israeli "conquest" was the consequence, not the cause.**

And, before 1967, how was violence against Jews justified? Well, if we had interviewed Palestinians in 1956, they would have argued that their violence was justified by "the problem of the Palestinian refugees". **But… if the Arabs had not declared war to destroy Israel in 1948, there would have never existed the refugees' problem. Once again, the consequence of the aggression was the motive for the future attempt.**

And, before 1948, how was violence against Jews justified? In many ways, but the most common was to affirm that the Jews stole the land of the Arabs. It was useless to prove to the Palestinian spokesperson that every piece of land where Jews lived had been purchased and, in fact, not stolen from the Arabs. Honest people do not "make up" the reasons and declare their wishes based on religious incentives.

77. What were the causes of the outburst of violence in 1936-1939?

A series of regional political events became the inspiration for the Arabs of Palestine to pressure the British by attacking them (1936-1939). In March 1936 there was a general strike in Syria, and although the French retaliation was hard on them, the government ceded and formed an Arab delegation that traveled to Paris to negotiate a French-Syrian independence agreement. This proved that the Arab economic and political pressure could end a fragile imperial administration. At the same time, on Mar/2/1936 the United Kingdom and Egypt agreed on the independence of Egypt. Allowing the British forces to remain in the Suez Canal area. **The Arabs in Palestine interpreted these events as a "weakness".**

During April of 1936, the Arab leaders of the British Mandate, led by Hajj Amin Al-Husseini (Great Mufti of Jerusalem), went on a general strike to protest against the Jewish immigration to Palestine. According to modern data from Israel, between 1933 and 1936, over 160,000 immigrants arrived legally and some more arrived secretly. According to Chaim Waxman, between 1931 and 1939, 225,000 people arrived. In 1931 the population of Palestine was 1,011,000 people, of which 174,000 were Jews (17%).

The Arabs were also protesting about the land purchase by the Jews because they feared they would become a minority in the territory, although it was precisely the Arabs that were selling the land. They demanded immediate elections, which based on their demographic majority, would have resulted in an Arab government that would have granted autonomy to the Jews, according to the Mufti's supporters. However, it would have avoided all Jewish immigration and would have made a retroactive review of all Jewish immigration since1918.

In 1936 the Arabs went on a general strike against the British. A month later, the leading group declared their refusal to pay taxes as an explicit opposition to Jewish immigration. The next step was violence…

78. What military actions did the Palestinian-Arabs perform between 1936 and 1939?

The Arab revolt against the British had two different phases: the first one was led by the urban and elite Superior Arab Committee and focused on two strikes and political protests. The second phase began by the end of 1937 and consisted of violent attacks against the British forces.

The military actions began sporadically and became more organized through time. A particular target was the TAP pipeline, which extended from Kirkuk to Haifa and was built a few years before. It was blown up in many points of its trajectory. There were also many attacks on the railways (including trains), Jewish settlements (like the Jewish massacre in Tiberias).

The violence began with a military attack on April/15/1936 against a convoy of trucks from Nablus to Tulkarm. The attack was carried out by followers of the deceased Al-Qassam, murdering two Jews: Israel Jazan and Tzvi Dannenberg.

Meanwhile, the British convened the Peel Commission to analyze the causes of the violence because during those months the violence reduced its savagery. After the rejection from the Arabs to Peel's proposal, violence started again during the autumn of 1937 and the British commissioner for Galilea (Lewis Yelland) was murdered in Nazareth. The violence continued throughout 1938 and started calming down in 1939.

According to official British data, the military and the police killed more than 2.000 Arabs in combat (1936-1939), while 108 were hanged and 961 died because of what they described to be "gangs and terrorist activities". In a British statistical analysis, Walid Khalidi estimated that there were 19.792 Arab victims with a total of 5.032 fatalities (3.832 were killed by the British and the other 1.200 died because of "terrorism"), and 14.760 wounded. These numbers are the result of the British-Arab conflict and not between Palestinian-Arabs and Jews.

79. What did the British do to repress the Arab violence against them?

During July 1936, Arab volunteers from Syria and Trans-Jordan led by Fawzi al-Kawukji, helped the Palestinian Arab rebels to divide their troops in four fronts, each one directed by a District Commander with an armed troop of 150-200 fighters. In a declaration by the Colonial Office in London (Sep/7/1939), the British declared: "This is a direct challenge to the authority of the British government in Palestine", and announced Lieutenant General John Dill as supreme military commander. By the end of September, 20,000 British soldiers were spread throughout Palestine to "defeat the Arab bands".

The main form of collective punishment used by the British to stop the Arab revolt of 1936-1939 was to destroy their goods. Some villages were reduced to rubble, such as Mi'ar in October 1938; many houses were blown and others destroyed inside. The largest act of destruction occurred in Jaffa on June/16/1936, when 220-240 buildings were destroyed leaving 6,000 Arabs without a home. **Brutal acts were carried out by the British during the la last part of the revolt, such as beatings, tortures and extra-judicial executions.**

One of the forms of repression of the Arab revolt of 1936-1939 was the construction of the Taggart forts, planned by Sir Charles Taggart, who also installed border fences and interrogation centers for the Arabs where prisoners were beaten and whipped on their feet, suffered electric discharges and what is now called "the submarine". **The Palestine Arab elite fled and later returned once the conflict with the British had ended. In 1948 they did exactly the same but this time they couldn't return, after the Israeli Independence War. The Arab revolt undermined the Palestinian combat spirit.**

80. How did the Jews react to the outrage of 1936-1939?

The Jews were worried because of the British measures that contradicted their Mandate again. The British government introduced measures to limit the transfer of lands from Arabs to Jews (1930s) even though they were easily circumvented by very willing buyers and salesmen. The Jewish settlement improved its quality and their Jewish union federations required Jewish labor (especially after the extreme massacre of 1929). In 1925 only 12.000 Arabs (5% of the population) worked for Jews, half of them in agriculture, while the other 32.000 worked for the Mandate authorities and the other 211.000 were independent or worked for Arab employers. The economic crisis favored the radicalization of the armed conflict.

Furthermore, it was discovered in October 1935 a shipment of weapons from Jaffa to the Jewish *Hagana* rising Arab fears. In parallel, the Jewish immigration also reached its highest point after Hitler's rise to power in Germany. Between 1933 and 1936 more than 164.000 Jewish immigrants arrived in Palestine, going from 175.000 to 370.00 people, the Jewish population rose from 17% to 27%.

In the summer of 1936, thousands of acres and crop fields cultivated by Jews were destroyed, civilians were attacked and murdered and, in some Jewish communities, like those on Beit-Shean and Acco, people fled to safer zones.

The attacks of 1936 to 1939 contributed to a major decoupling of the Jewish and Arab economies. The development of the economy and the Jewish infrastructure accelerated. Ben-Gurion had to affirm: "we could reward the Arabs for pushing us to our current creation". The Jews opened metallurgical companies to produce steel for armored vehicles and a company of rudimentary weaponry. Most of the important industries in Palestine were Jewish property and they were better positioned in commerce as in the banking sector than the Arabs.

81. What were the consequences for the Palestinian Arabs of the failure of their revolt?

The revolt resulted in a very important weakening of their recently-born leading class. Traditionally, Arabs had a tribal elite but not true leadership. Moreover, the disputes between the Nashashibi and the Husseini resulted in hundreds of deceased during the revolt of 1936-1939. As part of the attempts to reinforce Arab national ideas, they established a national anniversary date commemorating the Battle of the Horns of Hattin (Jul/4/1187, when the Ayyubid leader Saladin defeated the Crusaders to recover Jerusalem for the Muslim). The expansion of education, the development of civil society, transportation and especially radio broadcasting facilitated this "nationalism".

The insurgency was not successful, but it had a crucial influence on the War of Independence of Israel (1948) because it weakened the military capacity and the local Arab (Palestinian) incentive to go to war.

The Arab revolt also forced the main leader to exile, the Great Mufti of Jerusalem Hajj Amin Al-Husseini, who later aligned himself openly with Hitler.

The Arab violence against the British and Jews continued throughout 1938-1939. During the last fifteen months of the revolt, 936 people died and there were 351 murder attempts; 2,125 sniper incidents; 472 bombings; 364 cases of armed robbery; 1,453 cases of sabotage against the government and commercial spaces; 323 people kidnapped; 72 cases of intimidation; 236 Jews were murdered by Arabs and 435 Arabs were killed by Jews (mainly in self-defense).

According to the number of deaths during the Arab revolt of 1936-1939, 10% of the Arab Palestinian population, male and adult, ages 20-60, were killed, injured, imprisoned or exiled by the British.

82. Who was Izz Adin Al-Qassam?

During the 1930s, secret societies were formed in Palestine that promoted the armed conflict against the British and the Jews like the "Green Hand" group, which actively participated in the hills near Safe and was eliminated by the British in 1931. Another one was the Holy Fight Organization, led by Abed Al-Kader Al-Husseini, which operated in Hebron and would later play a more important role in the 1948 war and the Young Rebels, which acted in the Tulkarem and Kalkiyah zones in 1935.

In 1930, the sheikh Izz A-Din Al-Qassam (born in Syria) organized and established the "Black Hand" *(Al-Kaf Al-Asuad)*, an anti-Zionist and anti-British military organization. During his trips throughout the area, he gave extremist political and religious speeches, encouraging the farmers to form into gangs and attack the British government and the Jews. **After the Jewish massacre in Hebron in 1929, their activities increased and received a fatwa (permission) from the sheikh Badr al-Din al-Taji al-Hasani, Mufti of Damascus, allowing the attacks.** Al-Qassam recruited and organized the military training of farmers and by 1935 he had between 200 and 800 men who destroyed the trees planted by other farmers and the railways built by the British. In November 1935, two of his men murdered a police officer in a confrontation, which provoked the human hunt of Al-Qassam, who was shot and killed in a cave near Ya'bad. His grave is in the abandoned village of Balad As-Sheikh, the modern Israeli city of Nasher.

His influence is currently relevant. Hamas' rockets fired against Israeli civilians from Gaza are known as "Qassam" and the terrorist groups of Hamas are named after this Arab military leader Izz Adin Al-Qassam Battalion.

83. What was the Peel Commission?

Partition Plan by the Peel Commission, July 1937
(Source: un.org)

The Peel Commission (Royal Commission for Palestine, 1936) was an investigative commission led by Lord Peel to see about the causes of the unrest that began in 1936, three months after an Arab strike. On Nov/25/1936, Chaim Weizmann testified that there were 6,000,000 Jews for which "the world is divided into places where they cannot live and places where they cannot enter". Among the Palestinians, not only did the radical Mufti of Jerusalem declare, but also the ex-mayor of Jerusalem, Ragheb Bey Al-Nashashibi (who was a harsh rival of the Mufti among the Palestinians).

On July/7/1937, the Commission published a report and for the first time declared that the Mandate had become unviable, and recommended the partition of Palestine. After the publication, the Woodhead Commission was designated to design and recommend a real partition plan, which undermined the Jews compared to the one that was finally approved in 1947

As expected, the Jews accepted the partition proposal and the Arabs rejected once again any concession of territories to the Jews. They demanded that the British complied with their "promise" to create an Arab state. The Jews, led by Ben Gurion, accepted the partition idea, though not discarding that if there was a war conflict, their territorial possession could increase.

The Commission outlined 10 aspects: a mandatory treaty system between the Arab and Jewish states and the new government; a mandate of the holy sites; the borders; the need for inter-state subsidy; the need for British subsidy; the taxes and ports; the nationality; civil service; industrial concessions; and the exchange of lands and populations. It was the British, who in the midst of the Peel Commission, proposed the "transfer" of populations endorsed by some minor authors as a plan by the Jews.

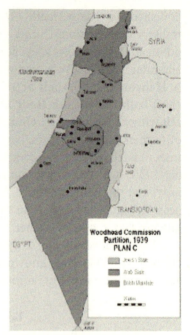

Proposal by the Woodhead Commission, 1939
(Source: ecf.org.il)

84. What is the McDonald White Paper of 1939?

As the inevitable war with Germany was approaching, the British politicians concluded that they needed Arab help, because the Jewish one "was secured". Prime Minister Neville Chamberlain said, "If one of the sides has to be offended, let it be the Jews instead of the Arabs". In order to "buy" calm among the Arabs, the British once again failed their international obligations.

After the ascent of Hitler and other anti-Semitic regimes in Europe, an increasing number of European Jews needed to flee towards the British Mandate of Palestine. The Nuremberg Laws of 1935 resulted in 500,000 stateless Jews.

The McDonald White Paper (1939), in reference to the Colonies Minister that fostered it, discarded the idea of dividing the Mandate into two states in favor of an independent Palestine governed jointly by Arabs and Jews, with Arabs keeping their demographic majority. The British would gradually associate Arabs and Jews to the government, so in ten years an independent state could be created.

Jewish immigration would be limited to a maximum of 75,000 people in the following five years, in order to maintain this minority in a third of the total population. **After the five years, no more Jewish immigration would be allowed unless the Arabs agreed to accept it.**

The purchase of new lands would be prohibited or restricted to the Jews, as a result of the natural growth of the Arab population (prohibited) and the maintenance of the level of life of the Arab farmers (restricted).

Now, let's ask ourselves: what would have happened if instead of closing the doors, the British would have allowed the European Jews to escape with their Jewish brothers in Palestine?

85. What was the reaction of Arabs and Jews to the McDonald White Paper of 1939?

The White Paper was received with great displeasure by the Jewish community of the British Mandate. Their spokespeople accused the British authorities of "betrayal" and "disloyalty", and to side with Nazi persecution by forbidding its victims to find refuge. The Yishuv (the Jewish community) went on a general strike and protests were held throughout the country. In defiance of the White Paper, the Jews established 12 new settlements in the Land of Israel during that May.

The Jews considered that the British were canceling the Balfour Declaration, although they denied it by affirming that a "national home" did not mean a Jewish State but an autonomy.

However, when World War II began (Sep/1/1939), the underground Jewish movements *Hagana* and Etzel (*Irgun*) decided to stop their sabotage operations against the British and focused on the Jewish settlement and illegal immigration to Israel. David Ben-Gurion, the main Zionist leader, affirmed: "We must help the British as if there were no White Paper, and fight the White Paper as if there were no war".

The Arab residents were opposed as well, demanding a total cease in the Jewish immigration, the cancellation of the Balfour Declaration and the San Remo Conference. The Mufti Amin Al-Husseini opposed because it did not provide them with a state of their own. This maximalist attitude (all-or-nothing) has characterized, since the 1920s, the Arab-Palestinian leadership.

In June 1939, the Mandate Committee of the League of Nations discussed the issue in Geneva and agreed that the policy of the White Paper

was incompatible with the interpretation of the Mandate of the League. The Committee recommended that the issue be discussed in the plenary of the League of Nations; the war began and the meeting was never held.

86. Did the Jews respect the boundaries of immigration stated in the White Papers of 1939?

The clear answer is: No. The Jewish operations to introduce illegal immigrants in Israel through land and sea (and since 1947 some were flown in) is known as *"Hapala" (or Aliya B)*.

Historians tend to divide the illegal immigration into three stages: the first one was between 1934-1939 when the Nazis came to power and other anti-Semitic parties, in parallel to the British limitation to extending immigration permits (certificates). Only between 1935 and 1937, 137.000 legal immigrants escaped from Hitler. However, another million people were waiting in Europe. At the same time, and in 50 boats, there were 21.000 Jews who were able to immigrate to Israel illegally. Around 12.000 were brought by the Revisionists Movement, 6.000 by the *Hagana and Hechalutz* and other 3.000 by various organizations.

The second period was between 1939 and 1945: Ben Gurion changed his position towards opposing illegal immigration and turned to support it after the Peel Commission (that is why the number of illegal immigrants brought by the *Hagana* during the first period was less than those from the Revisionists). A total of 27 ships arrived illegally to Palestine during World War II, bringing 17.000 Jews.

The third period, between 1945 and 1948: after the end of World War II, around 84.000 Jewish refugees entered Israel illegally. The British were able to stop most of the ships allowing some to stay regardless of the established permissions stated in the White Papers of 1939, while they deported another 52.000. At the same time, 250.000 Jews were in refugee camps or even in the concentration camps in Europe after suffering the Shoa.

Illegal immigration cost many lives. Around 2.000 immigrants were found dead after their ships sank or during their capture by the British Armada. During the three waves of illegal immigration, 115.000-132.000 Jews arrived in Palestine.

87. What was the Exodus ship?

The most famous illegal immigration operation was Exodus. In 1946, the members of the *Mossad Le-Aliya Bet* (Institution for Immigration B) of the United States purchased a cruise ship called President Warfield, renewed it and took it to Italy.

The Italians delayed the ship pressured by the British, and the ship was moved to the port of Sete (France), where it received its name, "Exodus from Europe 1947". The ship was loaded with 4,554 illegal immigrants, but the French authorities forbid its departure. Nevertheless, the ship sailed on July/11/1947, escorted by British destroyers.

When it was about to reach Israel, and after ignoring British orders, the ship was assaulted by British soldiers that escaped the tin cans thrown by the immigrants. The soldiers began to fire, killing an officer of the ship and two Jewish immigrants.

Because of the damage suffered by the ship, the Exodus was taken to the port of Haifa, and 4,552 Jews were deported in three ships that returned them back to France "to teach them a lesson" (instead of taking them to Cyprus). When they arrived at Port de Bouc in France, they refused to leave the ship and began a hunger strike. The British then decided to take them by force to Hamburg, in Germany, and leave the immigrants there.

The case of the Exodus was a difficult blow for the British prestige. About 200 journalists covered the issue, and after harsh criticism, the British stopped returning ships with immigrants.

Members of the investigating commission of the UN (UNSCOP) were present in the port of Haifa and witnessed how the immigrants were forced out of the ship and returned to Europe. The Exodus influenced the decision of the partition of Palestine (November 1947).

88.   What did the British do to stop Jewish illegal immigrants?

The British did not reduce their efforts in their fight against illegal immigration. In the military field, the British had one of the best intelligence services of the continent. That way, they were able to map almost every activity from the Aliya B organizers, locating their exit ports, transport routes for refugees and their mediums to buy supplies and gas.

As a result of the good intelligence they had, the British extended a patrol to Palestine, which intercepted the ships. These forces included patrol speedboats relatively light that moved throughout the Mediterranean Sea, airplanes of recognition and destroyers which operated in the border of the territorial waters of Palestine. They chased the ships, ramming them and blocking their way to the coast. Additionally, the British used radars to pick up the ships' movements (the most recognized headquarters was the Stella Maris in Haifa, where the base of the Navy was stationed in Palestine).

The British military forces also acted to avoid the dispersion of the immigrants among the civilian population. **When a boat was stuck, the British army would translate the immigrants to detention centers in Cyprus.**

In the political sphere, the British attempted to execute their diplomatic power over the governments in the countries the immigrants came from, exerting pressure to stop the boats. The Italian and French governments turned a blind eye to the illegal immigration deliberately, to sympathize with the suffering of the Jews after the Holocaust.

The British also attempted to impose a commercial embargo for shipping companies that took illegal immigrants. In this area, their success was partial as well. It is true that the big shipping companies did not help illegal immigration, but there were always some sailors that accepted to cooperate.

89.   Is it true that the Jews from British Palestine collaborated with the Nazis?

One of the most immoral arguments is to accuse Jews of collaborating with the same people that assassinated them in the gas chambers. However, was there some tacit agreement with Nazi Germany at the beginning of their government? Yes. We refer to the Transfer Agreement signed by the Jewish Agency and the Nazi authorities on Aug/25/1933. The German objective was to allow the Jews to sell their properties and goods located within German territory, before confiscating them, and to transfer their funds to Israel to help the legal immigration of Jews to Mandate Palestine.

This agreement resulted from a series of interests. The Nazis were interested in freeing themselves of the Jews (the decision of murdering them was adopted later on). The Nazi policy was to be free of its Jews *(Judenrein)* by purchasing their goods at low prices and besides, to stop the boycott organized by the American Jews against German exports. The Jewish Agency, on the other hand, wanted to increase the number of well-prepared and economically able Jews; the British expected them to increase their investment in the Mandate. If a Jew provided 1,000 pounds, he could receive an immigration certificate without discounting the amount set by the British for the Jews.

A German Jew who wished to emigrate to Palestine had to deposit his funds in German marks in one of the local financial institutions, inspected by the Jewish Agency; these funds allowed Jews to purchase German goods and machinery, the funds were transferred to the British Mandate and the owner would receive approximately two-thirds of the value deposited, receiving a British immigration visa.

With time, the agreement extended to other counties conquered by the Nazis such as Czechoslovakia and Hungary, as well as a similar agreement for Polish Jews.

90. What was the Jews' reaction to the Transfer Agreement of 1933?

The Transfer Agreement provoked harsh controversies amongst the Jews of the Yishuv (Jewish Community in Israel) and amongst those of the diaspora, because of the obligation to contact with the Nazis, an action that was interpreted as a cooperation with the oppressor. Others argued that the agreement breached the boycott organized against German products in many communities, emphasizing the U.S.

The main resistance was concentrated in some circles to the Revisionist Party (mainly represented by Abba Ajimeir). To moderate the critics, the mediator of the Sam Cohen agreement acquired part of the property of the Revisionist journal, influencing the contents.

On June/16/1933, the "Popular Front" published an article that accused those involved in a pact that "they sold themselves to Hitler because of greediness and richness", adding that the Jews "would know how to answer to those villains". The journal mentioned those involved, including Chaim Arlosoroff (Chief of the Political Department of the Jewish Agency and one of the negotiators). In the afternoon of that same day, Arlosoroff was murdered while walking with his wife on the beach of Tel Aviv. During the summer of that year, throughout the electoral campaign for the XVIII Zionist Congress, Zeev Jabotinsky (Revisionist leader) declared that "such agreement was despicable, shameful and horrible".

As a result of the controversy, the 19th Zionist Congress decided in 1935: "To promote the continuous German Jews' immigration into Palestine, the Congress requires that the Executive takes all the transference actions under his supervision". The Revisionist press attacked the Zionist Organization and the Jewish Agency as "Hitler's allies… who stepped on the Jewish honor with their bare feet".

A similar discussion happened in the 1950s when the reparations agreement was signed with Germany.

91. Is it true that Mahmoud Abbas, President of the Palestinian Authority (2019) denied the Holocaust and accused the Jews of collaborating with the Nazis?

"The Connection between the Nazis and the Leaders of the Zionist Movement 1933-1945" is the title of the doctoral thesis by Mahmoud Abbas, completed in 1982 for the Peoples Friendship University of Russia. In 1984 published his book in Arabic titled "The Other Side: the secret relationship between Nazism and Zionism"

The content of the thesis denies or relativizes the Holocaust, by affirming (with no shame) that the Zionist agitation was the cause of the Holocaust. In his 1984 book, Abbas rejected as a "myth" and a "fantastic lie" that six million Jews died in the Holocaust while stating that the real amount of Jews murdered by the Germans was "890,000" at the most or a "few hundred thousand". The number was exaggerated for political purposes, because "it seems to be the interest of the Zionist movement--- that led them to increase the amount [six million] to gain the solidarity of the international public opinion with Zionism".

In an interview in March of 2006 with the Israeli newspaper Haaretz, Abbas declared: "I cited a discussion between historians where several number of victims were mentioned... The Holocaust was a terrible thing and no one can affirm that I denied it".

In 2012, Abbas told Al Mayadeen, a television station of Beirut linked to Iran and Hezbollah, that he "defied anyone that can deny that the Zionist movement had links with Nazism before World War II". In 2013 he reaffirmed that "the Zionist movement had links to the Nazis". **On both occasions, he was referring to the Transfer Agreement.**

During a meeting of the Palestinian National Council in 2018, Mahmoud Abbas declared that Jews in Europe were massacred for centuries because of their "social role related to usury and banking".

92. What did the Jews do to become the majority in the Palestinian territory after being a minority?

A person inspired by the materialist dogma will say that "they became the majority because of the imperialist support". It began with the support from Great Britain to the Jewish aspirations referenced in the San Remo Conference and ended with the British ignoring their legal obligations (established in the Peel Commission of 1939). **The Jews became a majority despite the strict limitations set by the British.**

For the British, the Jews were unconditional against the Nazis and needed the support of the "conditional" Arabs. The British did not consider the Arabs as their enemies and the relationship between British, Arabs and Jews was not consistent during the Mandate.

If before Zionism there was a small community in Israel, mainly orthodox, the ideological strength and the increase in anti-Semitism in Europe promoted the five waves of immigration. The first one (1881-1903) brought orthodox families that created the first communities with the support of the philanthropist Baron Edmund de Rothschild. The second wave (1903-1914) created and developed cities with a small nucleus very idealist and socialist, which became the political leadership of Zionism from the mid-1920s. The third wave (1917-1924) was fundamental for the establishment of cooperative agricultural farms *(Kibbutzim or Moshavim)* and it happened after the Mandate. The fourth wave (1924-1928) was caused because of the anti-Semitic measurements and the crisis in Poland. The fifth wave (since 1933) came after Hitler's rise to power. The Jewish people in Israel increased from 20.000 souls in 1900 to more than 600.000 in 1948.

After the 1948 war, the Jews became the absolute majority in the recently created State of Israel because most of the Arabs remained outside their borders in a territory that represented a small part of Palestine from the British Mandate.

93. Is it true that Jews had a "solid military structure" for the War of Independence of 1948?

Such an affirmation is quite far from the truth, although, compared to the disputes between the Nashashibi and Husseini clans or the lack of Arab-Palestinian cohesion, the Jewish situation was very superior.

The military structure of the *Hagana* (Defense) developed at the rhythm of Arab violence, and not before. The semi-official *Hagana* was founded in 1920, after the pogrom of Jerusalem. Until 1929 it was a small and irrelevant organization, and it began to strengthen from the underground with the Arab revolt (1936) when it began to form combat groups and not just wardens. In its moment of major boom, it was a force of about 50,000 men and women, most of them without permanent mobilization.

The *Hagana* formed an elite unit, the *Palmach* (*Plugot Machatz* – "attack groups") created on May/5/1941. Originally, they were formed with help from the British to fight against a possible Nazi invasion to the Mandate. After the danger passed, it continued activating in spite of the British. In 1948 they had three combat brigades: aerial, naval and intelligence. From the Palmach, several leaders stood out, such as Moshe Dayan, Yigal Alon and Itzak Rabin. Being a Palmachnik was considered as a way of life.

The policy of the Jewish leadership was defensive (*Havlaga*). After 1929 a group decided to practice a policy considered as more dissuasive towards the Arab-Palestinian terrorists. It was the *Irgun Tzvai Leumi* (*Irgun*) or Etzel (National Military Organization), which rejected ideologically the use of terrorism. The Irgun had about 5,000 soldiers.

When in January of 1940 the *Irgun* decided to enroll with the British against the Nazis, a small group led by Abraham Stern separated and formed Lehi (Lohamei Herut Israel - Fighters for the Freedom of Israel), that believed that armed fight was the only way of attaining national independence. They were 500 soldiers.

94. Is it true that the Jewish clandestine forces cooperated normally to foster common objectives?

The relationship between the pre-state Jewish clandestine groups was complex. The ideological divisions were deep, especially between socialist-officialist *Hagana-Palmach* and the nationalist-Revisionists from *Irgun*. These last ones qualified the first ones as soft and the nationalists were called irresponsible fascists by the first ones.

After World War II, there was a brief period of cooperation to fight against the English in the frame of the Hebrew Rebellion Movement (*Tnuat Ha-Meri Ha-Ivri*), between 1945 and 1946. The leaders of the new movement included four representatives: two of the *Hagana* (Sneh and Galili), one of the *Irgun* (Menachem Begin) and one from the *Lehi* (Nathan Yellin-Mor).

During the Hebrew Rebellion Movement, big military operations were executed, emphasizing one that liberated 200 illegal immigrants from the detention camp in Atlit, sabotages on the railway and train stations during the Night of Trains, attacks against British Police stations, the destruction of eleven bridges during the Night of Bridges and the attempt in the King David Hotel in Jerusalem. In August 1946, because of Black Saturday (Operation Agatha

June/29/1946—the British imposed a blockade against Jewish cities and obtained documents that showed the involvement of the leader of the Jewish Agency with activities of the Hagana) and after the attempt in the King David Hotel, the coalition was dismantled and each one of the groups continued working independently.

This brief period of cooperation lived even when the official leadership turned in fighters of the *Irgun* and *Lehi* to the British. Between December 1944 and February 1945 (after the murder of Lord Moyne, British Minister for the Middle East, by two soldiers of the *Lehi*, Eliahu Hakim y Eliahu Beit-Tzuri), the Jewish official authorities decided to help the British to stop the dissenting forces (known as Saison – Hunting Season).

95. How institutionalized were the Jews near the War of Independence of 1948?

From its foundation, the Zionist movement understood that no one would grant them a Jewish state in a "silver plate". If the goal was to recruit immigrants, it was mandatory to purchase lands, develop institutions and the economy. During the British Mandate, a state was constructed within the mandate; this period was called "The State Underway" (*Ha-Medina She-Baderech*) In fact, the Jews developed several autonomous states at the same time before creating the State of Israel officially (1948)

Each Jewish ideological group developed services for their followers. If a person was a socialist, he deposited his money in the *Bank Hapoalim* (Bank of the Workers); if he was a member of the Hapoel team of his city, received medical attention from the Histadrut Ha-*Ovdim* of *Eretz Israel* (Workers Organization of Israel, founded in Haifa in 1920), and if he wished to participate in a military force he would enroll in the *Hagana*, the underground organization of the Jewish socialist movement.

On the other hand, if a person belonged to the Revisionist movement, he would deposit his savings in the Bank Leumi (National Bank), rooted for the Beitar of his city, received medical attention from the *Kupat Holim Leumi* (National Medical Service) and could enroll in the underground movement *Irgun Tzvai Leumi* (National Military Organization)

A person identified with liberal ideas opted to root for the Maccabean teams, deposited his savings in the bank Discount and received medical attention from *Kupat Holim Maccabi* (Maccabi Medical Service).

When the Independence was declared, Israel's Prime Minister, David

Ben-Gurion, declared that is was essential to change Kitatiut Le-Malajtiut (pass from sectarianism to officialism) forming national institutions such as one army (*Tzahal*)

The main feature of the "State Underway" period was construction. During the partition of Palestine, these constructions helped to recognize a Jewish state coexisting with an Arab state. At least, a Jewish State existed... *de facto*.

96. What was the institutional level of the Palestinians regarding the Independence War of 1948?

The Arab-Palestinian society was semi-feudal and had an organization that was more fundamental than the European-Jewish, based on clans that made enemies of each other (the dispute between the Nashashibi, the Hussein and others provoked a total of 10.000 deaths up to 1949).

The Arab narrative tends to affirm that they were not interested in improving the "Palestinian" living conditions but to obtain political and civil freedom to materialize their national rights. **It was not in vain when in the Partition of Palestine (1947) the Arabs could not translate into "facts" their rights given by the United Nations.**

The Jewish population increased to 470.000 people between both World Wars and the non-Jewish increased to 588.000 souls. In fact, the Arab population permanently increased by 120% between 1922 and 1947. The number of Arabs increased thanks to the improvement of the developed conditions by the Jews and the British. That way, the Muslim child mortality decreased from 201/1000 (1925) to 94/1000 (1945), life expectancy increased from 37 years (1926) to 49 (1943). From 1922 to 1947, the non-Jewish population increased by 131% in Jerusalem and 158% in Jaffa. The growth in the Arab towns was more modest: 42% in Nablus and 37% in Bethlehem.

The most important institution created by the Arab-Palestinians was the "Arab Higher Committee", the political organ of the community before the British Mandate, proclaimed as the "only representative of all the Arabs from Palestine". It was created in April/25/1936 by the initiative of Hajj Amin Al-Husseini, even though it was forbidden by the British authorities in September 1937 during the revolt against them. The Arab League reconstituted the Committee on November/10/1945 but had little relevance since the Arab-Israeli War of 1948, in which their helplessness was demonstrated. It was forbidden in Jordan (1948) and ignored by Egypt and the Arab League.

97. Is it possible to compare Arab-Palestinian and Jewish terrorism before 1948?

When dealing with the "terrorism" phenomenon, there are many non-sustained comparisons, similar to a coffee shop conversation. If the phenomenon is not defined, the analyses lack any sense. There is no simple definition of terrorism. However, for western academics, terrorism is: **"The use or threat of violence against civilians (non-combatting) to attain political objectives, with intention and within the framework of a propagandistic strategy"**.

In the previous sections, we described the intentional killings of 1920-1921 and 1936-1939. **In all these cases we described the intentional assassination of civilians to eradicate Jewish immigration and to impede the purchase of lands by Jews (both political objectives).** Instigation and the intentional assassination of Jewish civilians was the modus operandi of Arab-Palestinians.

Among the Jews, only one underground group could possibly be qualified as a terrorist, although most of their actions were not terrorist: *Lehi*, with its 500 soldiers.

Abraham Stern defined the objectives and combat methods of Lehi in a document called "Redemption" (*Ha-Tchia*). He said: "The land is the absolute possession of the people of Israel. The land must be conquered by force and not purchased with money, or obtained by political ways or favors of rulers or super-powers." "The Arabs of the land are foreign, their problem must be solved with a population exchange, but the main enemy is the British occupation regime". The murders of Lord Moyne or of Count Folke Bernadotte are two examples of intentional murders of civilians. Most of the actions by *Lehi* were guerrilla-style **(assassination of military to achieve political objectives)**.

Arab-Palestinian dominant behavior has been intentional murder; among the Jews, these were sporadic actions, not promoted or related to the official community leadership.

98. What happened at the King David Hotel in 1946?

To demonize Israel or relativize the Palestinian terrorism, it is usually argued that "the Jewish also committed terrorism" like in the King David Hotel (July/22/1946). The attempt in the King David Hotel, headquarters to the Military Command of the British Mandate of Palestine and to the Criminal Investigation of the Division of the British, was committed by the *Irgun Tzvai Leumi* (Etzel). The operation was against a military compound working at a hotel, transforming it into a military target 100% legal. **From the technical point of view, the operation should be qualified as a guerrilla" attack because it was a military target.**

In the south wing of the hotel, there were stolen documents by the British that incriminated the Jewish Agency (Operation Agatha). To blow it up, a man from the *Irgun*-Etzel entered the hotel dressed up with an employer's tunic, placing explosives in bottles of milk in the basement. A member of the *Irgun* (Gideon) yelled to the crowd: "Get out, the hotel is about to blow up". An operator called a warning to evacuate the entire building to avoid civil victims. The same person called the office of the Jerusalem Post and one last warning to the French Consulate nearby that was evacuated.

The British authorities of the Military Command ignored the warnings by answering: "We are not here to receive orders from Jews. We are the ones who give orders around here". The attack caused the death of 92 people, 16 of them were Jews. The south wing of the Kid David Hotel was destroyed.

The *Irgun* was accused of terrorism by the British and by the official Zionist leadership that had approved the attack. Even though the results provoked the death of innocent civilians it does not mean that it was a terrorist action since there is no intention nor was it the modus operandi accepted by the *Irgun*.

99. Why did the United Nations decide the partition of Palestine in 1947?

After World War II, the British economy was in a shaky state and could not afford to continue keeping 100,000 soldiers in Palestine. Besides, the simple idea of "colonialism" had lost prestige in the world. Forced instead of willing, the British decided to return the Mandate they had received from the League of Nations to its successor, the United Nations.

Moreover, the action of the underground Jewish movements (such as the attack on the Acco jail or the execution of the officers in Netanya) shook and humiliated Great Britain and reflected on the headlines of their newspapers. The British reaction towards the Exodus is another example of the British legitimacy crisis in the world public opinion.

In his book "100 Questions and Answers about the Palestinian-Israeli Conflict" journalist Pedro Brieger affirms: *"This fostered the Jewish revolt against the British, now with the support of the United States, one of the emerging powers together with the Soviet Union"*. Certainly, the U.S. government did not support the Jewish revolt against the British. This information is not correct. The support of the U.S. to Zionist activities consisted in tolerating Jewish leaders such as Golda Meir to carry out fund-raising campaigns among the U.S. resident Jewish communities.

The cause of the British leaving of Palestine can be summarized as follows: 1) They were economically bankrupt after World War II; 2) When the genocide of the Jews in the Shoa became known, there was an increase of sympathy towards the lack of a national Jewish home; 3) The loss of the prestige of "colonialism". However, the British did not want to withdraw; they were convinced that the Jews would be subject to death in the hands of the Arabs and would ask for the aid of the British.

PART THREE
- FLUCTUATING MODERNITY -

100. What was the UNSCOP and what did it decide?

The United Nations Special Committee on Palestine (UNSCOP) was created on May/15/1947 in response to the British government's request for the General Assembly of the recently created UN to "formulate recommendations by virtue of Article 10 of the Charter over the future government of Palestine". It was decided that the Committee should be formed by "neutral" countries, excluding the five permanent members of the Security Council.

The UNSCOP was formed by representatives of 11 nations (representatives from Peru, Guatemala and Uruguay among them). UNSCOP visited Palestine-Israel and gathered testimonies of Zionist organizations in Palestine and the U.S.

The Arab Higher Committee boycotted the Commission, explaining that the natural rights of the Arab-Palestinians were evident and could not continue being the objective if the investigations. Once again, the Arab-Palestinians acted according to the destructive premise of "all or nothing".

The report from the Committee from September/3/1947 recommended the end of the British Mandate in Palestine. It had a majority proposal for a Partition Plan in the two independent states with an Economic Union (CHAPTER VI) and a minority proposal for a federal union plan with Jerusalem as its capital (CHAPTER VII).

Most of the countries from the Commission (Canada, Czechoslovakia, Guatemala, Netherlands, Peru, Sweden and Uruguay) recommended the Partition into two separate states. This is the majority proposal. There was one abstention and three votes against, ironically tragic. Yugoslavia voted for a state formed by the two nationalities (only 36 years later Yugoslavia disappeared because of their impossible union). India and Iran also voted against.

The Zionist part accepted the Partition Plan, while the Arab part rejected both proposals. The proposal by the UNSCOP was taken to a vote in the General Assembly of the UN (voted on November 29th, 1947).

101. What did the General Assembly of the UN decide on November 29th, 1947?

The General Assembly of the United Nations gathered in New York and under the Brazilian Secretary General Osvaldo Aranha, approved Declaration 181, which recommended dividing the western part of the British Mandate into two states, a Jewish one and an Arab one (the term

Palestinian was not used). There would be an area under international control that included Jerusalem and Bethlehem. Both states had to contribute economically.

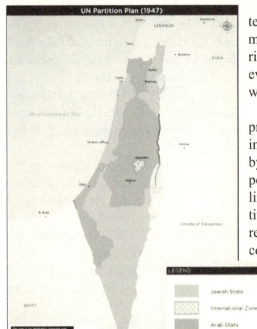

UN Palestine Partition Plan (1947)
(Source: Israel Ministry of Foreign Affairs)

The UN wanted to ensure a territory for the Jews to absorb a million refugees that were to arrive after the creation of Israel, even though 45% of the country was a desert (Negev).

Declaration 181 (based on the proposal by UNSCOP) was voted in favor by 33 countries, against by 13 and 10 abstained, and proposed some adjustments to the limits between the states. The partition would be in effect upon the retreat of the British, who did not contribute to the execution of the decision. The US and Russia were among those who voted in favor of the resolution.

In 1947, the United Nations had 57 member states (today 193). At present, it is impossible to think that a similar decision could have been adopted by such a shamelessly anti-Israel body.

Most of the Jewish inhabitants celebrated the plan although they criticized the lack of territorial continuity because the territory would be divided into three separate zones that made it not very viable (and hard to defend). David Ben-Gurion considered that if they were attacked the Jews could increase the borders.

The Arab leaders opposed the plan, arguing that it violated the rights of the Arab population, which was 67% of the total population at the time (1,237,000 inhabitants). The Arab League approved another resolution that rejected the UN's, threatening with armed intervention.

102. How did the Latin American countries vote on this Partition Plan?

The countries that stand out among the 33 (58%) that approved the Declaration 181 are Bolivia, Brazil, Dominican Republic, Ecuador, Guatemala, Haiti, Nicaragua, Panama, Paraguay, Peru, Uruguay and Venezuela. The one that stands out among the 13 countries (23%) that voted against it is Cuba. There were 10 countries (18%) that abstained. Among them are Argentina, Colombia, Chile, El Salvador, Honduras and Mexico.

The Latin American block represented 20 of the 57 states and, without their massive support, the Zionists did not have a real chance. Moshe Tov, chief of the Jewish Agency for South America, discussed after the State's establishment that the Brazilian chancellor had told him: "The General Assembly decided on the Partition because of the pressure exerted by the president of the United States".

Countries like Chile abstained because of the pressure exerted by the Palestinian community. Votes from some countries could be fundamentally explained by testimonies and bribery suspicions in diverse delegations. In a report sent by Lawlin Tomfson, director of Eastern Europe in the State Department, to Levi Handerson, he stated: "Mister Ballet said that a representative from South America changed his position from opposing to supporting the partition in exchange for 75 thousand dollars in cash. Another representative of Central America rejected the offer of 40 thousand dollars even though his government ordered him to support the partition. Mr. Ballet believes that a minister from that state bribed them from their own pocket".

Three Latin American characters were fundamental for the approval of the Partition: first, the President of the General Assembly, Osvaldo Aranha, who proposed the crucial vote because of Thanksgiving Day, allowing Zionists to reach the necessary votes. Previously, the representatives of Guatemala (Jorge Garcia Granados) and of Uruguay (Enrique Rodriguez Fabregat) from UNSCOP, were fundamental for drafting the Partition Plan.

103. What is the legal value of Declaration 181 of the United Nations General Assembly?

The final status of the British Mandate on Palestine was approved in 1922, and included section 25 that separated Trans-Jordan from the Mandate, therefore modifying the borders set in San Remo (1920). This decision was approved by the League of Nations, and even though it contradicted the Balfour Declaration, it was a legal action.

In 1936, the League of Nations adopted the Montevideo Convention (1933), according to which "recognition of a state is unconditional and irrevocable" (Article 6). When the British approved the White Paper (1939) they violated the laws of the League of Nations and the Montevideo Convention. **The League disregarded the legality of this White Paper.**

In 1945, the UN approved Article 80 (Chapter 12); Recognizing the rights granted to the different peoples recognized and, as a result, all decisions of the period 1920-1946 were in force. **Under these terms, the borders from the Jordan River to the sea and the national rights of the Jews to the Land of Israel were recognized by the UN.**

If the Arabs would have accepted the partition proposal (Declaration 181), reaching an agreement with the Jews, there could have been a new international rule of law. **In other words, if the Arabs would have accepted Declaration 181 (1947) it could have been legally binding.**

We must remember jurist Prof Steven Schwebel, ex-legal advisor of the State Department and president of the International Court of Justice of The Hague, stated: "The General Assembly of the United Nations can only, in principle, produce proposals with no legal effect, based on Article 10 of the Charter of the United Nations".

The legal status of Israel is not based on Declaration 181, which was only that, a "declaration".

103. If Declaration 181 lacks legal strength, why did the UN accept the State of Israel as a member in 1949?

The United Nations recognized the historical right of the Jews to Israel according to Article 80 (Chapter 12) that confirmed the continuity of the guidelines of the League of Nations (1920). **According to the article, the UN did not recognize "out of the blue" the right of Israel to exist, but ratified and validated a previous right recognized by the League of Nations.**

An advisory opinion from the International Court of Justice from June/21/1971 explained: "the last decision from the Assembly of the League of Nations and Article 80, Paragraph 1 of the UN Charter preserved the obligations of the Mandates". The International Court of Justice has always recognized that the Mandate survived the disappearance of the League of Nations.

When in 1949 Israel requested to be accepted as a member of the United Nations, this organization did not establish that the Jews "had rights" since that was already established in Article 80 (Chapter 12).

The process to be accepted as a member of the UN involves the candidate being a state that follows the premises of the Montevideo Convention (established borders, determined population, effective government and the capacity to establish international relations). Such guidelines are verified by the Security Council and later the UN General Assembly validates the acceptance with 2/3 of the votes.

On May/5/1949, the State of Israel became member number 59 of the United Nations, with 37 countries voting in favor of its inclusion, 13 against and 9 abstentions. The country that proposed with more vehemence the acceptance of Israel was the Soviet Union because at the time it expected that the socialist State of Israel would become part of its block.

105. How did the Arabs respond to the Palestine Partition Plan?

Argentinean journalist Pedro Brieger explains; "The Arab population of Palestine utterly opposed the partition, logically. They considered that their territory was being seized from them, that the United Nations had no authority to sentence the division and they had not even been consulted". Let's analyze this flawed statement. First, the argument about the UN seems strange, as it was the same western powers that created Iraq, Syria, Jordan, Lebanon or Saudi Arabia. **It is not logical to accept as "legitimate" artificial states created in the region by the powers, but at the same time, believing that it is "illegitimate" when it decides the future of a territory inhabited by Jews as well.** This double standard is unacceptable.

The second flaw is to affirm that "they had not been consulted". The Arabs refused to work with the investigation commission of UNSCOP. The Arab position impeded taking advantage of the opportunities set forth by the different negotiation processes, prioritizing the expulsion of the Jews and the interests of the new neighboring Arab states in the area. Why? Because the Arab-Palestinian identity was quite weak at the time.

Describing as "logical" without mentioning the most important reason impoverishes a serious analysis of the topic. The Arabs did not accept the partition because they thought they would defeat the Jews militarily. This was clearly explained by the Secretary of the Arab League, Azzam Pasha, to the negotiators of the Jewish Agency (Sep/16/1947): "The Arab world is not willing to reach an agreement... Nations never concede, they fight. You will never attain anything with pacific means or agreements. You may achieve something, but just by the force of arms. We will try to defeat you. I am not sure we will succeed, but we will try... But it is too late for pacific solutions".

106. How did the Jews respond to the Partition Plan of Palestine?

The Zionist movement was pragmatic and saw the opportunity in the Partition to found the Jewish state and open it to immigration, independently from the powers. If they were attacked, the Jews would defend themselves and would establish final borders after this confrontation. One of the principles of the Zionist pioneers like Theodore Hertzl: to create a refuge for all the persecuted Jews in the world. Pragmatically, David Ben-Gurion and the Jewish leadership of Israel accepted the Partition (181) ignoring the criticism from two ideological groups relatively small: the nationalist-Revisionists who aspired to create a Jewish state throughout the Palestinian territory received by the British in 1920; and the left-wing group who aspired to have a binational state together with the Arabs.

According to Palestine's Partition Plan, there would be 538.000 Jews and 397.000 Arabs within the Jewish state (even though there were more than half a million Jewish refugees that were waiting to enter the State of Israel). After dividing the territory, the UN took into consideration that the Jewish population would be of 1.300.000 souls after creating Israel. Approximately, 92.000 Arabs lived in Tiberias, Safed, Haifa and Beit-Shean and another 40.000 were Bedouins who inhabited the desert. The Arab State would have around 804.000 Arabs and 10.000 Jews. Jerusalem would remain as an international zone, isolating another 100.000 Jews from said city.

The fact that there is an Arab minority within Israel does not contradict the Zionist Project, which never defended the idea of an "ethnically pure" Jewish State. Some authors affirm that Zionism pretended to have said results but the accusation lacks factual evidence and only pretends to demonize the national Jewish ideal.

The plan was terrible and very defective for the Jews but they accepted it while the Arabs rejected it and began the war.

107. Was the partition of Palestine fair – Declaration 181?

There are three fundamental factors for the division of the land and not only that a general survey showed an Arab majority. The first, the land purchased by the Jews would be part of Israel; Arab private property would remain Arab. The second, the Jewish state would have to allow the absorption of nearly one million Jewish refugees arriving after the Holocaust. The third factor is related to the principle that the areas in which the Arabs were majority would remain under Arab control and the areas with Jewish majority under Jewish control. Jerusalem, with a Jewish majority since the end of the XIX Century, and Bethlehem, were left under international administration.

After the partition, the Jewish communities living in Arab countries were threatened and attacked, making almost a million people flee, most of them to Israel.

According to the Partition plan (1947), the Jews received a territory that was mostly the Negev desert, after showing an incredible capacity to develop agriculture in impossible conditions.

Let's analyze cold numbers: the original British Mandate included 120,000 km2, severed 76.5% of Palestine for the creation of a first Arab state called the Arab Emirate of Transjordan (Jordan). In 1947, the Jews received 55% of the 23.5% of the remaining land where they were the majority and possessed lands.

The partition of Palestine is a clear manifestation of the implementation of the principles of President W. Wilson and other progressive people. Moreover, in terms of potential farmlands, the distribution was unfair for the Jews. Apart from what they had already purchased, they were assigned 25% of farmlands. The rest, for the Arabs. The Jews only received good lands if they purchased them.

108. Up to what point was the creation of Israel a compensation for the suffering in the Holocaust?

The effectiveness of the independence of the State of Israel is a consequence of the accomplishment of the Montevideo propositions. In 1947-1948 the Jewish people from Israel dominated the territory of British Palestine; there was a specific Jewish population, the Jewish civilians respected their elected authorities (the Jewish Agency and the World Zionist Organization) who had the capacity to develop international relations. **Since the first immigration** wave (1881-1882) the Zionist ideal was constructive and the recognition/appreciation would come afterward.

If we were to compare said situation to the current Palestine, with Gaza dominated by Hamas and the territories A and B from the West Bank partially dominated by the Palestinian Authority, the "effectiveness" of the Palestinian State is debatable.

It's true, the genocide of six million Jews deeply affected the western world. Not only because some western countries executed the massacre but because many others were active or passive allies or allowed anti-Semitism to spread through its citizens. While the Nazi genocide was taking place, many countries limited access to Jews and even rejected ships with Jews in need of refuge. Vivianne Forrester, author of the book Western Crime, affirms that the European countries left the Jews "trapped in Hitler's mousetrap" and later, after the war, "keep them in fields for displaced people".

In Palestine, the British authorities restricted to a minimum the immigration quotas to avoid conflicts with the Arab population—whose leadership had sided with the Nazis.

That feeling of "guilt" helped increase the votes to approve Palestine's Partition Plan from November 1947. The hypothetical question would be: without the Holocaust, would there have been a Jewish State? **Surely yes, because this reality was under construction by the Zionist actions in the territory.**

109. Is it fair to say that the "guilt" for the Holocaust explains the current indulgence towards the State of Israel?

The Arab or pro-Palestinian narrative usually conveys two arguments: the Palestinians "paid the price" for the European Holocaust, and Israel enjoys impunity because of this genocide.

It is important to keep in mind that Palestinians were not oblivious to the Holocaust. The Palestinian leadership, led by Hajj Amin Al-Husseini, was an active ally of the Nazis, fostering Jewish murders: from the request to build gas chambers in Emek Dotan to the attempt to contaminate the waters of Tel Aviv.

In order to assess if there is indulgence towards Israel, we would have to compare the treatment given to Israel with that of other actors, both in international politics as in the media. In the United Nations, there is a very clear accusatory bias and non-indulgent attitude towards Israel. Some entities, such as the UN Human Rights Council should be a cause for shame to all the decent people of the world.

Regarding the media, when comparing the coverage of the Israeli operations in Gaza with the coverage of over half a million deaths and millions of refugees in Syria, the ethnic killings in Darfur or the totally null diffusion of the homosexual persecutions, women or Christians in the same countries that wish to destroy Israel, we can reject this alleged "indulgence". There are media that have acquired nefarious prestige for demonizing Israel. The vast majority of the Spanish media are a clear example of the obsessive bias against Israel.

In truth, the question should be another one: the obsession shown by most countries on the UN towards Israel, or by the world's media... **isn't it a demonstration that the lessons from the Holocaust have not been assimilated as should be expected?**

110. Is it true that between Declaration 181 and Israel's Independence they lived through a civil war?

The first part of the Independence War was the civil confrontation between the local Arabs and the Jews of the British Mandate, which extended from the day of the Partition to the Independence of Israel (May/14/1948).

The day after Declaration 181 (Nov/29/1947), seven Jews were murdered by Arabs in three different incidents: at eight a.m. three Arabs attacked a bus that was traveling from Natania to Jerusalem and killed five Jewish passengers. Then, another bus was attacked and one Jew died and at the end of the day, there was a murder in Jaffa.

In Jerusalem, the Supreme Arab Committee proclaimed a three-day general strike that would begin on Friday's Dec/2/1948 prayer. The attacks intensified and on Dec/11/1947, the correspondent of The Times in Jerusalem estimated that there were 130 deaths, from which 70 were Jews, 50 Arabs and 4 British.

The civil war centered on a fight for controlling the highways around the isolated and mixed cities. The combat in the mixed cities (Haifa, Safed or Tiberiades) was characterized by shots and attacks by Arab snipers. The Jewish forces made a considerable effort to maintain contact with the isolated settlements by sending convoys. The month of March 1948 was hard on the highways because of an attack on the convoy from Nebi Daniel (15 deceased and 40 wounded) when it was returning from Gush Etzion or the Yehiam convoy (46 deceased) on their way to the kibbutz.

That month's deaths created doubts about the capacity of the Jewish community to defend itself, which lead to a presentation of proposals to establish a trust in Palestine or new considerations before the UN. The Jews decided, instead, to execute the Plan Dalet.

111. What is Plan Dalet?

Many times this operation is shown with a certain negative mystic aureole. Palestinian historians describe a plan to conduct an "ethnic cleansing", with systematic expulsion, looting, fires, etc.

Plan Dalet (D) was developed to control all areas designated to the Jewish state by the Partition Plan to prepare for the invasion of the Arab countries once Independence was declared. It was the reaction of the Jewish leadership to two challenges: the rise of ideas such as the Trust, and the terrible losses after the attacks against the convoys (March 1948).

Plan D included the movement and organization of the Jewish forces in brigades and the planning of objectives to take control of concentrations of Jews (even those beyond the borders), creating blocks of settlements and dominating key areas before the expected Arab invasion. The premise was to avoid a confrontation with the British forces still stationed in Israel.

The most burning issue was that Jerusalem (and its 100,000 Jews) was still blocked by the local Arab forces. In order to open the access, Operation Nachshon was executed (Apr/4/1948), and for the first time, they took the initiative by concentrating forces in a brigade as if it were a regular army, with new weapons arriving from Czechoslovakia.

This Jewish initiative continued, and during April and mid-May of 1948 Tiberias, Haifa, Jaffa and Safed (cities assigned to Israel) fell under their domain.

The local Arab factor was defeated, the leadership disintegrated and most of the leaders fled. The escape movement began to transform Arabs into refugees as the local Arabs ceased to be a true military force. The Jews achieved most of the objectives of Plan Dalet.

112. Were there terrorist attacks during the civil war before May 1948?

The Arabs executed three major Jewish massacres. In the first one (Dec/31/1947) hundreds of Arabs murdered 40 Jewish workers (their workmates) in the Haifa refinery. The massacre was preceded by an attempt from the Irgun, where six Arabs were murdered because of an explosive can that was thrown at them. In response, the *Hagana* attacked the Arab villages of Balad Al-Sheik and Hawassa, killing around 60 Arabs. The Hagana also began kidnapping and torturing soldiers from the Irgun, and murdered one: Yedidia Segal.

The second massacre was in Kfar Etzion (May/13/1948) when the combined forces of the Arab League and local Arabs killed the 129 Jewish residents and soldiers of the Hagana that defended the kibbutz. Martin Gilbert affirms that fifteen prisoners were murdered after surrendering. Others speak of higher numbers. Apparently, it was about vengeance for what had occurred before in Deir Yassin and for the destruction of one of their villages months before.

The third case was the killing of the medical convoy of Hadassah (Apr/13/1948), perpetrated by Arab forces who set an ambush against a civilian convoy with medical and personal supplies for the Hadassah Hospital of Mount Scopus (located north of Jerusalem). Seventy-nine Jews, mostly doctors and nurses, were murdered in the attack, which was also perpetrated as retaliation for Deir Yassin.

From the Jewish side, historian Benny Morris assures that Israeli forces captured Jish (Gush Jalav) on Oct/29/1948 during the Jiram Operation and, after a "very hard battle", ten Moroccan war prisoners and other villagers, among them a woman and her baby (a total of around 50 people), were murdered by Israeli soldiers. The Prime Minister of Israel, David Ben-Gurion, issued an investigation but no soldier was taken to trial.

The remainders of a burnt ambulance in the road to Hadassah
(Source: Wikipedia)

113. What happened to the Arab village Deir Yassin?

The UN decided that Jerusalem (and Bethlehem) would be an international city, while 100,000 Jews (2,500 of the Old City) suffered an Arab blockade. Deir Yassin, a village located in a hill at the entrance of Jerusalem, was used to attack the Jewish aid convoys.

The Jewish leadership approved the attack against Deir Yassin (Apr/9/1948). David Shaltiel, commander of the *Hagana*, wrote to the leaders of *Irgun-Lehi*: "I learned that you are planning to attack Deir Yassin. I want to point out that capturing this position is a stage of our general plan. I have no objection regarding the operation, as long as you are able to occupy the village". One hundred and thirty-two soldiers of *Irgun-Lehi* attacked tens of armed Arabs hiding among 750 civilians. Many combatants, among them Iraqi soldiers, were disguised as women to shoot against the Jewish soldiers.

The *Irgun-Lehi* forces tried to warn the civilians that they were attacking, to try to scare them away, with a truck and speakers. Apparently, the truck did not reach the area and probably was not heard. On the day of the attack, at 9:30, five hours after the fire started, *Lehi* evacuated 40 elders, women and children and took them to a base in Sheih Bader- Why did they save them if they were planning a massacre?

A study of the Palestinian University Bir Zeit, based on Arab testimonials, affirms that 107 civilians died and 12 wounded, besides 13 "combatants". Four Jews died.

The Jewish authorities rejected the events of Deir Yassin and used them to discredit their ideological rivals. The Arabs exaggerated the events so the neighboring countries would send more forces against the Jews. **The events of Deir Yassin convinced many Arab-Palestinians that a massacre actually occurred, and they decided to flee the combat areas.**

114. What was the Trust Plan to postpone the Independence of Israel?

It is common to hear that the Jewish lobby in the United States controls local politics. A clear example of the contrary is that **the United States was about to retract from supporting the Partition Plan of November 1947 when it was already approved.**

The harsh events of March 1948 led to a shift in the politics of the United States. The State Department began promoting the idea that the Jews from Israel were not ready for independence and proposed to freeze the implementation of the Partition Plan. They say they feared that the Jewish community was not able to resist a massive Arab invasion.

In March 1948, the US demanded a new discussion in the General Assembly about the Israel matter. **This change in politics from the Americans was founded in ulterior motives: the State Department feared that if the United States supported the execution of the Partition Plan it could endanger their bond with the Arab and Muslim world, and they would lose their rights over petroleum and the air companies in the Middle East.**

The tension between the occidental and oriental blocks, in the Cold War times, was increasing during that year, which led the Americans to execute Realpolitik moves.

In March 1948, the United States offered to impose a temporary security regime led by the United Nations before they reached an adequate political solution. By establishing a trust they would postpone the establishment of the Jewish state for an indefinite period of time.

The leaders of the Zionist movement were opposed, just like the Soviet Union, who continued supporting the establishment of Israel. The resulting war and the decision of the Zionist leadership motivated them to abandon the idea of the trust plan.

115. Why did Israel declare its Independence on May 14 of 1948?

The Jewish leadership was doubting about declaring independence. Some of them were convinced that the Jewish army would not be able to confront an Arab attack and suggested to postpone the declaration and accept the trust offered by the US. Another position suggested forming a new "International Mandate" for two or three years until the situation was clearer and the area was more stable. The Chief of Staff (de facto) of the future Israeli Army, Ygael Yadin, said to David Ben-Gurion that the possibility of succeeding in face of an Arab invasion was 50%-50%.

Surprisingly, the British decided not to cooperate with the UN Partition Plan and withdrew their forces on May/15/1948 at 0:00 hours (they were supposed to leave on Aug/1/1948). This way, the British intended to maintain their influence and the dependence of the Jews on the British Crown. Curiously, that day was Shabbat (rest day for the Jews) and no Jew would be working in the port. It wasn't possible to declare the independence on that Saturday, either. The election that Friday and the precipitated advancement of the British retreat was seen as a show of the imperialist intentions and permanence of the government of "His Gracious Majesty"

On Friday May/14/1948 at 16.00, in the main hall of the Museum of Rothschild Street in Tel-Aviv, the provisional leadership of the Jewish community was gathered. In a brief and simple act, and in spite of the different Arab threats, the independence of the State of Israel was declared. This declaration would be in force starting at 0.00 of May/5/1948. David Ben-Gurion, who would be the first Prime Minister of Israel, was able to impose his position (6 representatives of the People's Administration voted in favor, 4 against, and 3 were absent). They had to take the opportunity to recover the Jewish independence in the land of Israel.

David Ben-Gurion reads the Declaration of Independence of Israel
(Source: Israel Ministry of Foreign Affairs)

116. What does the Israeli Declaration of Independence state?

The Declaration of Independence of Israel is a short text divided into three parts. The first part is "historical" and reviews the origins of the Jewish people, their contribution to humankind, the calamities they have gone through and the origins of Zionism. In this section, the Jewish right to the Land of Israel is explained, sealed with the recognition by the UN in the partition of November of 1947.

The second part is "operational"; it explains that the People's Council (the Parliament of 39 people), declared the end of the British Mandate and announced the Jewish State in Eretz Israel, to be known as the State of Israel. They announced that in October 1948 they would produce a Constitution and based on its rulings, they would call for elections. Also, the People's Council would be known as the "Temporary State Council", and its executive branch, the People's Administrations, would be the "Provisional Government of the Jewish State"

The third part is the "declaration"; it provides details about all the positive values that the State of Israel takes on as a democratic country, with a special call for peace and coexistence with the Arab locals and neighbors.

Those who signed the Declaration were not able to agree on the content written by David Ben-Gurion. For example, orthodox Jews were opposed to writing Tzur Israel instead of the presence and protection of God. The secular representatives rejected any kind of religious mention.

The abandonment of Palestine by Great Britain produces a political and legal void. The Declaration substituted this void, announcing that on May/5/1948 at 0.00 hours a new state would start to rule, known as the State of Israel. The Declaration formally announces the birth of Israel.

117. Is the Declaration of Independence of Israel considered a law?

After the State of Israel was declared as independent, discussions began on the consideration of the Declaration as a constitution or just as an educational-historical text. In 1953, an Israeli communist newspaper, *Kol Ha-Am* (The Voice of the People) published fake news that stated that Israel would provide 200,000 soldiers to the US to fight against the Soviet Union. The Minister of Interior decided to close down the newspaper, accusing it of being a threat to public peace. **The Supreme Court of Justice ruled that it was not clear that public peace was threatened, and since there was no law for this issue and there were two possible interpretations, the spirit of the Declaration of Independence was to be followed, which guaranteed freedom of speech.**

As we can see, when there is no existing law or jurisprudence as a reference, decisions are taken based on the spirit of the Declaration of Independence, although this is not a formal constitution. **If there is a law that formally contradicts aspects of the Declaration section and that is not contrary to a superior law, then said law is above the Declaration of Independence.**

The following case confirms the explanation above. A couple from a kibbutz of the youth movement Hashomer Hatzair were married in front of two witnesses without a rabbi and without signing a religious document. In other words, they married their own way. The new Rogozinsky family requested that justice recognize their marriage. The decision was, that according to the Law of Religious Marriage Courts of 1953, the competent authority for all matters related to marriages and divorced is the Rabbinic Court, and therefore, even though it could be seen as unfair, the Rogozinsky family must marry in the rabbinate if they want their marriage to be recognized as legal.

118. Why didn't Israel write a constitution? What is the Basic Law?

Israel does not have a written constitution (formal) but has a "material" one. A material constitution also discusses the functions and limitations of the

Powers of the State, on the rights and duties of citizens, but all these laws are not comprised in a text known as a "constitution".

The Declaration of Independence expresses the desire to produce a formal constitution. The election of a Constituent Assembly was held in February 1949, and not as ordered by the Declaration of Independence in 1948, because of the ongoing war with the Arab countries. The Assembly enacted the "Takeover Law of 1949" (*Hok HaMaavar* 1949), which stated that the Legislative Power of Israel would be known as the Knesset (Parliament) and they would be the "First Knesset". This way, they did not produce a Constitution as was stated in the Declaration of Independence.

The religious parties were among those who opposed a written constitution (the only supreme law is the *Halaha* – the Religious Law) and David Ben-Gurion argued that the conflict hindered enacting supreme norms for times of peace if they were living in a state of war in the country.

The discussion continued until Jun/13/1950, when the representative of the Progressive Party, Izahar Harari, was able to approve his proposal that a secretariat of the Knesset take on the role of Constituent Assembly and prepare a Constitution but "in stages". The Knesset would approve these "Basic Laws" (called *Hukei Yesod*).

The Basic Laws are written like a Constitution and in the future, they will have a superior rank to the common laws. If there is a common law that contradicts a Basic Law, the most recent law will prevail, but for two years. There are articles that are "shielded" (*Meshurianim*) and to change them, they must have the approval of a determined amount of representatives. At present, Israel has enacted 14 Basic Laws.

119. How did the War of Independence of 1948 develop?

The Secretary General of the Arab League, Azzam Pasha, threatened: "Personally, I hope Jews do not force us into a war, because it would be a war of extermination and a terrible massacre, only comparable to the devastation of the Mongols and the Crusades". The future chief of the PLO, Ahmed Shukeiri, affirmed that the invasion intended "the elimination of the Jewish State" and the Islamic University of El Cairo proclaimed a holy war against Zionism.

After declaring its independence, Israel was invaded by Lebanon, Syria, Jordan, Iraq, Saudi Arabia and Egypt. The best Arab army was the Jordan army, commanded by the British general John Baggot Glubb and armed by the British themselves.

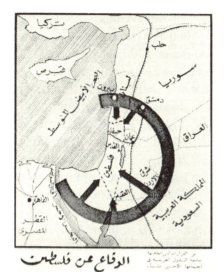

Arab attack plan published in the Arab press *(Source: Wikipedia)*

Although the United States had been a vigorous supporter of the partition resolution, the State Department did not want to provide weapons to the Jews. On Dec/12/1947, the US imposed an embargo on weapons in the region. Throughout the war, Israel was able to purchase arms to Czechoslovakia with approval from the Soviet Union.

The war of 1948 was divided into three stages: 1) May/18/1948 to June/11/1948: Invasion by three Arab armies and defense by Israel. 2) July/9/1948 to July/18/1948: After the cease-fire, the Tzahal attacks the Arab armies, taking over the area of lower Galilee and the path to Jerusalem. 3) From July 1948 to July 1949. The Arabs surrender and Israel carries out plans to protect its civilians, by dominating over lands from where it was being attacked.

Israel defeated the Arab armies and increased its territory in the framework of a defensive war, at a painful price: 1% of its population died in combat (6,373 deceased, 2,373 of them civilians). The territories destined to the Arab state were occupied by Egypt (Gaza) and by Jordan (West Bank), but no one protested or claimed against this injustice.

120. Why did Israel defeat the invading Arab armies during the 1948 War?

Because the Jewish civilians didn't have another option: either they defeated them... or they were murdered or expelled. From the military point of view, the Arabs were defeated because of their lack of coordination. It is not the same to fight for survival, as the Jews did, than to attack others based on "abstract" objectives led by corrupt leaders.

The Jews were poorly prepared for the 1948 War. The Hagana had 6 divisions (Golani, Givati, Carmeli, Alexandroni, Kiriati and Etzioni) and another 3 divisions of the Palmach (Harel, Yftach and Ha-Negev). During the war, another 3 divisions and a small air force (Force 101) were formed. There were 6,373 Israeli casualties in the war, 4,000 soldiers and 2,373 civilians. They fought 20,000 Egyptians, 18,000 Iraqis, 5,000 Syrians, 13,000 Jordanians and more...

The exact number of Arab deaths in 1948 is unknown: supposedly 2,000 Egyptians, 1,000 Syrians, 1,000 Jordanians, 500 Iraqis, 500 Lebanese and 3,000 more Arabs from Palestine... in total: around 8,000 people. Aref El-Aref, who also included the deaths provoked by discussions among Palestinian Arab clans, rounded the deaths to 17,000 (13,000 of them were Arabs from Palestine). The different Arab-Palestinian clans settled the scores among each other because during the direct war with Israel 3,000 of them died.

The Arab countries signed armistice agreements with Israel in 1949, starting with Egypt (Feb/24/1949), then Lebanon (March/23/1949), Jordan (Apr/3/1949) and Syria (Jul/20/1949). Iraq was the only country that did not sign. The cease-fire lines were military agreements and not recognized borders. However, in Lebanon's case, the cease-fire line was established in the international border of 1923 and with Egypt, the cease-fire line went through the 1906 border (except through the Egyptian occupation in Gaza Strip).

Blue- territories assigned to the Jewish state; pink- territory conquered by the Israelis because of the Arab aggressions. The green part was left for Jordan (West Bank) and Egypt (Gaza Strip) since 1949. *(Source: Wikipedia)*

121. Is it true that the Arabs were expelled intentionally during the war of 1948, and became refugees?

For years, the Israeli historiography assured that the Palestine refugees had fled, guided by their leaders, who requested to "allow the passage of the armies that would destroy the Jews". Historian Ephraim Karsh outlines: "In 1948 everyone knew that the Arabs had attacked the Jews, they were defeated and fled. Then, during the 50s they tried to erase their guilt by making up killings" (*the film The Curse of Hadrian*).

On the other hand, the Palestine narrative assures that "everyone was expelled in order to carry out a planned ethnic cleansing".

A pioneer in putting things in perspective, Benny Morris, in his book *The Birth of the Problem of Palestine Refugees 1947-1949* (written in 1988 and revised in 2004) *and 1948*: *The First Arab-Israeli War*, affirms that there was a combination of reasons: attacks by Israel and underground groups that coerced the Arabs, expulsion and effective acceptance of evacuation orders by the Arab leaders. In *1948* Morris argues that there was no expulsion policy although the high leadership of Israel ordered expulsions in response to local attacks. **"There are no documents to support this (an intentional expulsion) and apparently there was no such plan"** (*Morris in The Curse of Hadrian*)

The UN affirms that there were 711,000 refugees in 1948. According to Morris, the rich and wealthy Arabs (75,000-100,000) fled voluntarily (Nov/1947-Mar/1948) repeating the pattern of the 1936-1939 revolt and leaving their community without leaders. During April-July of 1948, 300,000 more left following their leaders, with no harassment by Israel. In July 1948, about 100,000 were expelled from strategic areas (Lod, Ramle)

Why would an Arab-Palestinian flee the combat zone? Possibly out of fear. **Maybe... because they thought that the Israelis would do to them what they had done to Israelis during the past killings, as happens when they execute acts of revenge among Arab clans.**

122. Are there testimonies from Arab leaders that confirm that their previous leadership caused the problem of the Palestine refugees?

In his memoirs (1972), the ex-Prime Minister from Syria, Khaled Al-Azam, wrote: "Since 1948, we were the ones who demanded the return of the refugees... even though we made them leave, we have disgraced the Arab refugees by encouraging them and pressuring them to leave... we have made them beg... we have participated in the decrease in morals and their social level... then, we exploited them to commit murders, provoke fires, everything for political purposes".

A leader of the National Arab Committee from Haifa, Hajj Nimer el-Hatib, said that the Arab soldiers in Jaffa mistreated the residents. "They robbed individuals and their homes. Life had little value and women's honor was violated. The state of these issues led many [Arab] residents to leave the city under the protection of British tanks".

There are too many testimonies about Arabs from Palestine fleeing by their own will. On Jan/30/1948, the Jaffa Ash Shaab newspaper reported: "The first Arabs of our fifth column abandoned their homes and businesses and went to live somewhere else. At the first sign of trouble, they leave to avoid sharing the weight of the fight". Another Jaffa newspaper, As Sarih (March/30/1948), criticized the Arab farmers near Tel-Aviv because they "embarrassed all of us by 'abandoning the villages'". Now, the Palestinian Arabs and their allies rewrite history due to political reasons, helped by certain academics.

The National Arab Committee of Jerusalem, following instructions of the Supreme Arab Committee (March/8/1948), ordered that women, children and elderly from many parts of Jerusalem abandon their homes: "Any opposition to this order… will be an obstacle to the holy war… and will interfere with the operations of the soldiers in those districts" (*1948*- Benny Morris).

123. Are there more testimonials of Arab leaders that recognize their faults for the Palestinian refugee problem?

"The Arab countries encouraged the Arabs of Palestine to leave their homes, temporarily, so they wouldn't disturb the invading Arab armies", published the Jordanian newspaper *Falestin* (Feb/19/1949).

King Abdallah of Jordan wrote in his memories that he blamed the Palestinian leaders for the refugee problem: "the tragedy of Palestinians is that most of the leaders were paralyzed with false and uncertain promises that they would not be alone; that 80 million Arabs and 400 million Muslims, instantly and miraculously, would run to their rescue". "The Arab armies entered Palestine to protect the Palestinians from the Zionist tyranny, but instead of doing so, they abandoned them, forcing them to emigrate and leave their homeland" (*Falastin A-Thaura*, March 1976)

The Economist reported on Oct/2/1948: "Of the 62,000 Arabs that used to live in Haifa, there are only 5,000-6,000 left. Several factors influenced this drain. There is no doubt that the most powerful factors were the announcements made on the radio by the Supreme Arab Executive, encouraging the Arabs to leave… It was clearly insinuated that the Arabs who would remain in Haifa and accept the protection of the Jews would be considered as traitors".

John Baggot Glubb, commander of the Trans-Jordan Arab Legion, said: "The (Arab) villages were frequently abandoned, even before they were threatened by the advance of the war".

The testimonies of 1948 (and immediate years) clearly confirm that the vast majority of the Arabs left encouraged by their own leaders and because of the natural fear of war and the "tribal revenge" they thought threatened their lives. **In time, the problem of the Palestinian refugees required a new narrative and re-writing history to adapt it to the need to demonize Israel.**

124. Are there individual testimonies that corroborate that the Palestinian Arabs were not expelled in 1948?

There are dozens of testimonies that prove that the cases of abandonment were voluntary in various places during the 1948 War (see in https://www.youtube.com/watch?v=JxfJxuOWAz0).

Fuad Khader from Bir Ma'in (central Israel), said to the Jordanian TV: "We left, those who made us leave were the Jordanian army because they were going into battle and we would be under their feet. They said: 'Leave. In two hours we will defeat them and then you can come back'. We left with what we were wearing, we did not pack anything because we were meant to return in two hours. Why would we carry our things? We are still waiting for those two hours to end today".

A refugee from Ein Karem (Jerusalem) said: "the radio stations of the Arab regimes repeated: 'leave the battlefront. In ten days or two weeks at the most, we will bring you back to Ein Karem'. We said to ourselves that it was a long time, two weeks was too much. That's what we thought then. And now, it has been 50 years".

What does the main interested party say about this problem? The President of the Palestinian Authority, Mahmoud Abbas, who, during the 1948 War, escaped his home in Safed (Tzfat), told the Palestinian TV that "the Salvation Army (Arab) retreated from the city of Safed in 1948, causing the Arab people to emigrate from Safed, just like from Hebron, and people were afraid that the Jews would avenge the massacres perpetrated by the Arabs in 1929 (Note: 65 Jews were murdered in Hebron, 18 Jews in Safed). In 1948, the people were terrorized and were forced to leave the city in a disorderly way".

125. Are there more testimonials about the Arab-Palestinians not being expelled in 1948?

The Jordanian former parliamentary, Talal Abu Ghazaleh, who left Jaffa during the 1948 war: "Cars with loudspeakers circulated the streets, demanding that people leave so the combats could succed. They spoke to us in Arabic so we would leave our homes: 'We –the Palestinians, the fighters – want to fight, and we don't want any impediment, so we ask you to leave the city (Jaffa) immediately'. All of us – me, my family, and the others – left as we could. We went to the port and boarded a ship".

Asmaa Jabir Balasimah wrote in his memoirs why he had left Kfar Saba (in the center of Israel): "We heard sounds of explosions and shots at the beginning of the summer in the year of the *Nakba* (1948). We were told that it was the Jews attacking our region and that it was better to evacuate the town and return after the end of the battle. And in fact, we were with those who left the pots on the fire, those who left behind their sheep herds, and those who left their money and their gold, supposing that we would return in a few hours".

Another testimony from Gaza, of a person who left the southern village of Mahdal (today Ashkelon): "My grandfather and my father told me that during the Nakba our district officer issued an order, that whoever stayed in Palestine and in Mahdal would be considered a traitor. The person issuing the order forbidding them to stay is guilty of it, in this life and in the life to come, throughout history until the Day of Resurrection. Because I left Dir Al-Qasi (north of Israel)) – We were told we would return in 'a week or two'". Those were the testimonials back then. Today… they re-write them.

126. Can we get "more confirmations" that the Palestinian Arabs were not expelled in 1948?

The Jordanian journalist, Jawad Al-Bashiti, writes: "In the Palestinian Nakba, the first war between the Arabs and Israelis had begun and the Arab Salvation Army said to the Palestinians: 'We have come to exterminate the Zionists and their state. Leave your homes and villages, you will return in a few days'. Mahmoud Al-Habbash added: 'The leaders and elites promised at the beginning of the Nakba in 1948 that the exile would not take long and that it would only last a few days or months, and then the refugees could return to their homes. Many had not left them until they believed the false promises given by the political leaders and elites'".

Once again, the President of the Palestinian Authority (originally from Safed), Mahmoud Abbas said: "To be honest, we were scared. My family decided- I was the eldest of those who left with my brother's wife and their two children- that they would move us… I only had two pairs of shoes, a new pair and an old one. I said: 'I will leave with my old shoes and I will leave the new ones for when I return…' We left with the hope of returning. We were taken to the east of Safed, to the Jordan River."

Ali Muhammad Karake confessed: "When we heard the news that the Jews were near the villages, the Arab Salvation Army- may Allah protect them-came and said: 'leave the village so that nothing happens to you like what happened in Deir Yassin. Leave, but don't go too far because they (the Jews) will stop here shortly'. The people left with nothing, not even bread, and they went to the mountains and were given tents".

127. What are the differences between a world refugee and a Palestinian refugee?

According to the Convention Relating to the Status of Refugees (1951), a refugee is "a person who is outside his or her country of nationality or habitual residence; has a well-founded fear of being persecuted because of his or her race, religion, nationality, etc.; this person is unable or unwilling to avail himself of the protection of his country, or to return there, for fear of persecution" (he does not accept or is not granted a nationality). This is the definition by UNHCR. **In this case, Palestinian refugees were the ones who fled the wars of 1948-1967, are still alive and were not granted citizenship from other countries.**

However, the 1951 Refugee Convention excludes the Palestinian refugees of 1948, "protected" and "assisted" by TWO pre-existing UN Special Commissions (UNCCP, for protection and conflict resolution, and UNRWA, for assistance and employment).

According to the surreal UNRWA, a person that lived in the British Mandate between Jun/1/1946 and May/15/1948 is considered a refugee. How is this brief period understood? An enormous amount of Arabs arrived in Israel looking for jobs offered by the British and the Zionists. **If they would have written the date as 1918, they would have "damaged the business" because there were 600,000 Arabs and not 1,800,000 like in 1948.** Surprisingly, and Arab is considered as a "refugee" if moved a few kilometers from his village to another one under Arab control. This is the most unusual definition of "refugee" in history.

At present, according to hereditary and SPECIAL parameters of UNRWA, they count over "four million Palestinian refugees" (others affirm 9 million), making them the largest population of refugees in the world. One out of every three refugees is "Palestinian" and about 60% of all Palestinians have an eternal refugee condition. What bad luck do all the millions of refugees of the world have, since they can't enjoy this DE LUXE REFUGEE status!

128. Is it true that the Palestinians have an organization for eternalizing the refugee status?

World War II created a terrible humanitarian crisis. Only in Europe, there were more than 16 million refugees and displaced persons. This massive problem was confronted by the International Refugee Organization (IRO), established by the UN General Assembly in December 1946 and transferred in January 1951 to the UN High Commissioner for Refugees (UNHCR), which was quickly expanded throughout the world.

There was an exception to this pattern: the Arab war fugitives from 1948-1949, who received their own agency to help, the UN Relief for Palestinian Refugees (UNRPR), established in November 1948 and transformed on May/1/1950 into the UNRWA (UN Relief and Works Agency for Palestinian Refugees). While the UNHCR (UN High Commissioner for Refugees) was created with an annual budget of $300.000, the UNRWA was established with a budget that "required the equivalent to approximately $33,700,000 for direct aid programs and constructions from Jan/1/1950 to Dec/31/1950". **In other words, the Palestinian refugees received 110 times more money than what was assigned to the rest of the refugees of the world.**

Recently, UNHCR had nearly 11,000 employees who received 17.2 million refugees (1,569 refugees per worker) and 65.6 million forcible displacements. The UNWRA had more than 30,000 employees that handled around 5.3 million "refugees" (176 refugees per employee). **In other words, the Palestinian "refugees" had 10 times more human resources than their equally less fortunate pairs in any other part of the world and 34 times more humanitarian support that what was given to the other displaced people in the world.**

The UNWRA was conceived initially as a transitory agency. However, its mandate was quickly affected for political motives, to pressure Israel, and the Palestinians inherited the status of indefinite refugees.

129. Are there relations and connections between UNRWA and terrorist groups?

In the sensational book *Roadblock to Peace. How the UN Perpetuates the Arab-Israeli Conflict: UNRWA's Policies Reconsidered*, David Bedein explains how UNWRA raises around 1 billion US dollars. We know that during the last few years, two schools of UNWRA in Gaza were used to hide rockets and two Israeli soldiers died as a consequence of a bomb set under a UNWRA clinic (2014).

Today, 99% of the 30,000 workers of UNRWA are Palestinians, the immense majority define themselves as "refugees". School books of the UNRWA (from first grade to high school), both in the West Bank (approved by the PA) and in Gaza (approved by Hamas) are loaded with demonizations about Jews, exaltations in texts and poetry on the myth of the "right to return", and of course, they glorify the path of Jihad and martyrdom.

Since 2000, the workers of UNRWA have participated in or assisted terrorist actions. For example, in 2002, Nidal Abad Al-Fatal Abdala, leader of Hamas in Kalkilya, served as a UNRWA ambulance driver and was arrested. That same year, Nahd Rashid Ahmad Atallah, a high officer of UNRWA in Gaza, who assigned funds to refugees, was arrested and admitted that during the previous decade, he handed part of those resources to family members of the wanted terrorists. Awad Al-Qiq, who worked as Principal and science teacher of a UNRWA school in Gaza, works at night as a terrorist building rockets for the Islamic Jihad as commander of their "engineering unit".

In Gaza, there are profound links between Hamas and the UNRWA schools. They organize Hamas ceremonies and competitions in the UNRWA schools; teachers designated by Hamas and UNRWA do not bother to check if the people that work for them are linked to terrorist organizations.

130. How many Palestinian-Arabs abandoned the combat zone in 1948?

By August 1948, after eight months of combat between Arabs and Israelis, the director of the Program for Disaster Relief in Palestine, Sir Raphael Cilento, established the number of refugees between 300,000-350,000 and the Report of the General Assembly by mediator Folke Bernadotte (Sept/16/1948) presented a slightly higher number: 360,000 refugees. Another report presented a month later by Bernadotte's successor, Ralph Bunche, elevated the number to 472,000, estimating the number of people that required aid from the UN for 9 months from Dec/1/1948 to Aug/1/1949 to 500.000.

In October 1948, the Arab League established the number of refugees at 631,967 and by the end of the month, the Arabs official numbers varied between 740,000 and 780,000. When the UNRPR began working in November 1948, they found around 940,000 refugees in their list of aid. **Officers from the United States consider that these numbers were extremely exaggerated, especially because there was not a substantial influx of refugees.**

Sir John Troutbeck, chief if the British Office for the Middle East in Cairo, had a first impression of the inflation generated by the number of refugees during a research mission in Gaza in June 1949. They informed London: "They have almost 250,000 refugees registered in their books. They admit, however, that the numbers are not trustworthy since it is impossible to stop the fraud in the implementation of returns. Deaths, for example, are never registered, nor the names are erased from the books of those who abandon the district secretly. It is also possible that some names are registered more than once to have additional rations."

The UNRWA began helping 711,000 Palestinian refugees; although today, the "refugees" (4th Generation!) are reaching 5.3 million.

131. What does the term Nakba Palestine mean?

The term *Nakba* was devised for the first time by Constantine Zureik, a Syrian professor of the American University of Beirut, in his book *The Meaning of the Catastrophe* (Nakba) *of 1948*. "The defeat of the Arabs in Israel is not only a failure or a bad step. It is a disaster in every sense of the word…".

Nakba translates as "catastrophe" and refers to the creation of the State of Israel. **After the Six-Day War, and especially after the book by Aref Al-Aref, the term was associated with the phenomenon of the Palestinian refugees (but that was not the intention of the author of the word).**

The official commemoration of that day was proclaimed for the first time by Yasser Arafat in 1998, on the 50th Anniversary of Israel. However, at the end of the 1950s, the 15th of May was known as the "Day of Palestine", described by the Arab-Muslim media as a day of international solidarity.

The *Nakba* is a day of national mourning for the Palestinians, their disgrace was the creation of Israel and that is why the day they chose was the Independence Day. The key is the symbol of the homes that the Palestinian grandparents left behind during the war, considering that "they would return" even though there is no legal obligation that sustains this. Israeli investigator Meron Benvenisti affirms that it was "the Israeli-Arabs that taught the inhabitants of West Bank-Gaza to commemorate the day of *Nakba*".

On Mar/23/2011, the Israeli Parliament approved a law in which the Ministry for Economy can reduce or terminate government financing to any Israeli NGO that commemorates the Day of *Nakba*.

The modern term is used as an attempt to balance the "moral charge" of the Holocaust, trivializing when comparing it to the Shoah.

132. Is it true that Jewish communities in Arab countries were destroyed during the 1948 War?

With the development of Zionism and the establishment of Israel, around 850,000-900,000 Jews were forced to leave Arab states, making them refugees. The process began in the 1930s, becoming more intense because of the Arab League's intention of destroying the State of Israel. It continued its violence in the 1950s and 1960s because of Pan-Arabism when the Jewish communities stopped existing.

These Jews were expelled and/or forced to flee their countries fearing for their lives. They were persecuted and there were numerous pogroms, although they did not attack their Arab fellows- not like the Palestinian refugees who fled after an annihilation war that their leaders and the Arab regimes had begun against the Jews.

This destruction, named by some as the "Jewish Nakba", provoked the disappearance of millennial communities like the Iraqi, established after the expulsion of the Jews from Babylonia (586 A.C.) or hundreds like those in the North of Africa (Morocco, Algeria, Tunisia), which nurtured from the Sephardic immigration in times of the Inquisition; or the Egyptian and the Yemenite communities, with roots prior to the destruction of the Temple of Jerusalem (year 70).

This destruction came together with a movement of refugees, larger in dimensions to the Palestinians, but affecting a group that had no part in the war. Israel absorbed these refugees with great difficulties. It was a large mass equivalent to the population of the recently created state, with a different culture and without resources – although in their countries of origin they were prosperous. The integration was not idyllic, but they are a key part of Israel today.

Regretfully, the Arab states not only do not want to pay compensation for those Jews who were expelled, but they also deny any recognition of the atrocity.

133. Is it true that there were more Jews than Arab-Palestinians displaced during the War of Independence of 1948?

This statement is correct. The official number of Arabs that fled or that were expelled during the Israel-Palestine War (1948) reach 711,000 people. On the other hand, the Jews that were living in Arab countries, that had not assaulted their country people, abandoned their homes reaching nearly 900,000 displaced people.

In 1948, there were 265,000 Jews in Morocco and in 1976 there were 17,000 left. In Algiers, during the same period there were 140,000 and then 400, in Tunisia there were 105,000 and then 200 left. In Libya from 38,000 to 20, in Egypt from 200,000 to 200. Iraq 135,000 to 400, Syria 30,000 to 4,350, Lebanon 55,000 to 1,000 and in Yemen 8,000 to no one left. So, in total, in 1948 there were 880,000 Jews living in Arab countries, then in 1976 there were only 25,620 people left, and at present, in the same countries, there are only 7,650 people.

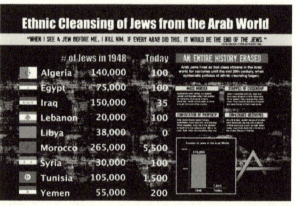

In Iran, since the Islamic revolution, the situation of the Persian Jewish community has been undermined. In 1990, 55,000 Jews left the country: 30,000 went to the US, 20,000 to Israel and 5,000 to Europe. However, the community has relative cultural autonomy, so in general, they are not victims of harassment or insults by the Muslims. The community has a representative in the Iranian parliament, Morris Mutmad. In July 2012 there were approximately 8,756 Iranian Jews left.

With the establishment of the State of Israel, and even before, most of the Jews of Turkey immigrated to Israel, a total of 55,500. Today there are only 17,400 Jews in Turkey.

Until November 2003, for example, 101 of the 681 resolutions of the UN on the Middle East conflict concerned the Palestinian refugees directly. **Not one of the resolutions addresses the Jewish refugees from the Arab countries, which were more, according to the numbers.**

134. How much money worth of goods and properties are the Jews claiming from the Arab countries?

The economic situation of various Jewish communities before 1948 was good. European colonialism led to increasing demand for rich professionals who had more knowledge and knew other languages for translation, contacts for commerce, the running of customs, banks and administration of money, professions in which the Jews performed a central role.

The quick voluntary or forced "fleeing" of the Arab countries made them leave most of their belongings behind. **The property left included territories, houses, businesses and stores, bank accounts and more. Most of the properties were confiscated by the state authorities or taken by others and were never returned to their owners.**

There are different estimations of the value of the Jewish properties left or confiscated. The difference between the estimations is because of the difficulty to calculate the total property of the Jewish refugees in numerous countries, as well as how to calculate the sums.

In 2007, the World Jewish Organization estimated that the total belongings left behind by the 900,000 refugees from the Arab countries equaled around 300 billion dollars' worth of value (amounts calculated in 2000) and the total estimated from the properties reached 100,000 square kilometers of land.

On the other hand, Professor Sydney Zabludof, an economist specialized in compensations to survivors of the Holocaust, **calculated that the total property was worth approximately 6 billion dollars (values from 2007), while that of the Palestinian refugees was worth 3.9 billion dollars.**

Even though it is necessary to conduct a deep study, little doubt is left that the Jews from Arab countries are owed more money and that in the frame of a solution to the problem of the refugees, those debts to them should be taken into consideration.

135. When did the War of Independence of 1948 end in territorial terms?

The Green Line between Israel and Jordan was the line for the cease-fire according to the Rhodes Agreements. The lines agreed in the armistice included almost all the lands assigned to the Jewish state in the framework of the Partition Plan, except a small area south of the Beit Shean valley. However, it included most of the area assigned to the Arab state according to Declaration 181. Also, Hamat Gader and Snir (north-east coast of the Galilee Sea) were left under Syrian control, although they should have been Israeli.

After being attacked, Israel added 5,700 km2 to what had been assigned in the Partition. At the end of the war, Israel had 20,770 km2, 77% of the Palestine Mandate after 1922 (about 27,000 km2) and 17.30% of the original Palestinian land (including Jordan).

Before the Partition, 7% of the land belonged directly to the Jews, including the land that was the property of the National Jewish Fund (KKL). The area that was added after the Arab attack was of good quality and relatively abundant in sediments. This duplicated the areas that were apt for agriculture compared to the areas set in the Partition, which included approximately 9,600 km2 of the Negev desert for the Jewish state.

In a few months, the Jewish population increased to 1,000,000, after hundreds of thousands of immigrants arrived in Palestine between Nov/30/1947 and the armistice of July 1949. The non-Jewish population (Arab-speaking) that remained in the State of Israel reached 156,000 people.

Eastern Jerusalem (including the Old City and the holy sites) and the West Bank were conquered by the Hashemite Emirate of Trans-Jordan and the Gaza Strip was occupied by Egypt. The other Arab state was not created.

136. What is Declaration 194 of the General Assembly of the UN?

Declaration 194 (Dec/11/1948) was adopted towards the end of the Arab-Israeli war. **The Declaration of the General Assembly has legal force only if those implied accept them as valid.**

Article 11 requires that "refugees wishing to return to their homes and live in peace with their neighbors should be permitted to do so at the earliest practicable date, and that compensation should be paid for the property of those choosing not to return and for loss of or damage to property which, under principles of international law or in equity, should be made good by the Governments or authorities responsible". In other words, the Arabs who recognize Israel must be compensated or allowed to return to their homes (this is not a legal obligation).

The Declaration also required the establishment of a UN Conciliation Commission to enable peace between Israel and the Arabs.

Of the 58 members of the UN (1948), it was accepted by 35 counties, with 15 votes against and 8 abstentions. **Significantly, the six countries of the Arab League represented in the UN and part of the conflict: Egypt, Iraq, Lebanon, Saudi Arabia, Syria and Yemen voted against the resolution. Therefore, it lacked legal value.**

Israel was not a member of the United Nations at that time but it opposed and it still opposes part of the articles. The Palestinians were not directly consulted.

Since the end of the 1960s, Article 11 has been dramatically cited since the Palestinians use it to argue an inexistent "right" of returning. The General Assembly reaffirms Declaration 194 every year since 1949.

In 2008, Ehud Olmert offered to allow 100,000 Palestinians the entry to Israel as part of a final peace treaty.

137. What is the situation of the Palestinian refugees in the Arab countries?

In 2018, Palestinian refugees and their descendants reached several million, divided between Jordan (2,247,768), Lebanon (504,376), Syria (630,035), West Bank (970,633) and the Gaza Strip (1,388,668).

The Palestinian drama was enhanced due to the policies of the receiving countries, that opted to confine them in refugee camps, denying them

citizenship – excepting Jordan, partially – in spite of the evident belonging to a similar socio-cultural group, and even though many of them descend from Egyptians, Syrians, Jordanians or Lebanese that arrived in Palestine in search for jobs.

The Palestinians in the best conditions are the Jordanians (almost 60% of the population is Palestinian). Two thirds of them are considered refugees and live in 10 refugee camps.

In Lebanon, only one fourth has citizenship, they are not free to work in many professions and in some of their camps, they lack education and sanitation services. Not always can they move freely. In the past, they have suffered killings in Sabra and Shatila, in the hands of the Maronite Christians.

In Syria, they do not have citizenship nor political rights, though they enjoy education and sanitation services, and others. Palestinians have been murdered within the war between the ISIS and the Shiites. **In 2016, about 30 Palestinians were murdered by ISIS at the Al-Yarmuk camp (2,000 of the 18,000 were able to escape).**

In Saudi Arabia, they do not have citizenship nor political rights (they cannot request it), but they have the right to work. In Iraq, many live in precarious camps of the UNWRA and were received partially during the days of Saddam Hussein, but later persecuted by the Shiites.

The Arab League ordered their members to deny citizenship to Palestinian originals (or their descendants) or refugees "to avoid the dissolution of their identity and protect their right to return to their country of origin".

138. Can we say there was an ethnic cleansing on Palestine?

The concept implies a systematic elimination or the forcible expulsion of a population for religious, ethnic or national motives and it is currently considered a "crime against humanity". The previous chapters show a war between two identities, sometimes between irregular armies, with military mistakes like in Deir Yassin, war crimes like the shooting of innocent civilians in Kfar Etzion, the intentional murder of civilians (terrorism) in the Mount Scopus Convoy, expulsions in Lod or Ramle and auto-motivated fleeing. Using the words "ethnic cleansing" in this conflict trivializes the phenomenon and its correct use becomes relative.

Israel does not qualify as ethnic cleansing the destruction of Jewish communities in Arab countries either, despite that in that case, there were no traces of Jewish life left while there were around 150,000 Palestinians still living in Israel, most of the remaining lived in their homes within the

British Mandate (or went to the West Bank or the Gaza Strip).

Ilan Pappe is a quasi-historian propagandist who constantly accuses Israel of committing such crime. Pappe himself said in an interview with Le Soir of Brussels (Dec/7/1999): "There will never be an objective historian. I care less about what happened than the way people see those facts. I confess that my ideology influences my historical texts. The fight is based on ideology and not facts."

Historian Benny Morris in *The New Republic said about The History of Modern Palestine: One Territory, Two People:* "Regretfully, much of what Pappe tries to sell his readers is a show. For those in love with subjectivity and dependent on historical relativism, a fact is not a fact and precision is unreachable."

139. Can a Palestinian that abandoned his land in 1947 return to it?

After the war of 1948, many Arab-Palestinians tried to return to their homes. Though the Israeli troops impeded the return of most of them, Benny Morris (2003) explains that between 1948 and 1950, the soldiers resettled between 30,000-40,000 Arabs in the new Israeli state. In a context in which the Arab community rejected the Jews and declared war, the reaction of the Jewish leaders should not be a surprise.

Up to now, many Palestinians do not acknowledge Israel's right to exist as the national state of the Jewish people.

The government of Prime Minister David Ben-Gurion organized the recolonization of the lands and distributed the properties they considered as abandoned. **In 1950, they approved the Absentees' Property Law, which managed the transfer of the Arab-Palestinians houses to Jewish hands. In the meantime, about 400 Arab-Palestinian villages were destroyed, creating a new reality. Thus, 64,000 houses of Arab-Palestinians were transferred to Jewish hands by 1958.**

The main objective was to avoid the demographic balance tilting in favor of the Arabs as the intention was to have a Jewish majority in the State of Israel.

There is no legal obligation to allow the return of the Arabs to the territories where they lived before 1948 (unless an international law is "invented"). All war conflicts in the world result in refugees. **The Palestinian case is special because they created their own disgrace by attacking Israel in 1948.**

The Arab-Palestinian insistence on returning to the exact pre-1948 geographic coordinates is just a mechanism to make a peace agreement impo-ssible. If the objective is to make Israel a bi-national state, forcing it to receive 5 million Palestinian descendants, an agreement will not be reached.

140. Is it true that Israel accepted compensation payment from Germany?

The Reparations Agreement between Israel and the Federal Republic of Germany was signed in Sept/10/1952, establishing that Germany would pay Israel the costs of "resettling so great a number of uprooted and destitute Jewish refugees" after the war. They would compensate them individually through the Conference on Jewish Material Claims against Germany because of the loss of Jewish properties as a result of the Nazi persecution. The money was essential during the economic anguish that Israel was living (*Tzena*). The unemployment was high, especially in the Maavarot (transitory camps) and the reserve of foreign currency was limited.

Nahum Goldmann, President of the Jewish World Congress, had been negotiating with Konrad Adenauer, Chancellor of Germany. Part of Israel's population considered it humiliating to accept German money (their leader was Menachem Begin). Ben-Gurion and his party's (Mapai) position was pragmatic: "There are two approaches", he said to the central committee of Mapai. "One of them is the ghetto Jewish approach and the other is an independent people approach. I don't want to chase a German and spit him in the face. I don't want to chase anybody. I want to settle and build here". Israel bought machinery and infrastructure that were essential for that time.

The business people calculated that because the absorption had cost 3,000 dollars per person, then 1.5 billion dollars was owed to Israel (14.5 billion currently). They also thought that the Nazis had stolen 6 billion dollars in Jewish property, but they underlined that the Germans could never compensate what they did with any type of material compensation.

The German Parliament (*Bundestag*) approved the agreement on Mar/18/1953 by a majority: 239 in favor and 35 against. In Israel, the opposition to the traumatic agreement reunited 15,000 people in Jerusalem (Jan/7/1952). However, the decision was accepted by 61 to 50 votes in the Knesset).

141. What is the Law of Return for the Jews?

Israel's Law of Return of 1959 stated that anyone who has at least one Jewish grandparent has the right to access an accelerated process to be granted Israeli citizenship. According to the racial Nazi laws, a Jew was "infected" because of having at least one Jewish grandparent and had to be eliminated because of it. Israel's Law of Return is the counterattack to the Laws of Nuremberg.

In order to access this right, the person must not have abandoned his link to his people (not professing any other religion), must not be a danger to national security and public health, etc. Even people married to Jews can be granted citizenship so families are not separated.

The person who immigrates is called an ole (he who ascends) and the person who leaves Israel is called *iored* (he who descends). The ascent and descent have the same positive and negative sense than repatriation and exile. The same concept appears in the Bible. People would ascend to Jerusalem, because it was located 800 above the sea level, while the villages on the coast or in the Jordan valley were physically "down".

The Law of Return for Greek descendants is in force only for Greeks; the Japanese Law, only for Japanese and the Bulgarian Law only for Bulgarians. The Law for Return to the national cradle of the Jewish people is valid only for the descendants of the Jewish people (the kingdoms of Judea and Israel). **There are 18 countries in the world that have a similar law. Denying this right only to Israel is discriminating.** A future Palestinian state will surely have a similar law and probably will not include the Jews that want to return to Hebron, Nablus, etc. (even though they lived there until the Arabs expelled them).

142. What principles does Pan-Arabism defend?

Pan-Arabism is an ideological movement that supports the political, social and economic unification between Arab people and states in the Middle East. They defend a secular, socialist and anti-Western identity. They argue that by expelling the powers (and Israel) they will rebuild their states. Some believe that it is about an extension of the *Umayyad* (VIII Century) where only one authority governed from Pakistan to Spain.

The idea was formulated for the first time in 1905 by Najib Azoury in The *Awakening of the Arab Nation*. Pan-Arabism was transformed into an executive idea led by Hussein Iben Ali, who according to his letters with McMahon (1915) intended to create a supra-national Arab reign.

A more concise version of Pan-Arabism than that of Hussein Iben Ali was formed in the 1940s in Syria by Michel Aflaq, founder of the Baath party, according to Italian socialist and fascist elements. The Pan-Arab ideology was the base of many attempts of uniting the National Arab States into a political entity. The most famous one was the United Arab Republic, which united Egypt with Syria (between 1958 and 1961) and included Druze, Sunnis, Shiite and Christian Arabs.

The term Nasserism acted as a synonym for Pan-Arabism since it discussed the politics driven by Gamal Abdel Nasser, President of Egypt, a Pan-Arab radical.

The Pan-Arab Party, Baath, is the current party governing in Syria. They also governed Iraq until the fall of the Saddam Hussein regime. The Pan-Arab movement reached its highest point in the 1960s decade, but the Arab defeat in the Six-Day War damaged deeply their support. In the 1970s and 1980s, the Pan-Arabism was substituted by the current Pan-Islamism.

The decadent Arab League (founded in 1945) demonstrates the Pan-Arab ideals.

143. Who was Gamal Abdel Nasser and what was his role in the Arab-Israeli conflict?

Gamal Abdel Nasser was president of Egypt since 1954. During the War of Independence, he was an intelligence officer with a rank of commander of the Sudanese brigade of the Egyptian army that invaded Israel. For several months he was under siege by the Israeli army to the Egyptian forces in Fallujah.

In 1952, Nasser commanded the military revolt against King Farouk. As a result of the coup, the British forces were withdrawn from Egypt and the government was then directed by General Muhammad Nagib. In 1954 Nasser expelled Nagib and became the *de facto* president.

The visibility of Nasser as the leader of Pan-Arabism was mainly due to his charismatic personality and his rhetoric abilities. This personality allowed him to transform failures into successes both in propagandistic terms as in the political sphere (such as his defeat in the war of 1956). Nasser nationalized the Suez Canal, united many countries of the non-aligned block, expelled the western powers, allowed a massive Soviet penetration in his country and at the same time, led Egypt away from liberalism.

Gamal Abdel Nasser

His ideology is stated in his book *The Philosophy of Revolution*, in which he presents the theory of the three circles: the Arab circle, the Muslim Circle and the African circle. Nasser envisioned Egypt as the leader of these circles.

Motivated by these guidelines, he transformed countries and organizations (the Arab League, PLO, etc.) into his personal puppets.

Gamal Abdel Nasser died of a heart attack on Sep/28/1970, seven weeks after agreeing on the end of the War of Attrition. A few years earlier he had been humiliated by Israel in the Six-Day War (1967). His successor in power was his peer official, Anwar El Sadat. Without Nasser, Pan-Arabism would have fallen...

144. Why were the Christians strong drivers of the Pan-Arab ideals?

Two Christians were fundamental in the development of Pan-Arabism. The first one was Najib Azoury (1870-1916), a Maronite Christian and the author of *The Awakening of the Arab Nation*. Azoury openly insisted on the Arab provinces breaking their connections with the Ottoman Empire. Besides the nationalist nature of the text, he showed anti-Zionist feelings. Some argued that Azoury only intended to incite the Europeans to overthrow the Ottoman Empire.

The second eminent Pan-Arab Christian was the Syrian Michell Aflaw (1910-1989), one of the main theoreticians of Arab socialism and nationalism and founder of the Arab Socialist Baath Party. He met his ideological partner in France, the Sunni Muslim Salaj Bitar, and both developed an essentially secular ideology. Their ideology revolves around the concept of an Arab nation, saying that it exists according to more cultural and linguistic identity than a religious one.

In modern times we can highlight two other Christians that defended the Pan-Arab postures. One of them is Copt Boutros Boutros-Ghali, an Egyptian diplomatic who was the Secretary General of the United Nations (1992-1996). Another Pan-Arab was Tarek Aziz, a Catholic Christian who was Vice-Prime Minister of Iraq during the Saddam Hussein period.

The Pan-Arab activism of the Christians in the Middle East is totally logical... although somewhat pathetic. If the factor of cohesion is that "they all speak Arabic", then they, who are all Christians, will form part of such identity. However, if the identity that unites them is religious, then the Sunni or Shiite Islam will be left out. Therefore, there are many times when they exaggerate their anti-Zionism, anti-Semitism or their anti-Westernism instead of defending the Christians from those who really attack them. The Christian Chilean-Palestinian Daniel Jadue or the Mexican-Maronite Alfredo Jalife Rahme show the same "pro-Christian Islamist" behavioral pattern.

145. Who were the Fedayeen?

The *Fedayeen* (literally, "adherent" that is the non-religious version of *mujahidin)* were occasional terrorists or trained by Nasser, acting from Jordan and Gaza during the mid-50s, violating the Armistice Agreement (1949) that forbade hostilities by paramilitary forces. However, Israel was condemned by the UN Security Council because of its counterattacks. Palestinian refugees hoping to revert the situation, or instigated by the countries that had been defeated in the War of 1948, would enter Israel, attack, and leave rapidly.

According to historian Martin Gilbert, during 1951-1955, the number of Israelis killed in terrorist attacks by the Fedayeen, sponsored by Egypt, reached 967; the attacks were carried out not only from Egypt but also from Jordan, Lebanon and Syria. This situation was totally unsustainable for Israel.

Fedayeen attacks in Tel Mond (1956)

Israeli diplomat Abba Eban explained to the UN Security Council (Oct/30/1956) the situation Israel was facing: "During the 6 years of the Armistice Agreement there have been 1843 cases of armed robbery, 1139 cases of clashes with Egyptian armed forces, 435 cases of raids from territories under Egyptian control, 172 of sabotage perpetrated by military units and Egyptian Fedayeen in Israel. As a result of these hostile Egyptian actions in Israel, 364 Israelis were wounded 101 deceased".

One of the cruelest actions by the Fedayeen was the attack on an Egged bus in Maale Akravim (the Scorpions Pass) in the road to Eilat on Mar/17/1954, in which 12 passengers died and only 2 survived. The attackers entered from Jordan. This action provoked strong retaliation by Israel. The Fedayeen were one of the causes of the war of 1956.

146. Why was Unit 101 of Ariel Sharon so important?

After the end of the 1948 war, the Israeli soldiers did not show any special military capacities. For example, they fled from various confrontations in the Syrian front.

In 1953, the Fedayeen infiltration adopted an organized character, which is why Prime Minister David Ben-Gurion went looking for the history student Ariel Sharon to command the new Unit 101. The 101 received special training (in the Sataf base) to retaliate and dissuade the Arabs.

In October 1953, after infiltrators from Jordan murdered a woman and her two children in Yehud, they executed their retaliation against the Arabs in the village of Kibiya, where the attackers had come from. **Sixty civilians, among them women and children, were murdered during the operation.** The Security Council of the United Nations condemned Israel, a country that tried to avoid the responsibility of the action, arguing that it had been an act of angry civilians (David Ben-Gurion declared that no soldiers had abandoned their bases during the night). The explanation given by Ariel Sharon was that the force did not know that there were civilians hiding in the blown-up houses.

Another action was the raid in Hebron on Dec/21/1953, where Meir Har-Zion directed a small force into an incursion on foot, forty-two kilometers through a mountainous route, up to the heart of Hebron to destroy the house of a pursued terrorist.

The Kibiya operation raised a discussion about morality. To contain them, Ben-Gurion decided to dissolve them by integrating the Paratroopers Unit after only five months of activity.

The contribution of the 101 was fundamental for the Israeli army. They transmitted an example of training, courage and efficiency in the execution of operations that was copied by the rest of the army.

147. Why did Great Britain, France and Israel join to weaken Nasser?

The Sinai War was a brief one (Oct/29/1956 to Nov/5/1956) in which Israel, France and England attacked Nasser's Egypt, after a series of severe aggressions by the Egyptian leader.

On Jul/26/1956, Gamal Abdel Nasser decided to nationalize the company that managed the maritime pass through the Suez Canal. This company belonged to French and English investors. Although Great Britain had been affected by Nasser, it was less interested than France to begin a war against Egypt. France wanted to stop Nasser, a strategic partner of the Algerian rebels. Great Britain had a military defense alliance with Jordan, a country that wanted to join Nasser in the war. On the other hand, Great Britain also wanted to weaken Nasser, who was leading a Pan-Arab nationalism that was threatening its position in Jordan and Iraq. That is how France and England became involved in the war.

From October 22 to 24 of 1956, the French convened Great Britain and Israel to a secret meeting to coordinate a military operation against Egypt. It was agreed that France would defend, from Israeli bases, against an Egyptian air raid. Israel would attack the Suez Canal and would immediately accept a French and British ultimatum to withdraw 20 km from the Canal in exchange for the freedom of circulation through the maritime passage. Supposedly, Egypt would reject the ultimatum, so the powers would attack the Egyptian airplanes on land.

The European forces entered lightly in the combat. A Soviet ultimatum, supported with a passive position by the United States (who were not informed of the attack), decreed the retreat of the allied forces from Sinai. Israel achieved a military victory, though it was partially defeated in the diplomatic field. In exchange for its military retreat, Israel demanded the opening of the Straits of Tiran and the participation of the UN Blue Helmets in the Sinai region.

148. What happened during Operation Kadesh – Sinai War of 1956?

After the coup that led Nasser into office in Egypt (1954), he signed a peace arms deal with Czechoslovakia in September 1955. Egypt wanted to exceed the military power of Israel and the Soviet Union (through Czechoslovakia) and to have a way into the Middle East. According to the deal, Egypt would receive 200 heavy and medium tanks, hundreds of artillery pieces, 150 war aircraft, which gave them a quantity advantage over Israel. **Israel did not have the resources to acquire weaponry but they knew they should give Nasser a preventive blow before his army learned how to use their new weaponry.**

After 1949, the Arabs adopted a "war doctrine of limited liability". According to this doctrine, the aggressors may reject an agreement and participate in a war to win, knowing that, even if they fail, they can insist on reestablishing the previous *status quo*. In 1956, Nasser was the one who threatened with starting a war.

In mid-1956, Nasser violated once again the Armistice Agreement (1949) by closing the Strait of Tiran to Israeli ships (under international law, blocking navigation is an act of war), limiting Israel's access through the sea.

On October 25th, 1956, Egypt signed a three-way agreement with Syria and Jordan that allowed Nasser to rule over the three armies. The blockage of the Suez Canal and of Tiran to Israeli navigation, together with the increase in the attacks from the Fedayeen and the aggressions of the Arabs, forced Israel to attack Egypt with the support of Great Britain and France on Oct/29/1956. At the same time, England and France carried out the Musketeer Operation to dominate the Suez Canal, even though their military participation was close to nothing.

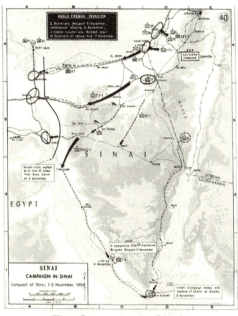

The Campaign in Sinai
(Source: Wikipedia)

149. Is it true that France helped Israel to develop a nuclear plant with military purposes?

The main promoter of the idea of equipping Israel with nuclear military capacity was David Ben-Gurion. **He believed that if the Arabs understood that Israel had nuclear capacity, they would abandon the idea of destroying it, and long-term peace would be achieved in the region**.

During October 1956 the French convened a secret meeting to coordinate a military operation against Egypt. In these agreements, France committed to construct a one-megaton nuclear reactor for Israel in Dimona (October 1957). The main architect of the signing and development of the agreement was Shimon Peres.

Those who opposed the idea argued that it was a very expensive project, that would confront Israel and the United States, or that Israel's safe-

ty was not based on attaining a nuclear bomb, but in avoiding the nuclearization of the region.

In 1963, with the arrival of Eshkol to the presidency and the pressure by President Kennedy, there was a change in the policy and the nuclear development was downsized to a lower profile.

Dr. Abner Cohen affirms that at the end of May 1967, during the "waiting period" before the Six-Day War, Israel was able to build an improvised nuclear device after intense activity.

The only alleged nuclear test directed by Israel is known as the Vela incident. On Sep/22/1979, US satellite Vela, built to detect nuclear testing, informed about a blaze, typical of a nuclear detonation, south of the Indian Ocean. According to journalist Seymour Hersh, this event was the third joint nuclear test by Israel and South Africa. The ex-Director General of the International Atomic Energy Agency, Egyptian Mohamed El-Baradei, considers Israel as a State in possession of nuclear weapons. It is estimated that Israel has between 75 and 400 nuclear warheads.

150. What is Israel's policy regarding the use of nuclear weaponry?

Despite not having concluding evidence, Israel is considered as a state with nuclear bombs. It is one of four countries with nuclear weapons that have not signed the Treaty on the Non-Proliferation of Nuclear Weapons (with India, Pakistan and North Korea). The Arab states, especially Egypt, have tried to force Israel to sign this agreement without success.

Israel maintains a "nuclear ambiguity" or "nuclear opacity" policy. Israel has never admitted to having nuclear weapons; instead, it has repeated throughout the years that it would not be the first country in introducing nuclear weaponry into the Middle East and does not determine if it will be the first country in creating, revealing or using nuclear weapons in the region. The first one in affirming this was Prime Minister Levy Eshkol in the 1960s. In the 1970s, Prime Minister Yitzhak Rabin affirmed that "we will not be the second ones either". During the Yom Kippur War (1973), the Minister of Defense Moshe Dayan suggested considering the use of doomsday weapons before the destruction of the Third Temple (Israel)".

It is suspected that Israel built its first nuclear bomb towards the end of 1960. It was not confirmed publicly by any internal source until Mordecai Vanunu, an Israeli ex-nuclear technician, revealed details of the program to the British media in 1986.

Currently, Israel possesses the capacity of launching missiles with nuclear heads through aircraft, submarines (like the German Dolphins) or the transcontinental ballistic missiles.

Sooner or later, some of Israel's Arab/Islamic enemies will probably begin magnifying their objectives and terrorist operations by using weapons of massive destruction. The Israeli strategy is based on scaring them and destroying their attempts through military or diplomatic actions (like when Osirak was destroyed in 1981).

151. Is the situation of Israel comparable to the plans of Iran to develop non-conventional weapons (2019)?

To develop nuclear weapons, a country needs "intentions" and "capacities". Capacities refer to three levels: the development of precise missiles that can carry non-conventional warheads, knowing how to assemble a nuclear warhead and the capacity to enrich plutonium or uranium – 25 kg at least at 93%. There are few doubts that the Islamic Republic of Iran has the capacity to complete these three stages.

When discussing Iran, we must focus on "intentions". On Apr/30/2018, Israeli Prime Minister Binyamin Netanyahu revealed stolen documents by the Mossad that proved Iran's secret nuclear arms program (Project Amad) and assured that Teheran was violating the 2015 agreement that limited its atomic program (55,000 pages and files stolen from a warehouse south of Teheran). It is true that some media demeaned this revelation. But this was not the case for intelligence centers and politicians of the world (it was one of the reasons that led the US to retreat from Agreement 6+1).

Iran's intentions are not "pure" if it was hiding the violation of its obligations. When we read the "declared and public intentions" of Iran, their wish to destroy other states stands out. Iran is involved in thousands of terrorist attacks throughout the world, by arming and training Hezbollah and Hamas, sustaining the genocidal Syrian President Bashir El-Assad and threatening other Sunni kingdoms of the Middle East. **In summary, the intentions of Iran are destructive and threatening and its technological capacity is dangerous**.

There is a fundamental legal difference. States are not forced to commit to international treaties. Israel has never signed the Nuclear Non-Proliferation Treaty so it is not bound to it, but Iran IS committed to NOT developing nuclear weapons (the treaty was signed during the reign of the Shah).

152. What is the Palestine Liberation Organization (PLO)?

In 1959, Yasser Arafat founded the Al-Fatah organization in Kuwait. For some, it was "another nationalist Pan-Arab manifestation". **This is an incomplete image because it lacks the religious factor: the victories of Mohammed during his caliphate are known as "Fatah".** The supreme objective of the Al-Fatah was the destruction of Israel. There was no Israeli domain over Judea, Samaria or Gaza, which is why they rejected all Jewish presence in the region.

In 1964, the Arab countries reunited in a conference in eastern Jerusalem to formally create the Palestine Liberation Organization (PLO), dependent on Nasserist Pan-Arabism. Their first objective was to destroy the Israeli national pipeline that carried water from North to South *(Movil Artzi)*. Once again, their objective was to destroy. **The PLO Charter (1964) spoke about the destruction of the "Zionist entity of Palestine" (Article 15) but not about the foundation of a Palestinian State.**

The PLO was an umbrella for various organizations, the strongest of them being the one of Arafat, who got rid of Nasserism after the 1967 humiliation. To achieve such unity, Arafat did not hesitate to eliminate rivals, like when after a failed conciliation reunion he threw Yussuf Orabi, a pro-Syrian Palestinian, off the roof of a building (1966).

Modus operandi: Besides kidnapping airplanes, the murder of Israeli athletes in the Olympics must be included, as well as the kidnapping and the killing of passengers of a bus passing through Israeli routes (including children) and bombs in different cities. **The civilian objectives prevailed over the military.**

In October 1974, the Arab League recognized the PLO in Rabat (Morocco) as the "only and legitimate representative of the Palestinian people". Then, Yasser Arafat was named "observer" in the General Assembly (UN). In 1993, the PLO was recognized by Israel as the only representative of the Palestinians, making them the leaders of the Palestinian Authority.

153. What is the National Charter of Palestine (1968)?

The National Charter of 1968 states (Article 9): "Armed struggle is the only way to liberate Palestine. This is the overall strategy, not merely a tactical phase" and Article 2 adds: "Palestine, with the boundaries it had during the British Mandate, is an indivisible territorial unit". Article 21 unfolds its violent wrath: "The Arab Palestinian people, expressing themselves by armed Palestinian revolution, reject all solutions which are substitutes for the total liberation of Palestine and reject all proposals aimed at the liquidation of the Palestinian cause, or at its internationalization" **Following this logic, negotiations to divide the land contradict the objectives of the Charter. As can be read, the conflict was not about the "occupation of the West Bank" (non-existent in 1964 when the PLO was created), being the armed fight the only way to destroy Israel.**

The National Charter underwent modifications, especially after 1967, when Yasser Arafat took over the command of the PLO. The organization adopted a less Pan-Arab path, palestinized the National Charter and demanded the conformation of Palestine instead of Israel.

Some see the Charter as a "declarative-historic document". When an Arab-Muslim leader declares something, it should be taken seriously, as his declaration is measuring the reaction of its followers (read Eli Avidar's *The Abyss*).

When Yasser Arafat recognized Israel, he wrote to Yitzhak Rabin that the articles of the Palestinian Convention that contradict the content of its Charter were "not valid and impracticable". The truth is, even though they voted to cancel the terrorist articles, they did not attain two-thirds of the council members for its annulment, as stated in the Palestinian Constitution. Therefore, the Charter is still in force, from a legal standpoint.

154. Who was Yasser Arafat?

Yasser Arafat was born in Cairo (1929). There is information that the Mufti Haj Amin Al-Husseini was his grand uncle.

As the founder of Al-Fatah (Kuwait, 1959), he succeeded Pan-Arab Ahmad Shukheiri as leader of the PLO after their defeat in 1967. In Nov/13/1974 he was received in the General Assembly of the UN as "chief of state" after 105 countries voted in his favor (an Arab-Islamic-Soviet-non-aligned alliance, together with other dictatorships). He appeared as challenging with his *Kefia* by saying: "I come with an olive branch in one hand and with a gun of the fighters for freedom in the other. Do not allow the olive branch fall from my hand".

The PLO began operating from Cairo and later moved to Jordan (at the end of the 1960s). They were expelled by the King of Jordan after Black September and then Israel expelled them from Lebanon in 1982, and later agonized from Tunisia after supporting Saddam Hussein in the 1991 War of the Persian Gulf.

After it was cornered and far from the power, the PLO decided to formally recognize Israel and declared that they would abandon the use of force. After signing the treaty, Yasser Arafat repeated several times that he had imitated the prophet Mohammed in their *Hudaybyah* agreement (628), *Hudna* (Truce) that he could violate if it favored Islam. In 2000, after rejecting the concessions of Prime Minister of Israel Ehud Barak (Camp David), he returned to terrorism and began the Second Intifada (2000-2005). He died in 2004.

Yasser Arafat with Muammar Khadaffi in 1977

Of the 5.5 billion dollars raised by international aid and taxes during 1994-2003, Arafat took great quantities. At the time of his death, his inheritance was in dispute. They had to convince and threaten his wife, Suha, to deliver Arafat's hidden money to the Palestinian people.

155. Why did Palestinians resort to violence?

Palestinians resorted to violence since the British Mandate when they opposed the Jewish immigration and the purchase of lands. The argument that came up when the Palestinian refugees tried to return to their homes (1948) or after the conquest of the West Bank (1967) lacks consistency.

Their motivation for such violence is sustained in their religious and nationalist principles. For Palestinian leaders, Jews are not a people, they are a false religion and were stealing Islamic holy land and destroying Muslim mosques. These accusations were supported by the "colonialist" development of the Jews of the British Mandate. **BWut there is another reason: their institutional and social weakness. When there is no social cohesion (due to tribal disputes) and lack of constructive capacity, the simplest way is to say "NO" to the Jews. A lot of strength is required to say "YES" and to relinquish**.

The "all-or-nothing" policy, developed by the Palestinians since the 20s of the XX Century, has condemned them to a momentary "small amount" (even though Palestinians dominate 100% of Gaza and Territories A and B of the West Bank). A materialistic vision would argue that "it's all about the occupation" and that they are violent because they have no other choice. **This type of accountability does not help Palestinians. The current Palestinians DO have a lot to lose, as they control territories and count on disproportionate international economic support.**

Israel is also to blame for the inclination towards violence of the current Palestinians. On one side, for not acting strongly to dismantle the then-emerging Hamas, believing it was a social alternative for the PLO. On the other hand, the contact and control of the Israeli Military Forces on Palestinian civilians have increased the humiliation sensation, and at times this has manifested as ignoble and violent behaviors by Israeli soldiers.

156. Why did the Six-Day War begin in 1967?

The "Six-Day War" was a continuation of the 1956 war. Why did it begin?

1) Syria, which had not been defeated in 1956, had a new military leadership that attacked Israel and tried to illegally divert the Jordan River to "dry Israel out". On Apr/7/1967, the Syrians attacked civilian tractors in Israel and, in an air combat, Israel took down six Syrian planes. Egypt had signed a mutual military defense agreement with Syria that needed immediate help from Nasser;

2) On May/17/1967, Egypt demanded the UN's peacekeeping forces evacuate the Sinai. Nasser knew that this was a *casus belli* for Israel;

3) Egypt sent seven divisions with 100,000 soldiers and 1,000 tanks to the Israeli border, violating the treaties after the 1956 war;

4) On May/23/1967 Egypt blocked the entry of ships to Israel in the Strain of Tiran, infringing the Maritime Laws of the UN, another "cause for war";

5) On May/30/1967, the pressure made Jordan join the Syrian-Egyptian alliance, giving the power of handling their military forces to Egypt. On Jun/4/1967, Iraq joined the offensive coalition;

6) The PLO and its allies from Arab countries increased their attacks against Israel. In 1965, there were 35 incursions against Israel. In 1966, they increased to 41. Only in the first four months of 1967, there were 37 attacks;

7) Nasser, Egypt's president, said clearly: "We will not accept coexistence with Israel... Nowadays, the problem is not the establishment of peace between the Arab states and Israel... The war against Israel has been in effect since 1948".

Israel's government did not want war and was afraid of it. The military considered that it was necessary to counterattack because without the surprise factor Israel could not survive.

157. What territories did Israel conquer in the War of 1967?

The war began on Jun/5/1967 when Israel launched "Operation Focus", a surprise attack against Egyptian aircraft and bases when they were still on land (they attacked at 8:00 am). Egypt lost 286 of its 420 combat aircraft, 13 of its most important airbases and 23 radar stations. This attack gave Israel an advantage in air superiority throughout the war.

A few minutes after the beginning of Operation Focus, about at 11:15 am, Jordan began a series of raids against the Israeli part of Jerusalem and an attack on the main buildings, among them, the Government headquarters. On Jun/5/1967, at 12:30, the Israeli air force attacked the Jordanian force, destroying most of it on land. In three days the Egyptian army was defeated, the Jordan army was destroyed in two days and the Syrian in a day and a half.

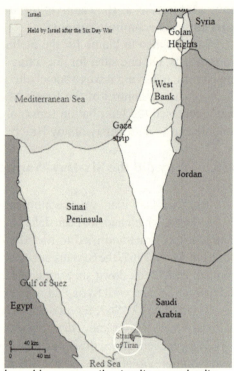

Israel increases the territory under its control by conquering the areas in orange.
(Source: Wikipedia)

The previous attack by the Egypt-Syria-Jordan alliance was defeated in just six days. About 15,000 Egyptians perished in the war and 5,600 were imprisoned. The king of Jordan declared that 6,000 Jordanian soldiers had died. Syria lost 1,000 soldiers. The Arabs ended with 45,000 wounded and 6,000 prisoners. On the Israeli side, 779 soldiers perished, especially on the Jordanian front. Additionally, 2,593 Israelis were wounded and 15 were imprisoned. From a territorial point of view, Israel conquered from Jordan the lands of Judea, Samaria and eastern Jerusalem, a total of 5,875 km^2. Israel conquered the Gaza Strip from Egypt (363 km^2) and the Sinai Peninsula (61,000 km^2). Also, Israel conquered the strategic Golan Heights (730 km^2) from Syria. Over a million Palestinians, contrary to the plans, were left under Israeli control in the areas of Judea, Samaria and the Gaza Strip.

158. Why was the Six-Day War in 1967 so important?

The 1967 war produced a change: it was the third consecutive Arab defeat (there is one more) but it was the second for Pan-Arabism. It was a mortal blow for Nasser's leadership. For the Arabs, the defeat had a devastating moral effect, which is why they call the combat *Naksa* (backward). If in 1947, the partition of Palestine had divided the emerging Arab nation, the Israeli expansion of 1967 was seen as a humiliation for the Arabs.

The 1967 war resulted in a qualitative change. Israel achieved what is known in military terms as "strategic depth" to stop being "in shooting range of the enemy", as it had been for the past 20 years. On the other hand, the capitals of the enemy countries were under the eyes of the IDF. However, Israel was not clear on what they were going to do with the conquered part.

The western vision was not unequivocal. Israel stopped mustering sympathy from the left (not communist) and the progressives. In 1967 it was perceived as an "occupying" power as they were seen in their colonial days.

The Palestinian issue acquired a new dimension because of the union of the mentioned factors and because of the thousands of Palestinians who went to live under direct Israeli military control. **The damages resulting from the Palestinian-Israeli military contact were perceived in the second and third generations of Palestinian-Arabs, those who had not known about the Jordan (and Egyptian) occupation and began the Intifada of 1987.**

After the Six-Day War, in August 1967, the Arab countries convened in Khartoum (Sudan) and issued a declaration known as the "Three NOs of Khartoum: No peace with Israel, No recognition of Israel, No negotiations with Israel". After 1967, there was much more to discuss about the Palestinian-Israeli conflict than the Arab-Israeli one.

159. What was the position of the United Nations in reference to the War of 1967? What is Resolution 242 of the UN Security Council?

The UN developed a peace project known as Security Council Resolution 242. It is based on: 1) retreat of the Israeli forces from the conquered territories in the Six-Day War; 2) end of the military actions, in respect of the right of all the countries of the area to live in peace in their territorial integrity; 3) solution to the problem of the Palestinian refugees in the framework of the peace agreements. The UN committed to send a mediator to negotiate a peace agreement, according to Resolution 242.

At first, Israel considered as negative the request to retreat from the conquered areas, although the official declaration (English version) did not say from "all the territories", allowing Israeli control over sensitive areas for its security. The Arab countries rejected it, although later Jordan, Egypt and Syria accepted it.

Possibly the highlight of this Resolution was its acceptance by the Soviet Union and the United States.

Although the Palestinians were not a part of Resolution 242, it became the framework for Israel's participation in the Oslo Accords (1993) with the PLO.

Resolution 242 of the UN Security Council is not legally binding, although Israel accepted it since December 1967. It does not lead to sanctions, as it is based on Chapter VI of the UN Charter that deals with "any dispute, the continuance of which is likely to endanger the maintenance of international peace and security ", compared to mandatory and binding resolutions related to Chapter VII, "threats to the peace, breach of the peace, or acts of aggression".

In December 2016, the Security Council approved Resolution 2334 (Chapter VI) that contradicts Resolution 242, setting a border (the Green Line) where there wasn't one before.

160. What was the attitude of the Israeli population towards the conquest of the West Bank and the Gaza Strip?

In the local front, the Israeli population "fell in love" with Judea, Samaria and Gaza. Some used to wander or did business around the area, while others found cheap workforce for their companies. Entire economic sectors, like the constructions, depended on the Palestinian workforce, which later became a problematic situation.

There was a wide Israeli consensus about the need to maintain control over parts or the entire territory. In 1967, Israel lacked "military strategic depth", which made the defense of the civilians more difficult. Now, the borders were much farther from the population concentrations.

Within some political parties, the victory of 1967 was understood as a messianic era. In general, the entire political map of Israel was clearly inclined towards the right. The Mafdal (neo-orthodox Zionist party) lived the most drastic change; its leadership passed to be slowly substituted by a new and activist one that defended the Jewish right over all territories.

On the eve of the Six-Day War (1967), there was an existential fear in Israel (they thought that 100,000 Israelis would lose their lives). The memory of the tough battles for Jerusalem in 1948, the fall and destruction of their Jewish neighborhoods and the pre-war fear, created a sensation of euphoria and omnipotence, that was the base of groups that perceived this development as part of a process of redemption

Strategically speaking, the Israelis fell in love with their air force; they developed an equivocal conception that there would not be any new attack without an Arab superiority in that matter.

Very few Israelis considered that the everyday military contact with a civilian population would produce damage in the defensive spirits of their soldiers, it would make the soldiers act as policemen and the Palestinians would feel humiliated by the Jewish presence in every facet of their lives.

161. What did the Israeli government decide to do with the conquered territories of the War of 1967?

In September 1967, the Arab League Summit held in Khartoum (Sudan) issued its "No to peace, No to recognition and No to negotiations with Israel". **The Israelis understood that there was no one to negotiate with, and therefore studied other options.**

The government considered that the Sinai Peninsula (Egypt) and the Golan Heights (Syria) could be used as exchange within a bilateral peace agreement. Israel returned the entire Sinai to Egypt (1979) and the territory claimed by Jordan was reinstated (1994). **To date, approximately 94% of the territories gained in the War of 1967 have been returned by Israel to its Arab neighbors during negotiations. This proves the disposition of Israel to make territorial concessions.**

Alon Plan *(Source: Wikipedia)*

The position of the governing Socialist Party was based on the plan of Minister Igal Alon. Because of security considerations, Israel was to prevent the penetration of terrorists from Jordan, by establishing bases and villages in the valley of Jordan, and the same was to occur in the first heights from the east, the central mountain range. The rest of the territory could be granted to an Arab authority. This is how the settlement of Kiryat Arba (near Hebron) was established and the 6,000 Israeli inhabitants living in the Valley of Jordan.

Moshe Dayan, Defense Minister at the time, believed that there was no possibility of reaching total agreements as Alon proposed, so he suggested allowing the Palestinians to live as Jordanians, passing freely to that country. Because of this policy, the Arab-Palestinians passed to Jordan via the Allenby Bridge. Both plans were carried out.

With the arrival to the government of the nationalist party Likud, a *de facto* policy was imposed in order to increase the Israeli control over the West Bank.

162. Do all Palestinians live in territories that were once occupied by Israel in 1967?

Most of the Palestinian concentration (more than four million, even though there is not a formal census), is located in the West Bank and the Gaza Strip. Currently, in the Gaza Strip, there is a *de facto* state governed by Hamas and another proto-state in Territories A and B of the West Bank.

A good deal of those who left after the 1948 War went to live in the numerous refugee camps in Lebanon, Jordan and Syria. Their situation is different from one country to another. They are alike because of how they have been used by their Arab brothers as cannon fodder without protecting them nor giving them rights. The Palestinian identity was perverted by their Pan-Arab leaders, starting with Nasser but following with the emirs of Kuwait or the presidents of Iraq.

More or less 20% of the Israeli population are Arabs (Palestinians); in other words, more or less 1.7 million. The Israeli citizenship that they possess allows them to enjoy civilian rights unknown to their Arab equals in the Middle East, and a superior economic status from the rest of the Palestinians that have not been integrated into the countries that, allegedly, fought for them in 1948 and generated their drama. **In Israel, we find Palestinian representatives in the Knesset, in the Supreme Court of Justice and in different tiers of the government and, currently (2019), there is an increase in the recruitment of Arab-Israelis in the security forces or in the national service (social volunteering linked to the army).**

The Palestinian conscience of belonging to one people had a late awakening and the dispersion was not so much of an obstacle but a unifying factor. The conformation of a Palestinian nationality was clearly motivated by the creation of the State of Israel and was developed after the Six-Day War.

163. What is the situation of the Palestinians living in Israel?

After the creation of Israel, about 150,000 Arabs were left within the country, most of them Muslims. At the time, they were about 15% of the population and today they are about 20%. The government decided to impose a military government over the Arab villages until 1966 because the Arabs were perceived as enemies, as they had fought against the Jews during the war of independence; a totally logical situation at the time.

As a result of this new reality, between 1948 and 1967 the every-day ties with the Palestinians were lost, beyond the Green Line. Israelis like to call them Arab-Israelis, though, at present, many of them refer to be called Palestinians with Israeli citizenship.

Most of them live in the north, around the previously Christian city of Nazareth (an economic center). Most of the population of Nazareth is Arab-Muslim and they usually harass their Arab-Christian co-inhabitants. They live in cities considered as "mixed", with Arabs and Jews, such as Haifa, Jaffa or Akko, the three on the Mediterranean Sea.

Near eastern Jerusalem, there are about 200,000 Palestinians, an area previously in Jordanian hands up to 1967. After the War of 1967, they were offered citizenship but rejected it almost totally. Since then, they have permits to work and enter Israel and they can vote in municipal elections, but not for Parliament. They are permanent residents. Parts of these neighborhoods of eastern Jerusalem are indirectly controlled by the Palestinian Authority.

At present (2019), there seems to be a tendency towards integrating the Arab-Israeli minority (especially Christians). A survey developed among Arab-Israelis by the Israel Democracy Institute (2007) showed that 75% of the population supported the State of Israel as a Jewish and Democratic State that guarantees equal rights to minorities.

164. What was the Attrition War? What do we refer to when we talk about the "Country of Persecutions"?

It was a long and hard series of battles in the border between Israel and Egypt and the Israel-Jordan border. President Gamal Abdel Nasser's reasoning to initiate the incidents was explained by Mohamed Heikal, an Egyptian journalist close to the regime: "If we succeed in inflicting 10,000 deaths, inevitably, they will be forced to stop fighting because they don't have reservists". The Egyptian president Nasser believed that "what was taken by force must be restored by force".

The war of medium intensity began on Jul/1/1967, when an Egyptian commando took their position in Ras el-Ish, 16 km away from Said Port, an area in Israeli hands since the cease-fire of Jun/9/1967. The Israeli revenge came on the night of Oct/30/1967 when commandos (*Sayeret Matkal*) that were transported in helicopters destroyed the main source of electricity in Egypt. Israel was attacked in bases and fixed positions (Bar-Lev Line).

During the Attrition War, there were 1,424 dead Israeli soldiers and another 3,000 were wounded. The Israeli Air Force lost 14 airplanes. Israeli historian, Benny Morris, sustains that there were around 10,000 deaths among Egyptian soldiers and civilians and that 98 airplanes were destroyed. However, the Egyptians did not publish any data. The Egyptians consider this battle as a victory because they were not defeated and so did the Israelis that controlled the Egyptian offensive aided by the Soviet Union.

The Attrition War was present in the Jordan border. The land of the persecutions (*Eretz Hamirdafim*) is the name given to the Jordan Valley and to the eastern part of the mountains of Judea and Samaria, the north of the Dead Sea. Until Jordan murdered Palestinians in Black September (1970), the terrorist commandos were struck down in hundreds of persecutions, when they penetrated from Jordan to attack Israel. Israel lost soldiers and officers that led these persecutions.

165. What is Black September?

The PLO fighters not only attacked Israel in the "Land of Persecution", they also intended to overthrow King Hussein of Jordan (they tried to kill him twice), considering him an ally of imperialism. The actions of the PLO created international complications for the King because hijacked planes were consecutively directed to Jordan by the Palestinians (1970).

The hijackings of Dawson's Field were three aircraft forced to land on Zerqa, their passengers were taken as hostages and the equipment was detonated on the field, before the international press. Hussein saw this event as the last straw and ordered his army to move forward.

On Sep/9/1970, Jordan began to bomb the Palestinian refugee camps. The Fedayeen were expelled one by one, until the last group of 2,000 Palestinian fighters surrendered when rounded up in a forest near Ajloun, on July/17/1971, thus ending the conflict.

The Black September Organization was created during the conflict to retaliate. The group took responsibility for the murder of the Jordanian Prime Minister, Wasfi Al-Tal (1971), and the murder of 11 Israeli athletes participating in the 1972 Olympic Games of Munich.

The number of Palestinians deceased was estimated by the Jordanians in 2,500, while Yasser Arafat estimated 3,400 deceased and 10,800 wounded. Israel estimated a higher amount: about 20,000. The Hashemite Dynasty ensured its rule over Jordan, while the Palestinian terrorists found a new place for their activities: Lebanon. The Jordanian forces reported 537 losses among their members.

After creating an institutional void and anarchy in Jordan, the PLO continued to do the same thing in Lebanon, participating in the civil war against the Maronite Christians. They stayed there until 1982.

166. What happened in the 1972 Munich Olympic Games?

Not all terrorism is identical: there is the "romantic terrorism" (*Narodna Volya*); "personalized terrorism" like ETA (they performed some indiscriminate actions); "indiscriminate terrorism", when the maximum amount of civilians are murdered intentionally; "suicidal terrorism" and, finally, "terrorism with unconventional weaponry" (biological, chemical, atomic). **The *modus operandi* of the PLO in the 70s and the 80s was the indiscriminate terrorism.**

There are people with an untuned moral compass that praise those who murder civilians intentionally (Leila Khaled or similar characters). The issue seems to exceed the circumstances of the Palestinian-Israeli conflict and links the value of violence with an act of heroism, diplomatic and political measures or acts of institutional construction, which tend to be seen by them as "weak and condescending". **This guideline of sanctifying terrorism makes the solution of a conflict more difficult since it can only be solved through compromise.**

One of the acts of terrorism by the PLO was the kidnapping of Israeli athletes during the Olympic Games in Munich (September 1972) to exchange them for 234 Palestinian prisoners in Israeli jails and the liberation of the founders of the Red Army Faction, Andreas Baader and Ulrike Meinhof, imprisoned in Germany.

They entered the athletes' bedrooms, murdered some of them and took others as hostages. The Israeli government rejected the negotiation with a self-proclaimed group "Black September", in memory of what happened in Jordan in 1970.

What began as a negotiation with the German authorities was followed by the relocation of the athletes to a military base in the outskirts of the city where, after a fire exchange, they were murdered. **The Olympic Games were not interrupted despite the murder of eleven Israelis.** After Munich 1972, the Mossad formed a special commando group to execute those responsible for the killings.

167. What is the importance of the War of Yom Kippur of 1973 for the Palestinian-Israeli conflict?

This was the last attempt to "erase" Israel via an open war with state armies. On Oct/6/1973, an Egyptian-Syrian alliance initiated a surprise attack on the Day of Atonement (Yom Kippur), while the Jews were fasting and pra-ying. The weakened Israeli defense forces, concentrated on the Bar-Lev Line, were easily defeated.

Raymond Aron (*Memoirs*) affirms that Egyptian President Anwar El-Sadat prepared an attack with a limited objective, in order to, as he later told Golda Meir, "not having to arrive on our knees to negotiate with Israel". But this affirmation was made later and did not represent the Syrian opinion.

Anwar Al-Sadat wanted to get away from the Russian patronage and approach the United States (Sadat called this *Intifah* – opening). In Israel, on the other hand, a concept had been created whereby the air superiority implied that it was illogical that the "weak" Sadat could attack them. This misconception made the intelligence coming from Egypt to be wrongly coded.

The doubtful limited objectives could have been true in the case of Egypt, though impossible to believe for the Syrian side in Golan. Syria attacked with 350,000 men supported by Iraq, Saudis and even Moroccans. **Sometimes it seems confusing that many are incapable to carry out their intentions, acknowledging their immediate limitations, as if they were abandoning their political-ideological program**.

Although the Israeli army recovered from this surprise attack and passed to counterattack, the war created a profound crisis in the State of Israel. The Arabs consider it a victory and call it the "War of October".

Since 1973, the Arab countries and the Muslims, including the Palestinians, have sought other ways to destroy or weaken Israel. For example, they pay and train terrorists of Hezbollah or Hamas, foster embargos and boycotts, and continue with a flagrant anti-Semitic rhetoric

168. Why do all the Jewish people in the world feel so linked to Israel?

The answer is simple: most of the Jews in the world feel a part of the Jewish people (it is possible to belong to more than one people, like the Chinese-Argentinian, the Italian-Chilean, or the Greek-Peruvian) and being Israel the national cradle of the Jewish people (80% of the inhabitants of Israel are Jewish), then the relation and the sentimental links are obvious.

For generations, the Jews from all over the world pray facing Jerusalem and in their prayers, they yearn for their return to Jerusalem or at least be buried there. Beyond the circumstances, Israel is a place where the Jews, as a nation, have reestablished their capacity of self-proclamation after centuries of building minorities in different places of the planet. There they can govern themselves and assume their national responsibilities.

The message that is transmitted to the Jews of the world is that they will never be massacred again since they count with a state. As such, their triumphs in wars, their multiple technological developments or the creative actions of the secret service of Israel are celebrated, as well as the kidnapping of the Nazi leader Adolf Eichmann in Argentina (1960) or the liberation of the kidnapped airplane in Entebbe (1976).

A certain part of the Jews from the world consider that Israel must be "the light for the rest of the nations", which is why their conduct must be exemplary. Their criticism towards all actions performed by Israel is very extreme (some even are obsessed to demonstrate others that they are not "that type of Jews"). On the other extreme, uncritical Jews stand out, unconditional to Israel, that condemn any negative judgment towards Israel, accusing any critic of being anti-Semitic. For the modern Judeophobe, these feelings of pride for Israel are usually qualified as "arrogant" or "racist". We know, those who hate, hate first and then find justification.

169. How can the US support to Israel be explained? Is it because of the Jewish lobby?

The US's support to Israel has not always existed, nor has it been unconditional. From 1948 to 1967, the assessment of the US State Department was that Israel would not withstand the threats to its existence, so they prioritized their relations with the Arab countries. Presidents George Bush (Sr.), Jimmy Carter or Barack Obama have been reticent towards Israel or have shown a certain hostility in many topics.

The influence of the North American Jews is important, especially during elections, as Jews donate 70% of the funds raised by the Democratic Party and 30% to the Republicans. Jews usually vote for the Democrats (over 70% since the 1920s), a party that during the recent years has developed a harsh anti-Israel branch.

One of the most influential organizations is AIPAC (American-Israeli Public Affairs Committee). Many of the 5,000,000 Jews belong to different pro-Israel lobby organizations, competing with other anti-Israel lobbies.

The US has other allies in the Middle East, and some of their relations (with Saudi Arabia) have created friction with Israel. However, Israel is still more predictable and trustworthy, being a vibrant democracy, and is an alternative in a highly unstable zone.

At present (2019), the vote of the 70 million Christians in the US belonging to the Bible Belt (Evangelic Christians) is more determining than the Jewish vote.

The economic support of the US to Israel is larger than other countries, but unlike the 70s decade, it has ceased to be determining for its economy. The US strategic support is still a survival issue for Israel, not only because of the immediate threats, but also because of the diplomatic estrangement it must face, and because of the influence of the US on some neighboring countries.

170. What is the Interim Agreement between Israel and Egypt?

The Interim Agreement (Sinai Agreement) was signed on Sept/4/1975 in Geneva between the governments of Anwar El-Sadat (Egypt) and Yitzhak Rabin (Israel). The agreement was reached after intense mediation by the US Secretary of State, Henry Kissinger, wishing to separate Egypt from the USSR.

Kissinger exerted pressure over Israel, threatening to stop sending weaponry and "reevaluating their bilateral relations" since Israel was not willing to give enough.

In the agreement, the parties were committed to not use threats nor force. The territorial part stipulated that Israel would withdraw to a 30-40 kilometers line to the east, including the steps of Mitla and Gidi in the Western Sinai. This area was transformed into a damping zone under the supervision of the UN forces.

Israel also withdrew from most of the oil fields in the Sinai, including Abu Rhodes (and the Shalhevet establishment, which was located there) and Belim. This strip became a demilitarized Egyptian territory and there were agreements between Israel and Egyptians in the parallel highway to the Gulf. The Egyptians promised in a letter to the United States that they would not intervene in a war between Israel and Syria, in case Syria was the initiator.

As part of this agreement, the US guaranteed to supply oil to Israel as a substitute for the evacuated oil fields in the Sinai and promised that, in case of a future war, they would prepare an emergency plan to supply military equipment to Israel in two months. It would also include agreements for the purchase of military equipment (F-15 airplanes and future F-16).

This interim agreement was important because it increased the trust between Egypt and Israel to proceed with the bilateral Peace agreement of 1979.

171. Why did nationalism defeat socialism in Israel in the 1977 elections?

The 1977 elections had two opposing processes in development since the beginning of the 60s; on one side, the process of the loss of popularity of the Mapai (Labor Party) in face of the growth of the legitimacy of the Herut (today Likud).

The fall of the Mapai or Ma'arach began with the second round of the "Embarrassing Issue" in 1960-1961 (the Lavon case, a failed sabotage operation of Israel in Egypt). The internal differences became more serious due to the negligence of 1973 (the surprise attack on Yom Kippur) when the founding fathers (Ben-Gurion, Levy Eshkol, Golda Meir) were not leading the party anymore.

The legitimating process of the Likud began with the development of Gahal (Herut –Liberals- 1965), and its later participation in the national unity government during the Six-day War – 1967), and continued with the organization of the Likud (1973).

The Herut of Menahem Begin had been declared by David Ben-Gurion as a legitimate party for the coalition. However, its position in the Israeli political spectrum was being increasingly accepted, especially after the Six-Day War, when the entire political map inclined to the right.

The Likud's legitimating process was reinforced by the support of the poorest. The Likud became a party supported by second-generation Sephardic immigrants that perceived that Ashkenazim and new immigrants were progressing while they were not.

These two opposing processes were catalyzed with clear tendencies: the downfall of the coalition after the arrival of the F16 to Israel (1976) and the different corruption cases among the leadership of the Ma'arach.

From 1977 to 2019, with the exception of brief government periods by the socialists or by Kadima (Sharon-Olmert), the Likud has been the governing party in Israel. (1977-1984, 1986-1992, 1996-1999, 2001-2006, 2009-2019).

172. What did the Egypt-Israel Peace Agreement of Camp David mean to the Palestinians?

On Mar/26/1979, Israel and Egypt signed two agreements. The first agreement was named Framework for Peace in the Middle East and was divided into two parts. On one hand, it was agreed that Declarations 242 and 348 would be the bases for regional peace. It was agreed that the West Bank and Gaza would have a Palestinian civilian autonomy for five years and, after this period, they would sign a final agreement with legitimate authorities. During the third year, they would begin negotiations for a final status. **Israel rejected the PLO as the Palestinian leadership but the 3+2 model was repeated in the Oslo Accords.**

The second part of the agreement stipulated a process of normalization that would be supported by the later signature of treaties with the other countries of the area.

The second pact centered on bilateral relations. Israel would abandon the Sinai up to the international border of 1906 (Egypt did not want Gaza back) and Egypt would recognize Israel by establishing diplomatic, economic and tourism exchanges. Egypt would ensure the free pass of Israeli ships through the Suez Canal. The total withdrawal (with the evacuation of colonies) would finalize in 3 years (April 1982).

Anwar Al-Sadat (Egypt) Jimmy Carter (USA) and Menahem Begin (Israel) during the signature of the Peace Treaty (*Source: GPO and Wikipedia*)

Sadat was interested in linking the bilateral peace treaties to a pro-Palestinian agreement, even though the Arab world considered Egypt as a "traitor" after what they did. Menahem Begin, in parallel, wanted to make clear that Israel would not renounce the West Bank nor the Gaza Strip. **However, he recognized that the Palestinians** had "legitimate rights" and committed to stopping to establish settlements during the peace process with the Palestinians. Begin and Sadat differed in regard to the future of Jerusalem.

The Egypt-Israel Agreement was the first occasion in which an Arab country would prefix their selfish interests to their Pan-Arab rhetoric.

173. What ideology replaced Pan-Arabism and why is Pan-Islamism so important today?

Pan-Arabism was mortally wounded during the 70s and continued its descent later. If you watch closely, the emerging powers in the Middle East are not Arab (Turkey and Iran). The only one that stands out is Qatar (because of its oil, gas and Al-Jazeera)

Pan-Arabism fell after the defeat of Egypt-Nasser in 1967 and the signature of the bilateral peace treaty between Sadat and Israel. The leader of Pan-Arabism (Egypt) was expelled from the Arab League in 1985.

The ideology that replaced Pan-Arabism was Pan-Islamism, in force at present. Pan-Islamism is a political idea that seeks the union of all Muslims in an Islamic State or caliphate. It is believed that the expression "union of Muslims" was used for the first time in 1872 by the writer and political activist of the Ottoman Youth, Namik Kamil. While Pan-Arabism seeks unity and independence of the Arabs regardless of their religion, Pan-Islamism advocates for union and independence of Muslims under the law of *Shaarya*.

The Islamic radical forces have done profound fieldwork since the end of World War I. During the 70s-80s two factors moved ideologists to complement the *Dawa* (social action and propaganda) with the *Jihad* (holy war and physical force). Besides the ideological influence of Sayd Qutb, the radicals witnessed how their pairs in Iran took over power in 1979. If the Shiites could do it, many thought, so could the Sunni. The Palestinian Islamic Jihad (1981) was influenced by the Shiite revolution. The second fact was the expulsion of Russian imperialism from Afghanistan by the Taliban during the 80s. If the Taliban Muslims could, they all could, so they thought.

174. How can we differentiate and analyze Islam schools?

Among the "universalist" intellectuals (wrongly named, from the left-wing) there are no great specialists in Islamist radicalism. **Not being a specialist in the tribal-religious Middle East is unacceptable.**

Within the "conservatives" we can differentiate two sub-schools: the first affirms that Islam is essentially radical because of radical theological premises. Important spokespeople are Robert Spencer or the activist and writer Ayaan Hirsi-Ali.

The second school of thought argues that the Islamic religion does not have to be radical, which may be moderated and reformed as others have been, even though the main agenda, especially in the Middle East, is dictated by the radicals. Among other noticeable spokespeople, there is Bernard Lewis or the analyst Daniel Pipes. The author of these lines is part of the latter sub-school.

On one hand, it is false that the Islam "is as radical" as other monotheistic religions and that there is no relation between the theological bases of the Muslims and their radicalized manifestations. Yes, the agenda of the religion has been kidnapped by radicals, but this will change.

What is the basis for essentialism? The 114 revelations (*Suras*) divided between those from Mecca and from Medina, which are those that impose the case of contradiction (abrogation principle – *Naskh*). Those from Medina are more radical (read revelations number 9 and 47, that are from Mecca). The *Hadiths* (conduct based on actions or sayings from Mohammed) can also be very radical.

The pre-Modern Muslims developed *Hiyal* (tricks) and other gimmicks for maintaining the intention of the law but relieving its implementation. Daniel Pipes calls this "The Medieval Synthesis". The modern Islamic radicals are "purists" and try to impose the law exactly as it is written. Nowadays, we are living the prime of "purism", the consequence of the deep crisis that the Islam suffered after World War I.

175. What deep factors motivated the rise of Islamic radicalism?

The current crisis did not begin exactly with WWI, but with the penetration of modernity in the Middle East. We could date it with the attack of Napoleon to Egypt in 1798. This challenge dispersed the Muslims in opposing directions during the following two centuries: westernization or Islamization. Some Muslims, impressed by western progress, intended to minimize the Islamic law replacing it with western customs, reducing the influence of religion, increasing women's rights and equality between believers and non-believers. The most notorious example was the foundation of Turkey by Kemal Atatürk. Today, we see how the same Turkey recedes towards the formal *Shaarya* with Erdogan's government.

Penetration of modernity occurred traumatically for Muslims, with the fall of the last Muslim empire, the Ottoman Turks, during World War I. Suddenly, some Muslims observed, stunned, how those that were supposedly inferior to Islam, the *Dhimmi* Christians of France or England, were imposing their foreign superior technology and customs before an Islam that had come to a standstill in the XII Century. The Islam, conquerors of the world, who had imposed their scientific and philosophical superiority, now seemed like a cartoon of itself.

One of the first people to react to the humiliation after WWI was a school inspector called Hassan El-Banna, who in 1929 formed the association of the Muslim Brotherhood. The motto was simple: if we develop social actions and propaganda (*Dawa*) we can bring back Muslims to the origins, in Arabic *Salaf*, to behave as the *Rashidun* did, the first four Caliphs and their followers. Violence was always present as an option but only when success was ensured or when it was essential to act in such a way.

176. How many Muslims feel close to the ideas of the Islamic radicalism (2019)?

The fourth edition of the Global Terrorism Index (Institute for Economics & Peace), with data from 163 countries, offers compelling data: in 2015, four terrorist groups that allegedly represented the original Islam generated 74% of the murders from terrorism. They murdered 17,741 human beings in only a year, much more than all the Palestinian casualties in every war against Israel from 1920 up to now. In addition, the other countries gather 72% of the casualties from terrorism: Iraq, Nigeria, Afghanistan, Pakistan and Syria, all of them Muslim. In 2000, the Islamist groups conducted 251 attempts around the world. Fifteen years later, in 2014, the number increased ten times that amount: 2,572 attempts.

It is probable that the following affirmations are correct: 1) the minority of the 1,600 million Muslims in the world think radically. The numbers are around 10% and 25% but it all depends on the parameters used to define radicalism.

Is someone who wishes to destroy Israel an Islamic extremist? No. There are anti-Semites that act in the same direction. Every person who wishes to imitate exactly Mohammed's behavior? Probably.

2) Even though they are a minority, there are not few people. If only 0.5% of the Muslims are radicals, we are talking about 800,000 human beings; 3) In the Middle East, the radicals dominate the agendas and are supported by

rich kingdoms like Qatar, Saudi Arabia or Turkey; 4) a tiny minority of these radicals execute terrorist attempts; 5) on the other hand, the great majority of the terrorist attempts are produced by Muslims and are performed in the name of Islam.

The Malikite and Hanbalite schools (30% of Sunni) are the most radical. The other 15% of the Islam is Shiite, like Iran, Hezbollah or Assad... How many of these 140 million Shiites are radical? It is hard to say...

177. What does it mean to a radical Islamist that all the west is Yahiliyah?

Yahiliyah ("ignorance") is an Islamic concept that refers to a period before the advent of Islam. It is the "Age of Ignorance". In modern times, several Islamic thinkers have used the term to criticize what they perceived as the non-Islamic nature (secular) of the public and private life in the Muslim world. Pakistani philosopher Abul Allah Maududi affirmed that modernity is the "new *Yahiliyah*". The radical groups justify the armed fight against secular regimes as a Jihad against *Yahiliyah*.

In modern times, *Yahiliyah* is television, democratic elections, gender equality, theatres, etc... For Hamas or the Islamic Jihad, Israel is a *Yahiliyah* state that contaminates Islam.

The term Yahiliyah is used in several passages of the Quran (33:33) "Stay in your houses and do not flaunt your finery like the former days of pagan ignorance" or (48:26) "When those who disbelieve had set up in their hearts zealotry, the zealotry of the Age of Ignorance...".

The concept of modern *Yahiliyah* attained great popularity because of the work developed in 1950 by Abul Hassan Nadvi, a student from Mawdudi, titled *What did the world lose because of the decadence of the Muslims?* In Egypt, Sayid Qutb popularized the term *Yahiliyah* in his influential work *Maalim fi-al-Tariq* (milestones). For Qutb, "...the main duty of Islam in this world is to replace the *Yahaliyah* in the leadership of mankind, take over leadership in its own hands and fulfill the particular way of life that is its permanent characteristic".

Why do they attack France? Because it is the cradle of the French Revolution. England? Because it is the cradle of democracy. The United States? Because it is the main cultural exporter of *Yahaliyah*. Within the Gaza Strip, some accuse Hamas of *Yahaliyah* for participating in the parliamentary elections of 2006.

178. How does an Islamic radical divide the world?

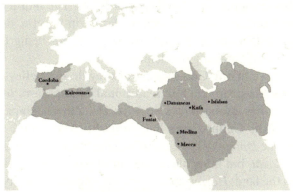

In green, the House of Islam (includes El-Andalus – Spain); in white Dar El-Harb *(Source: Wikipedia)*

For a radical, the world is divided into two parts. One is the House of Islam, *Dar El-Islam*. The idea of a geographic-religious division is not mentioned in the Quran nor in the Hadiths, but it was suggested for the first time by the Sunni jurist Abu Hanifah, founder of the Hanafite School.

Dar al-Islam is the land controlled by the Muslims during the first three caliphates: the conquests of Mohammed (until 632), from the orthodox Omiya Caliphates (until 750). In the House of Islam, the *Shaharya* was imposed as a law, an idealized period of the history of Islam to which they wish to return to. A good Muslim cannot, in any way, renounce the re-imposition of the glory of the House of Islam. There is one truth, Islam, and in the future, everyone will be *Dar al-Islam*. Israel is unacceptable because it occupies *Dar al-Islam*.

Facing the House of Islam, there is *Dar al-Harb* (literally "House of War"), which is the land inhabited by non-Muslims who they will have to fight if they attack Islam or if the sole truth is imposed via *Dawa*. The aggression could also be through the cultural exportation of their *Yahiliya*. The *fiqh* establishes that the non-Muslim regions belong to Islam, as well as the goods of those who profess other non-Muslim religions and must be returned to its law when circumstances allow it.

Sometimes, *Dar el-Hudna* (truce) is used. It is a territory in which an agreement of non-belligerence has been signed between battles.

This division in the world comes from classic Islam and, currently, it is used in an aggressive way and with political-religious purposes by Islamic fundamentalists.

179. How does a radical Islamist divide humanity?

The only truth is Islam and it is the one that is expressed by Muslims (that is how a radical thinks). Pagans face the Muslims, those who do not believe in one God alone. These people cannot live together with Islam. The murder of pagans in hands of radical Muslims has been seen in Darfur, in Nigeria, or more recently in Syria when ISIS murdered hundreds of Yazidi for being a pre-Islamic religion they accuse of "praising the demon".

Jews and Christians believe in one God alone, but they do not believe in Allah and Mohammed as his prophet. For traditional Islam, Jews of Christians, and sometimes other monotheists such as the Zoroastrians, are *Dhimmis*, the property of the Caliphs, and live under his protection.

Typically, the "people of the *Dhimmah*" are exempt of the military service and the religious tax, called *Zakat*, but in its place, they must pay a per capita tax, called *Yizia*, and a tax on the land, *Haray*, apart from obeying the authority of the Caliph or the Sultan. Also, they have the right to practice their faith (although with severe limitations), they cannot reconstruct or build new churches or synagogues in Dar Al-Islam, they cannot sound the *shofar* or church bells, they cannot ride on donkeys or horses or use swords, as these humiliate Muslims, they must use identification signs on their clothes, and although they can use their own judges for civil issues, such as matrimonies, divorces and successions, if the Caliph considers it appropriate, the son of the *Dhimmi* can be educated in the Islam.

The laws of the *Dhimmah* were imposed as a measure to convert Jews and Christians to Islam, but not by force.

Now, a radical would say: how do these *Dhimmis* of Israel dare to impose a Jewish state in *Dar-El-Islam*?

180. Is it true that there are no universal values for Islamic radicals?

For an Islamic radical there are laws within Islam and others outside. Consider "robbery". Islamic law is notable for imposing harsh punishments and the most famous one can be amputation for robbery: "And (as for) the male thief and the female thief, cut off their hands as retribution for that which both committed, a punishment by way of example from Allah. And Allah is All-Powerful, All-Wise." (Quran 5:38). What happens when someone steals from an enemy of Islam? The answer for a radical would be "it is possible". The Quran has laws for the distribution of the booty of war, demanding that one-fifth must be destined to Allah and charity work (Quran 8:41).

Consider the concept of "peace" for a radical. Peace exists within Islam and it is known as *Sulha* (forgiveness) while for the non-believers there can only be *Hudna (*truce) imposed as Mohammed did with the tribe of Quraysh in Hudaybiyah between 628 and 630. The *Hudna* can be violated if it favors Muslims. Does Israel have a *Sulha* or a *Hudna* with Egypt? The University of Al-Azhar said it clearly: a *Hudna.*

Here is another example lacking truth. When the Shiite Muslims were persecuted by the Sunni, they developed the doctrine of *Taqiyya* or hiding, where they could lie to save themselves. Currently, we see an exaggeration of the *Taqiyya* among the Sunni as well as in the Shiites, when they exploit the use of lies, especially before the *Dhimmi.*

The phrase of Jesus "all things whatsoever you wish that men should do to you: you should do unto them..." (Matthew 7:12) appears as well in Judaism when the wise Hillel summarizes Judaism in the same phrase. The value is universal. When there are norms within the faith and others outside, we are close to radicalism.

181. Is it true that imitating Mohammed in all his actions and sayings increases the tendency towards radicalism?

For Islam, Mohammed is a *Rasul* (they transmit his message through a book), and not only a Prophet. Mohammed is the last prophet of Allah on Earth, he is the "Seal of the Prophets" and after him, there will not be any new revelations. Before Mohammed, 24 prophets preached on Earth, who new part of the truth; among them, Abraham, Ishmael, Yitzhak and Yaakov, Jethro, kings David and Solomon, Elijah and Elisha, Jesus and John the Baptist. Mohammed is the last Prophet and the possessor of all the truth. As the superior authority of Islam, he guides the prayers.

If a person wishes to follow exactly each action by Mohammed as a sacred mandate, then this is an Islamist behavior. Why? Because the behavior of a leader of the VII Century cannot be adapted to what is accepted in the XXI Century.

If Mohammed is perfect, no one can joke about Mohammed because revenge can be brought upon the person as happened with the satiric diary *Charlie Hebdo.* Mohammed married 13 women. His third wife was called Aisha, the daughter of the First Caliph of Islam, Abu Baker. In the Islamic writings, her name frequently appears, preceded by the title "Mother of the Believers" (*Umm al-Mu'minin*). Traditional sources affirm that Aisha married Mohammed at age 6 or 7 (he was 53), and the marriage was consummated when she was 8 or 9, in Medina. Someone that considers such conduct is "imitable" will legitimize marriage with a minor or pedophilia. Another example can be seen when telling the truth to a non-believer.

182. What is the Jihad Islamic Organization for Palestine?

Established in Gaza (Palestine) in 1981, its main objective was the destruction of the State of Israel and the establishment of an Islamic Palestinian State. The organization's flag has a verse of the Quran: "And those who do *jihad* for us, we shall guide them to our paths. And God is with those who do good". It has been labeled as a terrorist organization by the USA, the European Union, United Kingdom, Japan, Canada, Australia, New Zealand and Israel.

The Islamic Jihad was founded by the Palestinians Dr. Fatji El-Aziz Shqaqi, a doctor from Rafah, and the Sheik Abed Awda, an Islamic preacher from the Jebalya fields. **They were originally members of the Muslim Brotherhood but were seduced by the successful Iranian Revolution (1979). Today, they collaborate and compete with Hamas in Gaza and have connections with Hezbollah.**

The Shqaqi branch was expelled from Egypt in 1981 after the murder of President Anwar El-Sadat and later reestablished in Gaza. The Islamic Jihad began its armed operations against Israel in 1984. They executed various attacks in Israel. The first one was a suicide attack against a 405 bus from Tel-Aviv to Jerusalem in 1989, murdering 16 Israeli civilians. During the Second Intifada, they multiplied their suicide attacks.

Shqaqi was a key piece in the creation of the Alliance for the Rejection of the Palestinian Forces that in January 1994, had conformed a coalition of eight groups of the PLO (among them the Popular Front and the Democratic Front), the Islamic Jihad and Hamas, which rejected the peace process of Oslo. Shqaqi was murdered in Malta in 1995, he was replaced by Ramadan Salaj for 23 years and then substituted by Ziad Najalah because of his illness in 2018.

The armed wing of the Islamic Jihad is the Al-Quds brigades, which are active in the West Bank and Gaza, with their main bastions in the cities of the West Bank: Hebron and Jenin.

183. Why did Israel invade Lebanon in 1982?

After being expelled from Jordan in 1979 ("Black September"), the PLO set their base in Lebanon, creating an independent zone, Fatahland (Land of the PLO), from where they attacked Israel.

Lebanon was suffering from a long history of religious confrontations between Maronite Christians and Muslims, in a political system that maintained a delicate ethnic equilibrium. It all came down in 1975 in a bloody civil war, plagued with mutual massacres that resulted in an important Christian emigration.

During the 1978-1981 period, there was an increase in the military attacks from the south of Lebanon to Israel. The most renowned were the attacks to the coastal road (Mar/3/1978), the assassinations of Naharia (Apr/12/1979) and the attack to the daycare center of Kibbutz Misgav Am (Apr/7/1980). The PLO also attacked in other countries. On Oct/20/1981, a car-bomb exploded in the Synagogue of Ambers (Belgium). In April 1981, an Israeli diplomat was murdered in Paris.

The previous military operation in Lebanon (Litani, 1978) could not eliminate or distance the PLO bases of the south of Lebanon, from where they launched Katyusha rockets against Israeli civilians.

The situation was being exploited by Syria to increase its dominium over a country it considered indivisible from Great Syria. Syria installed missile bases in the center of Lebanon, supporting Muslims from there. The PLO, previously confronted with Syria, now had Israel as a common enemy, who publicly supported the Maronites led by Bashir Gemayel. The Israel-Maronite alliance had consolidated during the 70s decade, especially during 1975, when Israel allowed the passage of Maronite workers to Israeli territory via "the Good Fence".

This is why the main goal of Israel was to eliminate or weaken the base from where terrorist attacks were made against its civilians.

184. What are the baseless interpretations of the reasons for the 1982 Lebanon War?

The first argument lacking seriousness is that Israel wished to destroy the bastion of the PLO in the south of Lebanon to appease the "emerging rising in the West Bank-Gaza of the Palestinians". Israel did not foresee in 1982 what would become the Intifada (1987) nor did the PLO provoke the movement.

In 1982, the coexistence between Israelis and Palestinians was shown in half a million Palestinian employees working every day in companies with and for Israelis, the purchase of vegetables and furniture in Gaza and the West

Bank from Israeli families, religious and leisure tourism, etc. In 1982, the Muslim Brotherhood continued developing their propagandistic and benefactor actions (*Dawa*) and the violence at the time was minor.

Second, war is wrongly explained as a demonstration of the strength of Israel after the 1973 failure. Between 1973 and 1983, the Israeli military forces destroyed the nuclear base of Saddam Hussein in Iraq (Osirak) and they executed the brilliant operation in Entebbe (1976). Maybe there was an excess of trust. To say that a war was beginning to strengthen the trust in the people is a weak argument.

Finally, it is argued that it was to "weaken the left-wing Muslim-Druse-Palestinian front in Lebanon to crown a right-wing Christian-Maronite minority under the leadership of the Israeli tanks and change the correlation of internal forces" (Brieger, 2000). Are the Muslim political organizations considered as "left-wing" because they affront the Great Satan (USA) and the Small Satan (Israel)? False. **The Muslim-Druse-Palestinian front was not "left-wing" nor the Christian-Maronite "right-wing", since the conflict was not a translation to "Marxist materialization", but a fight for power with ethnic-religious basis and motivations.**

185. What was the strategy of Israel in Lebanon in 1982?

The Israeli Army had two programs to deal with Lebanon, the *Oranim* (Cedars) Programs. The short program dealt with an operation of no more than two days in which the Tzahal would enter the south of Lebanon and eliminate the PLO bases in a 40 km radius, the distance from which the Russian-made missiles, Katyushas, would not reach the Israeli populations in the north of the country.

The "Wider *Oranim*" was adopted by Ariel Sharon (designed by Minister of Defense by Ezer Weitzman in 1979). This was a more ambitious program where not only would they eliminate the PLO from Lebanon, but from Syria as well. Defense Minister Ariel Sharon thought that Israel could help the Maronites take possession of Lebanon and later win the elections. The Maronite forces of Gemayel would collaborate with the Israeli army, and at the end of the battle, Gemayel would be named president of Lebanon and would sign a peace agreement with Israel. Sharon believed that the Palestinians would escape to Jordan, where they would overthrow the government of King Hussein and form a Palestinian state; no doubt an ambitious program that was rejected by the Israeli government.

In 1982 the government adopted the Small *Oranim* program. Once the confrontations began, the situation could not be controlled by the government. Minister Sharon requested authorization to extend the operation towards the north and even requested authorization to carry out actions that were already in development. In the book *Begin in the Government*, by the secretary of the Prime Minister, Arieh Naor, the author implies that Ariel Sharon deceived the government and Prime Minister Menahem Begin. Sharon's work ended after Sabra and Shatila.

186. What happened in the refugee camps of Sabra and Shatila in Beirut?

During the 1982 invasion, the Israeli army occupied the south of Lebanon and Beirut (even though there were neighborhoods that were still under Muslim forces). The civil war had already cost more than 100,000 lives.

Israel was able to impose Bashir Gemayel as president of Lebanon, who was immediately murdered by Syrian intelligence with an explosive placed in his headquarters in Beirut (Sep/14/1982). He was replaced by Amine Gemayel, who was slowly getting closer to Syria.

The Maronite branches wished to avenge the murder of Bashir and they entered the camps of Palestinian refugees in Sabra and Shatila, west of Beirut. On Sep/16/1982, the Maronite forces murdered 700 or 800 Palestinian refugees, according to Israeli sources, 2,000 murdered according to the Palestinians.

It was not the first Christian-Palestinian massacre: **in the Massacre of Damour (Jan/20/1976), the PLO forces entered a Christian village, killed civilians massively (around 600), desecrated a cemetery, painted a portrait of Arafat in the wall of a church, destroyed buildings and the rest of the village was evacuated.**

The Sabra and Shatila massacre began a series of important protests in the world and in Israel (what Damour could not incite). They accused Israel, as an occupying power, of being responsible for "everything that happened in that city". The State Commission of Investigation (*Kahan*) was formed, which established that in Feb/7/1983 that there was no evidence that the Israeli army had directly participated in the massacre and that the officials did not act to stop the event, even though they knew what was happening. The Commission suggested that the Minister of Defense, Ariel Sharon, should be dismissed from his duties (as it happened). The Commission also criticized Prime Minister Begin, Chancellor Yitzhak Shamir and the authorities of the army.

187. When did the Hezbollah arise in Lebanon?

Hezbollah was created in 1982 to expand the Shiite Islamist revolution sponsored by Iran and to defend the Shiites in a dismembered Lebanon. Iranians considered that the expansion of the Revolution would ensure the permanence of the regime. In Lebanon, there was already a Shiite Islamist group called *Amal* (Hope) founded in 1974, as a response to the Palestinian invasion (after Jordan).

The average materialistic person would affirm that Hezbollah was created because of the Israeli occupation of Lebanon. The Israeli presence increased the legitimacy of violent people to carry weapons, but it was not the cause. Proof? In December 2018, Israel discovered a series of tunnels built by Hezbollah to attack Israelis, but there was no Israeli presence since May 2000, and in any case, the aggression of the tunnels was done.

The origin of the problem was the incapacity of the Lebanese state to monopolize the use of force and become responsible for violent actions made from their territory. The official Lebanese army (in Sunni hands) could not cope with a Hezbollah armed by Iran.

In 1992, Hezbollah ran in the first parliamentary elections and became a key party in Lebanese politics. This fact should not surprise: a terrorist Islamic group is not only a military arm, it also has a social action and propaganda section (*Dawa*), religious and political authorities, and media specialists in Islamic terrorism, who consider that it is artificial to separate their action in independent departments.

The EU the US, Australia, Canada, England, the Netherlands, France, Israel, Bahrain and Egypt consider Hezbollah or its armed branch (as if it could be separated) as a terrorist organization.

Hezbollah, the Iranian armed branch, has attacked in Argentina and expanded its influence in Latin America, where they found a base for action in the Venezuela of Chavez.

188. What is the Security Strip in the South of Lebanon and the Southern Lebanese Army?

After expelling the PLO from Lebanon, Israel withdrew from parts of the occupied territory between 1983 and 1985, but kept partial control of the region in the border known as the "Security Strip in the South of Lebanon". It was initially coordinated with the self-proclaimed Free State of Lebanon, which executed a limited authority over the southern areas of Lebanon until 1984, as well as with the Southern Lebanese Army (derived from the Free Lebanese Army), conformed by Maronite Christians (led by Antoine Lahad) armed and trained by Israel.

The purpose of the Strip, declared by Israel, was to create a space to separate border settlements from the north, away from the terrorists in Lebanon that were shaping up to become Hezbollah.

The Strip included approximately 10% of the Lebanese territory, housed around 150,000 that were living in 67 villages of Shiites, Maronites and Druze. In the central zone of the Strip was the Maronite city of Marjayoun, which was the capital of the Security Strip. The residents that remained in the security area had a lot of contacts and received diverse services from Israel.

Even though the Strip was officially formed in 1985, throughout the years it became a war zone for battles between Israel, Maronites and Hezbollah.

On Feb/16/1991, the leader of Hezbollah, Abbas Musawi, was killed by missiles launched by Israeli helicopters. His successor was a harsher leader, Hassan Nassrallah. Among other things, Hezbollah avenged the murder of Musawi by blowing up the Embassy of Israel in Buenos Aires (Mar/17/1992).

A total of 256 Israeli soldiers died in combat in the south of Lebanon (1985-2000). In May 2000, Israel's Prime Minister, Ehud Barak, withdrew the Israeli forces from the Security Strip to the international border.

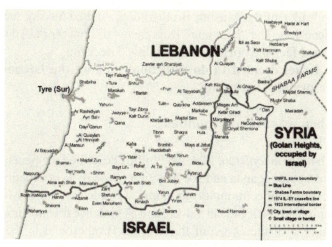

The Security Strip *(Source: Wikipedia)*

189. Is it true that Israel created Hamas?

To affirm that Israel created Hamas would discredit the ideological basis of the Muslim Brotherhood. It is true that Israel closed its eyes before the growth of Islamic fundamentalism when the phenomenon was not very known.

Moshe Arens, Minister of Defense of Israel (1982-1984) said: "For a period of time, without a doubt, we felt that it was a healthy phenomenon to stop the PLO. There was even an attempt to encourage the fundamentalists against the PLO, as I was informed when I took office. In fact, we didn't do anything to stop them". There was a problem with the conception: **For Israel, every person who was not involved in terrorism or violent acts did not receive the attention of the security services. There was never a clear policy regarding fundamentalists.**

For the first 10 years (1967-1977) the Internal Intelligence Service (Shabak or Shin-Bet) did not personally persecute or control the leaders of the Muslim Brotherhood. Israel thought that it was only a religious movement. Members of the Muslim Brotherhood that lived in the West Bank were considered allies to King Hussein, which is why they were seen as less dangerous.

In 1979, the Israeli army named Yitzhak Segev military commander of Gaza. Segev, who served in Iran a few years before the fundamentalist coup, warned about the danger of what he was seeing in the streets of the Strip, affirming that it looked similar to what he had seen in Teheran. Segev tried to weaken the leader of the Muslim Brotherhood, Ahmed Yassin, tempting him with his friendship. The "bear hug" from Segev did not work. Additionally, it was an isolated fact and not a strategic political decision.

When Israel decided to do something to stop the Islamism, it was weak and especially... very late.

190. When was Hamas founded?

In her book *Londonistan*, Melanie Phillips described the penetration steps of Islamism: 1) propaganda and social action (*Dawa*); 2) occupation of public spaces; 3) creation of community autonomy: 4) violence against Muslims who do not comply with their radical values, and 5) violence towards non-Muslims.

An example of the *Dawa* of the Muslim Brotherhood in the 80s: a social-religious survey among Palestinians in 1984 in the West Bank and Gaza showed that 69% qualified themselves as religious or very religious. They were measuring religiousness according to how many times they prayed every day, if they fasted during Ramadan, etc.

Regarding the level of "internal violence", in 1986 the group *Al Maghar* was formed (the Honor). This was a secret group dedicated to identifying collaborators with Israel and people dedicated to selling alcohol or that were organizing prostitution activities. Sheik Ahmed Yassin drew a religious sentence (*Fatwa*) in which he affirmed that "any person who is interrogated and recognizes having collaborated with Israel or dedicated to prostitution, must be executed according to the mandates of Islam". Between 1986 and 1987, around 900 Palestinians were executed by *Al Maghar* in Gaza.

The evolution of violence against Jews happened slowly. On June/15/1984, the security forces of Israel searched the house of Sheik Ahmed Yassin and discovered a hiding place where the leader of the Muslim Brotherhood was hiding 22 guns, 11 M16 rifles, 30 Kalashnikov rifles, 5 Uzi machine guns. In May 1985 he was freed after 11 months in prison. Immediately, he organized an internal security service (counterespionage) of the Muslim Brotherhood (*Al Maghar*).

The final step to violence (and the change of the name to *Hamas* – Effervescence), came after the start of the Intifada (Dec/9/1987), although their Foundation Charter was signed in April 1988.

191. Does Hamas defend anti-Semitic arguments in their political platform?

The Hamas Charter confirms what was discussed in the initial question: Article 2 – the conflict with Israel is religious and political: the Palestinian problem is a Muslim religious-political issue and the conflict with Israel is between Muslims and "unfaithful" Jews.

The Charter is filled with anti-Semitism, the Jewish people have only negative traits and their intentions are to conquer the world. The Jews are presented as deservers of humiliation and a life full of misery. In the document, they include anti-Semitic myths such as *The Protocols of the Elders of Zion* (Article 32), which refers to the Jewish control of the media, the cinematographic industry and education (Articles 17 and 22). These myths are repeated constantly to make Jews responsible for the French and Russian Revolutions, for all the wars (local and worldwide): "No war has taken place without Jews behind it" (Article 22). The Charter demonizes the Jews, describing them as brutal in their behavior, as Nazis, even to women and children (Article 29).

It is important to deepen in the Nazi influence over the modern Islamic anti-Semitism. Hamas is one of the manifestations of this type of anti-Semitism.

On May/1/2017, Hamas published a political document where they tried to move away from the anti-Semitism that is found in their first document. They highlight that Hamas is not fighting against the Jews for their Judaism, but against their occupation and Zionist project. "Anti-Semitism and Jewish oppression are phenomena related to European history, not to Arab and Muslim history. The Zionist movement is a dangerous example of the settled occupation that has happened in the world and should end in Palestine as well."

The NGO Palestine Media Watch offers thousands of movies that reflect the anti-Semitic DNA of Hamas.

192. Why did a Palestinian revolt begin in 1987, known as Intifada?

On Dec/8/1987 an Israeli military truck crashed against another one transporting Palestinian workers. The rumor was that the event had not been accidental, because the brother of the driver of the military truck had been murdered in Gaza some time before.

The main reason for the outbreak of the Intifada of 1987 was that the descendants of the conquered people in 1967, that had not known the Egyptian occupation over Gaza, or the Jordanian occupation over the West Bank, had grown under Israeli control during 20 years and the consequences were felt.

The PLO did not bring on the Intifada in spite of the accusations of the Minister of Defense of Israel at the time, Yitzhak Rabin, or Prime Minister Yitzhak Shamir. It was about the discontent of the base, which facilitated the reinforcement of a group that had been doing their ideological-social work (*Dawa*), Hamas.

The famous "War of the Rocks" was broadcasted internationally by television, where street battles between Palestinians and members of the Israeli Defense Forces were shown. Palestinians attacked by throwing rocks and other objects while the soldiers responded with rubber and lead bullets, or with police persecution. The violence declined in 1991 during the Gulf War and modified its course with the Oslo Accords (Sep/13/1993) and the creation of the National Palestinian Authority.

Since Dec/9/1987/ until the Oslo Accords, 1162 Palestinian and 160 Israelis lost their lives during the First Intifada (approximately 50% were Israeli civilians, confirming it was not a confrontation against the military, only)

What was the influence of the First Intifada? The international image of Israel fell even lower (after Lebanon 1982), and since then the Israeli governments have understood that the *status quo* of the Palestinian issue cannot be maintained or is playing against Israel.

193. What influence did the Persian Gulf War 1990-1991 have over the Palestinians?

In August 1990, the President of Iraq, Saddam Hussein, occupied Kuwait and argued that the territory belonged historically to Iraq. In 1961, the western powers had created a puppet country (Kuwait) to control their oil. Behind these arguments, there was the Iraqi necessity of exploiting Kuwait to solve their damaged economy after their war against Iran (1980-1988).

Saudi Arabia refused to facilitate the rehabilitation of Iraq, Syria was interested in getting close to the west after the fall of the USSR and Jordan tried to keep a neutral position; a coalition against Iraq had been confirmed, led by the United States, which was the "sheriff" of the world after the Soviet fall.

To break this coalition, Saddam Hussein conditioned his withdrawal from Kuwait to Israel's withdrawal from the West Bank and Gaza. Iraq threatened to attack with chemical missiles to demonstrate that their war was a pro-Palestinian crusade.

Yasser Arafat and the PLO welcomed the intentions of Saddam Hussein and positioned themselves openly in favor of Iraq. This situation would confront Arafat with Saudi Arabia, the main economic collaborator of the PLO. **The support of Arafat to Saddam Hussein was a political and economic suicide.**

On Jan/15/1991, the ultimatum ended for Iraq to withdraw from Kuwait and on Jan/17/1991, the allied attack against Iraq began.

During the Gulf War, there were 39 Scud missiles launched at Israel that resulted in material damages with a value of several million dollars. Saddam Hussein did not charge these missiles with chemical heads, a situation that would have pushed Israel into war. Only one Israeli citizen died and three other people died of heart attacks.

The Palestinians went to the roofs of their houses to celebrate, rooting for the missiles that were heading to Israel. On the other hand, American batteries (Patriot) proved not to be very effective to destroy the Iraqi missiles.

194. What was the meaning of the Madrid Peace Conference of 1991?

When the Gulf War ended, the Middle East discovered that it had formed a coalition with Israel, Syria, Lebanon and Jordan in the same block. The main interested party in strengthening this block was the United States.

The peace conference of Madrid gathered the diplomatic corps of the Arab countries, represented by the Foreign Affairs Ministers, and the Israeli commission led by Prime Minister Yitzhak Shamir. The Palestinians were represented by a joint Jordanian-Palestinian commission because Israel did not accept the presence of the PLO.

In Madrid, there were groups of bilateral negotiations. The meeting did not lead to formal agreements although it was clear that a peace process was underway. After two months, the commissions continued meeting in Washington (some advances were achieved in the negotiations between Israel and Lebanon).

At the time, Israel was focused on receiving a great mass of Jews from the ex-Soviet Union that were arriving as new immigrants. During this period Israel received over half a million Jews, over 10% of the Israeli population. The migratory wave was also coming from Ethiopia. Thanks to a fantastic operation, the Israeli Air Force and El-Al organized an air bridge of 36 airplanes that moved 14,000 Ethiopians to Israel ("Operation Solomon").

Israel needed the funds to finance this project and expected the United States to sign bank guarantees for 10 billion dollars to access international loans. The North American government declared that it was not willing to allow the funds to be used for new colonies, pressuring the Israeli government to comply with the Madrid agreements.

As was evidenced in 1975 (Intermediate Agreement), the US opted to pressure its direct ally moved by its hegemonic interests.

195. What were the reasons that made Yitzhak Rabin and Yasser Arafat recognize each other?

The PLO was suffering from a constant weakening. In parallel, the fundamentalist groups (Hamas, Islamic Jihad), were performing a socio-political task that attracted the Palestinian masses. Without money and separated from Tunisia, Yasser Arafat's position was defined as a "political coma".

Arafat escaped death again on Apr/7/1992 when his airplane from Air Bissau crashed in the desert of Libya during a sand storm. Two pilots and one engineer died; Arafat was wounded.

The reasons that motivated Yasser Arafat to recognize Israel were evident: he was politically dead and separated from Palestine, not having many choices.

In 1974, the labor minister Aharon Yariv and his pair Victor Shem-Tov (Mapam) wrote a formula (Shem-Tov-Yariv) that specified that if a state or group abandoned their use of force and recognized Israel, the Jewish State would have to negotiate with that partner.

On Sept/9/1993, Yitzhak Rabin received a letter from Yasser Arafat in which he committed to: 1) the PLO would recognize Israel's right to exist; 2) he would accept UN Resolutions 242 and 338; 3) he committed to finding a solution to the Arab-Israeli conflict in peaceful terms; 4) he would abandon the use of force and terror; 5) he would take responsibility for the actions of all the members of the PLO; 6) he would make sure that the articles in the Palestinian Charter that advocated for the destruction of Israel would be considered as annulled and would be taken to their final cancelation in the Palestinian National Assembly (that did not happen).

These declarations responded positively to the "Shem-Tov Yariv" principles of the Labor Party. The PLO was considered by the Israeli government as the official representative of the Palestinian people. **Yitzhak Rabin deeply despised Yasser Arafat. However, for Israel, the alternative to the weak Arafat was the ascending Islamist Hamas.**

196. What are the Oslo Accords? What is the Palestinian Authority?

In Oslo (Norway), there were secret meetings between representatives of the PLO and Israel led by Shimon Peres's right hand, Yosi Belin, and other diplomats and academics.

On Sep/9/1993 the "Principles on Interim Self-Government Arrangements" (Oslo A) was signed in the gardens of the White House.

According to Oslo A, there would be autonomy in Gaza and Jericho, and the power would be transferred in Judea and Samaria. A formula was also agreed to hold elections to legitimize the Palestinian Authority, a body that would negotiate the final agreements. An important part of what was agreed in Oslo was linked to an economic collaboration between Israelis and Palestinians (as requested by Declaration 181).

There would be an intermediate transition period of 5 years, and after the first three years the dialogues would start again for a final agreement that would include paramount topics such as the future of Jerusalem, the status of refu-

gees, the Jewish settlements in the territories and the final status of the Palestinian Authority (they were copying the model 3+2 of Camp David, 1979)

If the autonomy in Gaza and Jericho began on May/4/1994, negotiations for final status had to begin in May of 1997 and the final agreements would be in force starting May 1999. The Cairo Agreement was signed on Aug/29/1994 to establish what powers would be forwarded to the Palestinians (in this Agreement Yasser Arafat simulated to sign the contract and he had to be pressured by Mubarak who humiliated him in Arabic, "sign, dog!")

On Jul/5/1994 the President of the Palestinian Authority and of the PLO, Yasser Arafat arrived at the Gaza Strip. In 1995 (Oslo B) the control over the Palestinian Authority would increase and, secretly, Yosi Beilin would reach a final agreement with Palestinians that was never presented to Yitzhak Rabin.

197. What was the Palestinian reaction to the Oslo Accords?

When "Oslo" began, the Palestinian support was massive. Saeb Erekat, a Palestinian business leader, affirmed that more than 80% of the population supported the agreement. For the Palestinians, the "Oslo spirit" was to receive an independent state in the West Bank, Gaza and eastern Jerusalem. Yitzhak Rabin preferred to focus on "building trust on both sides" delaying the crucial issues (Jerusalem and the refugees).

Some organizations of the PLO and Islamist groups (Hamas, Islamic Jihad), were energetically opposed to the Oslo Accords. This alliance against the recognition of Israel was known as "Rejectionist Front".

Two days had passed since the signature of the Oslo Accords when more frequent terrorist attacks occurred by the fundamentalist groups opposed to Oslo. **From October 1993 until December 1993, Israel suffered a series of ten attacks that killed 14 Israelis.**

After the Cave of the Patriarchs massacre, from February 1994 until January 1995, terrorist attacks increased resulting in 60 Israelis murdered. There are some who affirm that the suicidal attacks from Palestinians began after "Baruch Goldstein", but it is false. The first occurred in the Mehola Crossing (Apr/16/1993) when a Palestinian bomb car detonated between two Israeli buses. The author was a Hamas terrorist and caused one death and eight wounded.

The more destructive attacks occurred in Tel-Aviv when a terrorist from Hamas blew himself by carrying 20 kg of explosives on Bus 5 that went through the center of the city. That day, Oct/19/1994, 22 Israelis were murdered and 46 wounded. Previously, two terrorists of the Islamic Jihad committed suicide in the Beit-Lid crossing, where Israeli soldiers were waiting for the bus. That day, Jan/22/1995, 21 Israelis were murdered and 34 wounded.

From Oslo A to Oslo B, the Palestinians executed 10 suicidal attempts murdering 78 Israelis.

198. What was the Jewish reaction in Israel to the Oslo Accords?

After signing the agreement in Washington (1993), the Oslo Accords were discussed for their approval in the Knesset (parliament). The coalition achieved 61 votes with 50 opposing.

Those who opposed Oslo considered that signing a pact with a professional terrorist like Yasser Arafat was dangerous for Israel. The Israeli public and the media, mainly agreed with the peace process.

The opposition accused Rabin of conceding to a Palestinian state. Israeli Prime Minister Rabin, at first, opposed a totally independent Palestinian state and to hand over all of the West Bank, Gaza and eastern Jerusalem. Moreover, in more than one opportunity he affirmed to be willing to cancel Oslo if the Palestinian attacks continued.

In October 1994, Prime Minister Yitzhak Rabin, the Minister of Foreign Affairs, Shimon Peres and the President of the Palestinian Authority, Yasser Arafat, were awarded the Nobel Peace Prize.

On Feb/25/1994, on the day of the festivity of Purim, an orthodox Jew, settler of the town of Kiryat Arba (close to Hebron), named Baruch Goldstein, entered the Mosque of the Patriarchs with several grenades, an M-16 rifle and several charges, and opened fire indiscriminately against the worshippers, murdering 29 and wounding over 120. When he ran out of ammunition, he was beaten to death by the survivors.

The massacre created a strong rejection among most of the Israeli society and Prime Minister Rabin read a condemning statement in the Knesset, adopting judicial and administrative measures against extremists.

For the majority of the Israeli society, the Palestinian suicidal attacks were the price that had to be paid to achieve peace. When the attacks increased, support to Oslo descended.

199. What is Israel's legal basis to build settlements in the West Bank and in Gaza?

There are Israeli experts in international law, like Orna Ben-Naftali (Faculty of Administration) and Eyal Gross (University of Tel-Aviv) that oppose the legalization of any Israeli settlement beyond the Green Line. On the other hand, others argue that since Israel conquered those territories in a defensive war (Six-Day War 1967), it has the right of control until there is a peace treaty and even keep part of the West Bank, for example, Prof. Julius Stone, jurist Prof. Eugene Rostov, ex sub-Secretary of State of the United States (one of the authors of Resolution 242), jurist Douglas Feith, jurist Prof. Steven Schwebel (legal advisor of the State Department of the US) and later, president of the International Court of Justice in The Hague. The physical situation has been described in questions 4-5.

One of the central arguments, defended by the ex-presidents of the Israeli Supreme Court of Justice Shimon Agranat and Meir Shamgar, is that since there has never existed a Palestinian state and that Jordan illegally annexed Judea and Samaria (West Bank) the territories possess an "in dispute" status. **The Jewish settlements beyond the Green Line are located in territories "in dispute" that do not possess legal-private owners (territories from the British Mandate that were later under the Jordanian domain).**

The central discussion is if the Fourth Geneva Convention applies in the West Bank as well. The Convention (Article 2) applies to the occupied territory by a State that is a party to the Convention over another State party to the Convention. Israel defends that, given that the West Bank was not legally in the hands of Jordan, the Convention does not apply. **However, Israel decided that since 1967 they would voluntarily apply the humanitarian spirit of the Convention over the Palestinian civil population.**

200. What are the Oslo B Accords?

In the Oslo A Accords (1993) the parties committed to increasing the autonomy of Palestine after a year. On Sep/9/1995, the Interim Agreement on the West Bank and the Gaza Strip was signed in Washington, known as "Oslo B". **The objective was to reduce the friction between Palestinians and Israelis. This agreement was made to reinforce the position of Arafat in the territories while competing with the Islamist opposition and within the PLO.**

Israel committed to withdrawing from 6 main Palestinian populations (Jenin, Nablus (Shechem), Tulkarem, Kalkilya, Ramallah and Bethlehem and other smaller populations). These would be Territories A (under Palestinian military-civilian control) and added Territories B (Palestinian civilian control and peripheral Israeli security). Both A + B represented 40% of the West Bank.

After 22 days, free elections would be held for the Parliament and Executive Power. On Jan/29/1996, the elections were held with 68.5% participation of the Palestinians of Gaza. In eastern Jerusalem, they voted by mail. Yasser Arafat obtained 88% of the votes, leading him to the Executive Presidency of the Palestinian Authority, with a parliament with 65 of the 89 positions in hands of the PLO. While this was happening, the Palestinian suicidal attacks multiplied (a few days before the signature of Oslo B, Bus 26 exploded in Jerusalem, a work of Hamas, resulting in 5 fatal victims).

The situation of Arafat was complicated. The situation of Israel was even more so. Arafat did not want to be seen as "the slave of Israel" combatting his Islamists and other extremists. Others affirm that Arafat did not oppose ideologically to terrorist violence. On the other hand, the Israeli government was the one to accept Yasser Arafat as the partner for peace.

201. How did the assassination of Yitzhak Rabin destroy the peace process with the Palestinians?

The Oslo B Accords were approved by the Knesset (Oct/5/1996) with a 61 to 59 majority. Since then, the Israeli governments have tried to reach a majority among the Zionist representatives to approve territorial concessions (for example, in the Disengagement from Gaza in 2005).

More violent protests added up to the manifestations against Oslo A after the signature of Oslo B. Orthodox rabbis from the US and Israel sentenced Yitzhak Rabin to death for "betraying Jewish interests".

On Sept/13/1995 a nationalist manifestation ended with a confrontation between 2,000 protestors and 1,500 policemen. The leader from the opposing Likud, Binyamin Netanyahu, paraded through Raanana leading the march, and his followers carried a black coffin with an Israeli flag and painted "Rabin kills Zionism". Netanyahu has been accused of inciting violence or not denouncing soundly that the protestors showed Rabin dressed in a Nazi uniform and screamed "Death to Rabin".

On Nov/4/1995, after finishing a manifestation in favor of the peace process, a law student of 26 years of age, Ygal Amir, murdered Israel's Prime Minister, Yitzhak Rabin.

In the documentary "Oslo Diary", the main architect of Oslo, Yosi Beilin, explained that his team had reached a final agreement with the Palestinians that would be presented by Rabin a few days after the manifestation and that the same pact was rejected by Shimon Peres (who replaced Rabin) after considering that he did not have the legitimacy to do so.

Would Yitzhak Rabin have accepted Beilin's proposal? Hard to know. The truth is that after the assassination of Rabin, the Palestinian terrorist attempts increased (between November 1995 and May 1996, 59 Israelis were murdered in 4 attacks) turning the Israeli vote to Binyamin Netanyahu.

PART FOUR
- INTIFADA AND DISARRAY -

202. Is it true that Israel and Syria were about to sign a peace agreement?

The Israeli negotiators declared that Israel accepted withdrawing from the Golan Heights (conquered in 1967) in the context of a peace agreement, dealing with four key issues: 1) the withdrawal distance; 2) when and how long would the withdrawal last; 3) the stages of the withdrawal process and the link with the process towards normalization (as with Egypt, Israel was requesting a prolonged phase); and 4) agreement on security issues. The murdered Prime Minister Rabin declared that if a peace agreement were to be negotiated with Syria including a significant withdrawal from the Golan Heights, the agreement would have to be submitted to a referendum before signing it.

On Dec/8/1999, President Clinton announced that Prime Minister Ehud Barak and President Hafez El-Assad (represented by the Syrian Foreign Affairs Minister Farouk A-Shara) agreed on another round of conversations in Shepherdstown, West Virginia (January 2000)

In Shepherdstown, Ehud Barak accepted that Israel would return to the limit established by the British Mandate, controlling all of the Galilee Sea (including 10 meters to the east) and the Jordan River. Syria rejected this proposal, demanding the withdrawal of Israel up to point before the Six-Day War (in 1948 Syria conquered lands that weren't part of the Partition of 1947), allowing to "access" the Galilee Sea. Hafez El-Assad died on June/10/2000 and was succeeded by his son, Bashar.

In April 2007, Prime Minister Ehud Olmert emphasized that even though Israel was interested in a peace agreement with Syria, this country is part of the axis of evil and a power that fosters terrorism throughout the Middle East. After that, the civil war in Syria began, and today this country is indirectly controlled by Iran.

203. What was the unilateral withdrawal of Israel from the south of Lebanon?

A key issue of the electoral campaign of Ehud Barak (1999) was the promise to withdraw the Israeli Forces from the Security Strip, considering that the solution would come with a peace agreement with Syria.

In Shepherdstown (January 2000) Barak did not achieve an agreement with Syria and opted anyway for a unilateral withdrawal from Lebanon.

The Israeli authorities explained that since 1982, 1,216 Israeli soldiers had died there (654 during the Lebanon War of 1982 and 562 in the Strip) and 3,750 wounded. Unofficial data accounted for 660 deceased of the Maronite army of the south of Lebanon (*Tzadal*).

As the withdrawal approached, the southern Lebanon army began to disintegrate and many of its members fled to Israel. This process accelerated the decision to withdraw on May/24/2000, six weeks before what was originally planned.

Against Israel's desires, the Lebanese army did not deploy in the area. Instead, Hezbollah took over Israeli equipment and uniforms and had the Arab world believe that they had defeated Israel. On May/26/2000, the leader of Hezbollah, Hassan Nasrallah, gave "the spider web speech" in Binth G'bel ("Israel is weaker than a spider's web").

Israel withdrew to the international border, an act acknowledged by the United Nations. The town of Ghajar was divided in two: the northern part in Lebanon, and the southern in Israel. The Shaaba Farms are considered by Israel and the UN as Syrian territory although the Hezbollah and its allies usually demand that it is turned over to Lebanon, justifying their violence on this dispute.

Even though Israel announced it would respond strongly to any violation by Hezbollah, its responses were focused on concrete facts such as the kidnapping and murder of three soldiers of the IDF in Mount Har Dov (Oct/7/2000).

204. What peace plan was negotiated by Ehud Barak and Yasser Arafat at Camp David in 2000?

Ehud Barak offered Arafat 73% of the West Bank and the Gaza Strip. In a period of 10 to 25 years, the Palestinian area would have to expand 90-91% (94% including Jerusalem). As a result, Israel would have to dismantle 63 settlements beyond the Green Line.

The West Bank would be separated by a road from Israel to the Dead Sea, with free passage for Palestinians, though Israel would maintain the right to close it in case of a security crisis. In exchange for the attachment of part of the West Bank (the settlement blocks), Israel would cede a small part of the Negev to the Palestinian state. **The argument that the Palestinian State would be totally non-viable is, technically speaking, false.**

The Foreign Affairs Minister of Israel, Shlomo Ben-Ami, explained that Israel offered to divide Jerusalem; the east for the Palestinian State and the west for Israel. The Old City would be divided: the Jewish and Armenian neighborhoods (and the Wall) for the Jews and the rest for the Palestinians.

Yasser Arafat told Bill Clinton that he did not believe that there had been a Jewish temple in the Temple Mount, rejecting any kind of Jewish presence on the site (the Palestinians even consider the Wailing Wall as a Muslim site, because Mohammed "tied" his horse there when he traveled to Al-Quds)

At Camp David, the Palestinians kept their position regarding the "right of return": this had to be accepted by Israel even though there is no such "right". According to the Israeli proposal, there would be an international organization to deal with refugees and Israel and other countries would be members of said organization. In a later stage, during the Taba negotiations, before the 2001 elections, Israel offered the entrance of 100,000 Palestinians for several years.

What did Israel ask for in exchange? The end of the conflict. The Palestinians rejected the offer.

205. What was the main negotiators' opinion over the failure of Camp David 2000?

President Bill Clinton accused Yasser Arafat: "I regret that in 2000 Arafat missed the opportunity to bring that nation into being and pray for the day when the dreams of the Palestinian people for a state and a better life will be realized in a just and lasting peace." He also accused him of not presenting a counter-offer to those by Barak and Clinton.

Ehud Barak defined Yasser Arafat's behavior as a "disoriented act to demand so many Israeli concessions as possible without having the intention to reach a peace agreement or ending the conflict". After his return to Israel, Ehud Barak said "there is no partner for achieving peace in Palestine" and this sentence severely damaged the hopes of those who supported Oslo.

Dennis Ross, the envoy sent by the United States for the Middle East and key negotiator in the summit, summarized in his book *The Missing Peace* the lack of will of Arafat to sign a final agreement with Israel that would end the demands from the Palestinians, particularly their right of return. For Ross, Arafat really wanted "a solution of one state covering historical Palestine". **Ross also cited Saudi Prince Bandar while they were negotiating: "If Arafat does not accept what is available now, it won't be a tragedy, it will be a crime".**

Robert Malley, Clinton's collaborator in the negotiations, said in an article in *The New York Review of Books* (Jul/8/2001) that the failure of the Camp David summit should be divided between the three leaders that were present: Arafat, Barak and Clinton, and not blame only Barak as some barely sustained analyses assert.

206. What was the reason for the Al-Aqsa Intifada?

The Second Intifada can be explained with two facts: 1) the decision of Yasser Arafat to reject the proposals by Clinton and Barak to form an independent Palestinian state that would finally put an end to Palestinian claims. According to the well-known analyst, Ehud Yari, "Yasser Arafat preferred to continue being the Palestinian Saladin than the president of a poor country that would have to acknowledge the existence of Israel"; 2) The sensation, among the Palestinians, that Hezbollah had defeated the Israeli Defense Army in the south of Lebanon (because of the unilateral withdrawal), and therefore, "it was possible" to defeat the Israeli army. It was a psychological impulse.

The Second Intifada was planned previously. Mamdouh Nofal, the authority of the security forces of the Fatah, prepared to begin violence after the failure of Camp David. "He (Arafat) said to us: 'Let's go to combat! We have to be prepared'. When Ariel Sharon visited the mosques, Arafat said to us: 'Ok, this is the moment to act'" (David Samuels, "In a Ruined Country", *The Atlantic,* September 2005). Marwan Barghouti, leader of the Intifada, acknowledged that the Intifada was under preparation; the events of Al-Aqsa worked as an opportunity due to the religious mobilization of the Palestinians, as had happened before during the times of the Mufti and as would happen later with the stabbings of 2015.

On Sep/28/2000, Ariel Sharon visited the Temple Mount and on Sep/29/2000 the massive protests began. Palestinians and soldiers fought each other in the Al-Aqsa Mosque, resulting in 7 deceased Palestinians and 70 injured Israelis.

If the first Intifada of 1987-88 was characterized by stone-throwing against soldiers and tanks; this time it was an armed combat, with Palestinian suicidal attacks as the main feature during the revolt.

207. Is it true that Ariel Sharon's visit to the Temple Mount began the Intifada?

On Sept/28/2000, Ariel Sharon, leader of the nationalist opposition party *Likud,* visited the area near to the Al-Aqsa mosque (one of the most venerated by the Muslims).

President Clinton had promised that, in the frame of an agreement, the Jews would be able to visit the Temple Mount. Ariel Sharon wanted to "test" said promise.

Israel's Prime Minister, Ehud Barak, believed that by approving the visit he could neutralize the opposition by demonstrating that the government assured such a sensitive subject.

"Barak ordered the chief of Shabak, Ami Ayalin, to inform and request approval from Jibril Rajoub, with a special request to facilitate a pleasant visit [...] Rajoub promised that this would happen as long as Sharon abstained from entering in any mosque or praying in public [...] A group of Palestinian dignitaries protested the visit, as well as three Arab representatives in the Knesset. With the dignitaries observing from a safe distance, the Shabab (youth mob) threw rocks and tried to surpass the Israeli security to reach Sharon and his surroundings [...] However, Sharon's behavior was dignified and calm. He did not pray, did not give any declarations, nor did anything that could be interpreted as offensive to the Muslims' sensitivity..."

Later, and considering what had happened, the chief of the Palestinian Security in the West Bank, Jibril Rajoub, negated that he had effectively promised what he had really promised. Many Israeli analysts affirm that the terrorist attacks began earlier. A day before Sharon's visit, on Sept/27/2000, the Israeli Sargent David Biri was murdered by a house bomb in Gaza.

Currently, very few journalists argue that the Second Intifada began by Ariel Sharon's visit to the Temple Mount.

208. What were the consequences for Palestinians and Israelis after the Al-Aqsa Intifada?

According to the Israeli NGO Betselem, 668 civilians and 305 Israeli military lost their lives. There were an additional 47 "non-Israelis". There were 144 suicidal attacks carried out by 161 Palestinians, resulting in 515 deceased and 3,428 injured. Betselem registered 3,329 deceased Palestinians, not including the suicides nor those who suffered accidents when manipulating explosives. There were also 192 Palestinians that died at the hands of the Palestinians themselves. According to the Palestinian Central Bureau of Statistics, a total of 3,891 Palestinians died, 776 of them under 18.

The government of Barak blamed Yasser Arafat for the Intifada. After attacks such as the lynching of two soldiers in Ramallah (Oct/12/2000), Barak bombarded empty infrastructures of the Palestinian Authority. In February of 2001, Sharon defeated Barak in the elections. He began a policy of neutralization and detention in the *Mukata* of Yasser Arafat and destruction of the infrastructure of the Palestinian Authority under Operation Defensive Shield (2002- after the attack at Hotel Park in the night of Pesach).

For Palestinians, the "militarization of protests" moved the agenda of Hamas ahead of the others. Arafat freed the prisoners of Hamas and fostered attacks.

The international public opinion supported the Palestinian claims and accused Israel of disproportionate use of violence. After the death of Yasser Arafat (Apr/11/2004), Mahmoud Abbas rejected the militarization and opted for other options to promote his interests.

The Al-Aqsa Intifada (2000-2005) destroyed the spirit and perseverance of the Oslo negotiations. Since 1993, the strategy was to "create trust among the parties" to approach common postures to guide towards a final agreement.

At present, the dominating spirit is "mistrust". After Al-Aqsa, regional initiatives began to be considered to solve the Palestinian-Israeli conflict. Another dominating vision since then considers that the conflict cannot be solved, but only managed.

209. Why did Israel build a security barrier between Israel and the West Bank?

Israel began to build a Security Barrier to stop the infiltration of Palestinian suicidal attacks. A large part of the attacks was carried out by crossing the Green Line on foot. In 2001, 31 suicidal attacks were registered, resulting in 84 Israelis deceased; in 2002, there were 47 attacks resulting in 225 murdered and in 2003, an additional 22 attacks resulted in 142 victims. **After these events, and due to the barrier, the attacks were significantly reduced.**

The Security Fence was a project planned by the Israeli left-wing, adopted and carried out by the right-wing led by Prime Minister Ariel Sharon. Its construction was approved on Jun/23/2002. **Once the project as a whole is completed, the part made of concrete will be 6%, about 30 km.** The concrete parts were made to avoid attacks from buildings on the Pales-

The Green Line
(Source: Wikipedia)

tinian side on vehicles circulating on the Israeli side (snipers). **Therefore, the correct name is "Security Fence"**.

The complex consists on the following components: a fence with electronic sensors to alert on infiltrators; a trench (up to 4 meters deep); a two-lane paved road for patrols; a tracing strip (a sand path to detect footprints) parallel to the fence; six lines of barbed wire, one above the other, that mark the perimeter of the complex. All the installation has an average width of 50 to 70 meters, though in some parts it reaches 100 meters. There are 45 open doors for Palestinians with appropriate permits (of a total of 84).

The countries of the political forum (UN) considered (Resolution 2334/2016) that there was a border where there had never been one (the Green Line). This is a political decision that should be reviewed in terms of its legality. The fence was constructed before Resolution (2002).

210. Why didn't Israel build the fence on the Green Line? Is it true that the fence is illegal?

The fence runs on parts of the Green Line, but it is not built exactly above it. The Israeli argument is that the fence and the Green Line are not borders, therefore their location depends on their effectiveness in defending civilians.

Considering that the armistice line (1949-1967) was not, nor was it ever, a border (it was "politically" declared in December 2016), the construction of the fence in territories under dispute is logical. **Palestinians who consider that the location of the fence violates their rights can sue Israel in Israeli courts to modify the tracing. On more than 60 occasions the Israeli army has been forced to modify the layout**.

The Palestinians rejected the construction stating that its layout surrounded cities and cultivated fields, and obstructed their mobility. For the Palestinians, one of the main problems was that their economy was sustained on the penetration of illegal workers to Israel, so the fence became an obstacle for the free passage of Palestinians.

In 2004, the International Court of Justice of The Hague discussed the topic. The revision was taken to the General Assembly, although 22 western democratic countries rejected the right of the Court to judge a "political" issue, and not a legal one. The Court of Justice of The Hague said that the land of the West Bank was not Israeli territory (they disregarded the autonomy set in Oslo A-B), and therefore Israel did not have the right to establish a defensive fence in "its own territory". **This is an advisory resolution and lacks legal** force. The sentence was harshly criticized by the western democracies, as it determines that a country cannot build an internal security fence if it were to need one. This was interfering with the sovereignty of a country.

211. Why do some people qualify the fence as a "Wall" and refer to the Berlin Wall?

As explained in the previous question, almost all the layout of the separation fence is made of wire, so we could wonder why journalists like Pedro Brieger ask themselves "why did Israel build a wall taller than the Berlin Wall?" (see question 56)

The comparison of the label can only be used to associate the Israeli case with a wall condemned by history. This is a manipulation (intentional?). The Berlin Wall was not built to avoid suicidal attacks, but to impede citizens from escaping their supposed "paradise".

In his book *100 Questions about the Palestinian-Israeli Conflict*, the Argentinean journalist writes: "Throughout hundreds of kilometers the wall is partially built of concrete and in others of barbed wire. The concrete parts are 8 meters high, duplicating the disdained Berlin Wall". If this author wrote correctly, he should write than 96% of the fence is made of wire, so his comparison to the Berlin Wall becomes void. He continues: "The wire parts look like a border between two countries with a fence in the middle of about 3 meters - in many parts electrified – and on both sides, there are roads for military vehicles... As there are more parts made of wire than concrete, and to avoid comparisons with the Berlin Wall, Israelis talk about a 'security fence'". **The wall is called a fence... because it is made of wire in almost all its layout. The fence has electronic sensors (it is not electrified as he describes), designed to alert the Israeli forces of infiltration attempts.**

As the cement blocks are almost exclusively in the surrounding areas of Jerusalem, journalists (most of them working on site) feel "more comfortable" filming cement than wire.

212. Why did Hamas win the elections of 2006?

The deterioration of the Oslo negotiation process was one of the "achievements" of Hamas. The objective of the Islamic terrorism was triple-fold: a) convince the Israeli population that achieving an agreement with the PLO-PA would not bring peace, as the Hamas and other Islamic groups are "uncontrollable"; b) provoke a reaction from Israel to affect the credibility of the process among the Palestinians themselves; c) show themselves before the Palestinians as an authentically combating group, compared to a "compromising" PLO-AP.

The death of Arafat, the lack of authority of his successor Mahmoud Abbas and the lack of capacity to govern after Operation Defensive Barrier (2002), undermined the leadership of the PLO leading the Palestinian Authority.

The US administration pressured Israel and the Palestinians to hold free elections, allowing the participation of Hamas, after the death of Arafat. On Jan/25/2006, Hamas won the Parliament elections, the same ones it had boycotted in the past. We must remember that for a fundamentalist, elections are a manifestation of *Yahiliyah*.

Hamas defeated the PLO in those elections for two reasons: 1) the Palestinian failure in the Second Intifada. They did not defeat Israel. 2) The endemic corruption of the Palestinian leaders of the Palestinian Authority. The level of corruption of the PA bureaucracy, that managed the international funds they received and the funds provided by Israeli taxes, was scandalous.

This victory was presented to PLO followers as a circumstantial event. However, the level of support obtained by Hamas in Gaza and the West Bank during confrontations with Israel, suggests that the support came from deep within. **The growth of Hamas should also be seen in the context of the rise of all the Islamic movements throughout the region, with no relation to the Oslo process**.

213. What was the Second Lebanon War of 2006?

It was a confrontation of 34 days between Hezbollah and Israel. It lasted from Jul/12/2006 to Aug/14/2006, formally ending on Sep/8/2006 when Israel lifted the naval blockade over Lebanon.

Since June 2005, Hezbollah tried three times to kidnap Israeli soldiers. In July 2006, they achieved it when two Humvees that were patrolled on the Israeli side of the border, were attacked with anti-tank missiles. The ambush killed three soldiers and two others were kidnapped (Ehud Goldwasser and Eldad Regev).

Israel's Prime Minister Ehud Olmert gave Hezbollah an ultimatum, declaring that the "ambitious" Israeli objective was to destroy Hezbollah. The Israeli army lacked the necessary preparation for this mission, sustaining exaggeratedly their military force in the aviation. Meanwhile, Israeli civilians were exposed to the shootings of missiles from Hezbollah.

The Winograd Investigation Commission harshly criticized the government and the army for the decisions adopted in the war.

Israel attacked the military objectives of Hezbollah and the Lebanese civilian infrastructure such as the Rafic Hariri International Airport of Beirut, which was used by Iran to massively arm Hezbollah. After attacking through the air, Israel launched a terrestrial invasion, imposing an air and naval blockade. In contrast, Hezbollah launched between 3,970 and 4,228 missiles to Israel. It is calculated that there were 1,191 Lebanese and 165 Israeli deaths.

On Aug/11/2006, the Security Council (UN) approved Resolution 1701 that determined the Israeli withdrawal, the disarmament of Hezbollah and the deployment of the Lebanese Armed Forces and the United Nations Interim Forces in Lebanon (UNIFIL) in the south. Of these three conditions, the only one accomplished was the Israeli withdrawal.

There has not been another direct war between Hezbollah and Israel (2019) since the Shiite militia was immersed in a war to keep Bashar El-Assad in Syria.

214. What are the practical consequences of the coup of Hamas against the Palestinian Authority?

The Muslim Brotherhood and other radical Islamic groups were always stronger in Gaza than in the West Bank. In 2001, Hamas launched about 500 rockets and mortars against Israel. Between 2001 and 2004, there were 45 people killed, including 30 Israelis, 4 foreign workers and 10 Palestinians wounded by mistake.

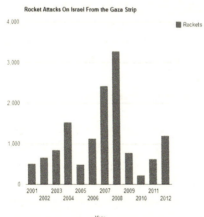

Rocket attacks on Israel from the Gaza Strip (by year)
(Source: Wikipedia)

The coup by Hamas against the Palestinian Authority (June/13/2007) in Gaza resulted in two phenomena: first, Hamas monopolized the distribution of the humanitarian aid, receiving tax funds because of the traffic in the Rafah-Egypt tunnels. This way, it destined part of their budget to build rockets and tunnels. In 2007, Hamas was launching 2,300 rockets and by 2008 it was more than 3,000 rockets per year.

The second effect was creating an open confrontation between Hamas and the PLO, an ideological-political conflict that reached its maximum expression in 2019 when Abbas asked Israel to cut the electricity it sells to the Gaza Strip or to suspend the 100 million dollars in taxes that Ramallah (Abbas) had to supply to Gaza (Hamas).

The coup in Egypt, which returned the military to power led by Abdel Fatah A-Sissi, strangling, even more, the blockade against the Islamist Hamas.

Officially, the international community disregarded the authority of Hamas. The US and the EU demanded that in order to acknowledge Hamas, it had to comply with three conditions: acknowledge Israel, acknowledge the treaties signed by the PLO and the cease of violence. Hamas rejected these conditions.

The strategy of Israel was to weaken Hamas with the legal blockade, rejecting to impose all its military capacity to eliminate the Islamist government. Netanyahu's government (2009) considers that the costs of such an operation overcome its benefits. Besides, such an effort would not guarantee the effective control of the Palestinian Authority over Gaza.

215. What weapons does Hamas use against the Israeli population?

At the end of the war in November 2012, the leader of Hamas, Khaled Mashaal, established the strategy of Hamas to destroy Israel based on two main and complementary elements: the army and politics. Mashaal suggested that the military superiority of Israel could be beaten by tactical military advantages, benefiting from Israeli vulnerabilities, reducing their military options through the use of political-legal tools and with the help of western left-wing organizations which "defend" the human rights.

It is important to point out: launching rockets against a civilian population, intentionally, is a war crime.

At the beginning of Operation Protective Edge 2014, the Israeli Defense Forces estimated that around 10,000 missiles filled the storages of Islamic Hamas/Jihad. Many of those rockets were provided by Iran and Syria or stolen from the Libyan arsenal.

The Iranian war vessels delivered their weapons in the port of Sudan or Syria and from there they were introduced to Gaza through the tunnels crossing the border between Egypt and Gaza, specifically with Grad rockets and M-302 mortars. Sometimes, the trucks that transported the weapons were intercepted and destroyed by Israel.

The rockets included: 1) short distance (15-20 km): 1,000 units of self-produced rockets (15 km), 2,500 units of contraband rockets (15 km), 200 self-produced Grad rockets (20 km) and 200 contraband Grad rockets (20 km); 2) medium-range (up to 45 km): 200 self-produced Grad rockets and another 1,000 improved contraband Grad rockets (45 km); 3) medium to long-range (up to 80 km): more than 400 self-produced rockets. 4) long-range (100-200 km): about ten rockets. **These are not rudimentary rockets.**

It is possible to suppose that currently (2019), Hamas possesses, at least, the same amount of rockets as in 2014.

216. What are the tunnels that Hamas and Hezbollah build to attack Israel?

Tunnels have been part of Gaza for decades. In 1989, the brain of Hamas, Mahmoud Al-Mahbrouh, used one to escape the Israeli Defense Forces. During the mid-90s, they built tunnels from Rafah to Egypt and used them for smuggling, from cigarettes and weapons to fuel, farm animals and even cars. "I was amazed by the underground tunnels used to smuggle terrorists", expressed in surprise Ban Ki-Moon when he visited one in October 2014.

On Oct/7/2013, the Israeli army discovered a mega-tunnel from Gaza to Israel, 18 meters deep and 1.8 km long. The tunnel, exiting in the Ein Ha-Shlosha kibbutz, had taken two years to build and required 800 tons of concrete molded with 25,000 bricks. This tunnel was equipped with electricity and enough cookies, yogurt and provisions to maintain its occupants for several months. Israel estimated that Hamas had invested approximately 10 million dollars in the tunnel. Its discovery proved that Hamas was building a network of tunnels to infiltrate Israel massively.

Operation Protective Edge 2014 exposed and focused on this network of tunnels, eliminating one of the strategic assets of Hamas and preventing a devastating surprise attack behind Israel's defense lines. Israel destroyed 32 tunnels that could have resulted in thousands of civilian deaths.

By the end of 2018, Israel destroyed about ten tunnels built by Hezbollah in the north, thanks to a special (and secret) technology developed to destroy tunnels. It is possible to assume that Hezbollah has built many more tunnels than what has been found to date.

217. Since when have the Palestinians recognized the State of Israel?

The first strategic-ideological change from the PLO towards Israel was adopted in 1974 with the approval of the "Plan in Stages". According to this plan, the main Palestinian objective was to create a State (West Bank-Gaza?) to destroy Israel militarily from there. Some considered this plan as a "moderation" from the PLO.

In November 1988, the National Palestinian Council (Algeria) declared the independence of the Palestinian State. They sustained that there should be a regional agreement based on the UN's Charter and its resolutions. That way, the declaration was ambiguous in regards to the recognition of the State of Israel. Any explicit affirmation of the exposed process was avoided and was limited to suggesting the approval of the resolutions of the United Nations, which implies the acceptance of the existence of the State of Israel.

After suffering a "political coma" (after the Gulf War 1991), the PLO decided to commit to the Israeli premises "Shem-Tov Yariv", accepting Israel and renouncing the use of force for the solution of conflicts. Because of this, the Oslo peace process began. However, the terrorist articles of the PLO Charter (1968) were never canceled (26 clauses) and the return of the terrorism was the strategy of Yasser Arafat and the PLO during the Intifada of Al-Aqsa (2000-2005).

Currently, due to the fact that the conflict for the Palestinians is essentially religious, the Israeli government (led by Netanyahu) demands the recognition of Israel as "the national home of the Jewish people" that, according to Islamic theology, symbolizes the acceptance of the end of the conflict. Among the opposition parties to Israel's government, not all agree with the need for such demand.

Mahmoud Abbas and other Palestinian leaders affirmed, several times, that "they will never accept Israel as a Jewish State" and that, apparently, is because they reject ending the conflict.

218. Does Hamas acknowledge the State of Israel?

Assuming that Hamas is a practical movement that "accepts Israel" has no basis. There are no important differences among experts in the Middle East regarding the Hamas Charter (1988): it is Islamic fundamentalist, Sunni, anti-Semitic, terrorist and anti-west.

Specialist Eli Avidar advises in his great book *The Abyss* (*Ha-Tehom*), to pay attention to what is publicly written and declared in the Arab Is-

lamic culture, as it is the most important thing. It is possible to watch thousands of films on the Hamas television (see the site *Palestine Media Watch*), and see that the alleged declarations of "accepting Israel" does not exist.

In the official TV channel of Hamas, the Vice-Minister of Religious Affairs of Hamas, Abdallah Jarbu, denied the human condition of Jews; he described them as microbes and exhorted Allah to "annihilate this dirty people that has no religion or conscience". Hamas author Mukhlis Barzaq writes that the destiny of the Jews must be "total murder, total extermination and the eradication of perdition".

On May/1/2017, Hamas renewed its 1988 Charter (in 36 articles), so the question would be: does the 2017 Charter replace the 1988 Charter? What changed? 1) There is no mention to the connection Hamas-Muslim Brotherhood; 2) the Islamist aspect is not highlighted – for example, there is no mention of the land of Palestine as *Waqf*, Islamic provision, as in the Charter of 1988; 3) the document tries to separate Hamas from the evident and sublime genocidal anti-Semitism that impregnates its original Charter; 4) they continue supporting Jihad and armed fight to free Palestine.

While the Palestinian Authority acknowledges Israel, though not as the "national Jewish home", Hamas does not acknowledge Israel or the Jews as a people with rights.

219. Why did an ex-Prime Minister from Israel say that "if I would have been born Palestinian I would have joined a terrorist organization"?

These declarations were made by Ehud Barak, Prime Minister of Israel from 1999 to 2001 on Mar/5/1998. He said it a year and a half before he received the rejection of his offer of creating two states and the beginning of the Second Intifada. **It was a time where big efforts were made to maintain the spirit of the Oslo Accords, despite the violent sabotage from Hamas and the deterioration of the mutual trust between Israelis and Palestinians.**

Barak's declarations were a message for the Israeli society about the need to reach historical commitments in exchange for peace and, at the same time, maintain a lucid and empathetic view over reality.

The laborist ex-Chancellor Shlomo Ben-Ami, in his book *Scars of War, Wounds of Peace,* described the emotional consequences for the Palestinians produced by the attacks and combats against them from "Zionist" soldiers before and after 1948.

The expressions of Barak or those of Ben-Ami are proof of the level of maturity of the Israeli side. Both, Barak and Ben-Ami, judged that Arafat's rejection of the Israeli proposals from the year 2000, was marking the turning point in the expectations that the Palestinian side would move towards peace commitments.

It would be useful to have symmetric examples of the declarations and comprehension of the Israeli motivations in the Palestinian field. Normally, these end up in assassination or in a *fatwa* or religious decree that authorizes the execution of the "traitor".

One of the reasons why Barak did NOT become a terrorist is that Zionism opted for constructive pragmatism. The other reason is that the Jewish pragmatism derived in that sympathies for terrorism were forcefully repressed and not encouraged.

220. Are the Palestinian suicidal attacks the main obstacle for peace?

Suicidal attacks have a strategic mission: to make adequate defense and prevention impossible because terrorists can attack in many places with no warning and not much logistics. From a propaganda point of view, the attacks attempt to undermine the morale of the enemy by showing its vulnerability. But indeed, it damages the Palestinian image in Europe and other "markets" that must be conquered, by glorifying murderers of defenseless people, showing a scale of values different from the "western" ones.

Palestinians did not "invent" the genre, not in the Middle East or in the world. *Shahada* attacks, or martyrdom, are sustained on an Islamic theological conception. It comes from the promise of 72 virgins and the acceptance of the *Shahid* (the martyr) in Paradise together with 50 family members. The modern "inventors" of religious martyrdom were the Iranians (in the war with Iraq 1980-1988); they distributed keys "to open the doors of Paradise" to children in exchange for them to detonating mines and to allow the passage of Shiite tanks.

The Palestinian suicidal attacks **did not** happen at the same time as the Oslo process but **fostered the frustration** over the peace agreements. The relevant fact is not that the suicidal attacks appeared 30 years after the occupation (1967), but that they happened precisely when the peace process was starting.

Perhaps the suicidal attacks are not the main obstacle for peace if they were isolated phenomena product of the frustration of individuals and not a policy promoted by the leaders who pay pensions and lifetime subsidies to the families of the murderers. They glorify and stimulate these acts.

The main obstacle for peace is the lack of mutual recognition and the need to make painful concessions to end the conflict. Palestinian terrorist attacks are a manifestation of the lack of recognition.

221. What is the Palestinian position regarding violence and suicidal attacks?

The violence of the Islamist groups (Hamas, Islamic Jihad) did not stop because of the Oslo Accords. Instead, they grew. It is debatable whether the PLO-PA didn't stop this violence because of its incapacity, for fear of being labeled as "traitors", or because of political speculation of counting with a group that did their dirty work without being directly involved. Regretfully, there is enough evidence to support each thesis.

Among the Palestinians, we can identify four positions: 1) those who oppose any type of violence; 2) those who say that they can only attack Israeli military; 3) those who support attacking every Israeli living beyond the Green Line; 4) those who believe that every Israeli is an invader and make no difference between adults, elderly people or children.

The existence of four positions describes a certain internal debate but does not ponder each one (a very fluctuating fact) and, less so, if it is not clear which is the official position from the recognized authorities. **The official authorities (Palestinian Authority 2019) revere, glorify and promote the third group.**

The Palestinians tend to affirm that their main support are the NGOs. Regretfully, the Palestinian pacifist groups are weak or non-existent and have little to no power within the Palestinian streets. Criticism towards violence has been silenced and a critical mass has not been formed to question whether "violence" (called "resistance") should be an accepted norm.

The acceptance of violence as a way to solve disputes has been formed by years of indoctrination and incitation. Moreover, that norm has mutated to the point where the differences between Hamas and the PLO (Palestinian Authority) are solved with violence. Educating and inciting violence provokes... violence.

222. How does Palestinian violence affect Israelis?

Psychosis is an illness. In the case of Israel, the illness would be to accept as natural the terrorist attacks against civilians and to not act against them. Imagine your family living around the Gaza Strip and having to constantly count to 15 to run to an anti-bomb refuge. Think about the uncertainty of sending your child to school on a bus and to have to consider the possibility of its explosion because of the work of a "Palestinian martyr".

In the modern State of Israel, the natural thing is to go to the supermarket or to any public building and wait to have your bag checked to make sure no one is hiding a weapon or a bomb. This practice used to scare away tourists, though now it is more frequent in important European centers.

Israel has had to face attacks since the beginning of the XX Century, so it has accumulated quite an experience. On the other hand, many Israelis feel frustrated when they see media coverage sympathizing with Palestinian violence or when they witness the demonizing of their country by any rookie with no proper information on the conflict.

Violence influences the votes in an election. For an average Israeli, the Prime Minister candidate has to offer two things: Peace and Security. In general, the average citizen feels that the right-wing enjoys a halo of Security, while the left-wing has the halo of Peace. When a left-wing candidate promises both things, like for example the ex-chiefs of state Ehud Barak or Yitzhak Rabin, they increase the possibility of a socialist triumph. When the population feels that there is no partner for peace or they live through days of physical violence, peace talks become less popular and the possibilities of a nationalist victory increase.

223. Why would a Palestinian decide to commit suicide to murder Israelis?

Analysts distanced from Islamic thinking affirm that the socio-economic reasons are the cause of radicalism. Many others distanced from the subject speak about "the Israeli occupation". The evidence rejects this argument. **There is a level of frustration, a wish of popularity and there are even economic incentives, but the option of suicide is based on religious motivations.**

Those who commit suicide are offered the entrance to Paradise, where there are vegetables and fruit trees with rivers of wine and honey. On Earth, it is forbidden for a Muslim to touch a woman if she is not his wife but in Paradise, he will have 72 virgins (*Jourin*) mentioned in the Quran with black eyes, from 30 to 33 years old, with permanent makeup, who do not drink nor eat and are always clean (they do not menstruate) and the superior part of their chests are as clear as a mirror. The description of Paradise appears in the book *El J'ana Wanna Inua –Paradise and the blessings it possesses*.

He can bring 50 members of his family and it is one of the reasons why there is family support. How do we know if they believe in this? Remains of people who have committed suicide have been found with their genitals covered with a cloth or metal sheet, to use in Paradise. In the burials of a suicidal individual, they clean his forehead because "he is now with the 70 virgin women" and making an effort. Paradise has a musk-like smell that can be perceived 40 to 70 years walking. Hundreds of participants of the burial procession affirm that they have "smelled" such an aroma.

What is hell like? In *The Tortures of Hell,* they explain that the person falls for 70 years until crashing against the bottom, and later floats among boiling sulfur and excrements of others.

In Arabic, this is known as "Seduction (Paradise) and Intimidation (Hell)".

224. How does Israeli violence affect the Palestinians?

The frustration that Palestinians feel is comprehensible. In the end, when Israel responds to the launch of rockets from Gaza, it is the citizens that suffer the reaction. The same can be said about the military controls that complicate the free movement of Palestinians in the West Bank.

A recurrent argument is that "thousands" of Palestinians are subject to "administrative arrests". An authorized military commander can issue an order for the administrative detention lasting 8 days. Administrative arrests are subject to a judicial revision by a judge of a military court, and the rulings are subject to the Superior Court of Justice (a world-wide prestigious institution). The order is valid for up to 6 months but can be renewed.

According to the numbers of the Penitentiary Authority of Israel, in December 2015 there were 584 detained Palestinians from the West Bank. Generally, the use of administrative detention is against Palestinians or Israeli Arabs that are suspects of terrorist activities, though also against Jews identified with the radical right-wing for acts of terror or instigation against Palestinians.

Israel's internal intelligence service (Shin Bet) explained that during 2018, 50 terrorist attacks were dismantled, planned from the West Bank (not from the Gaza of Hamas... from the West Bank of the Palestinian Authority). Israel suffers the dilemma of all western democracies: to stop terrorists as a preventive measure or to do so only after the attacks.

Violence against Palestinians can be also seen in the destruction of olive trees. The magnitude of this phenomenon is lower but indisputable. During the period 2005-2009, 69 Palestinian suits were processed regarding this issue. The Israeli "establishment" and its media condemn such behavior. This author considers that all cases should end in having the Israeli aggressor in jail.

225. Is it true that there are Palestinian cities surrounded by a wall?

It is important to affirm that there are not "several" Palestinian cities surrounded by a wall but only one: Bethlehem. Bethlehem suffers a more critical situation and is partially isolated because its shared border with Jerusalem confronts Jewish and Palestinian neighborhoods. The decision of building a cement wall in Bethlehem or even in parts of the border with Ramallah is used to dissuade the possibility of snipers or because there is not enough terrain to build a security fence (that needs at most 100 meters to build the entire structure). There are many graffitis and drawings in rejection to the wall in the internal part of the wall that faces Bethlehem.

Certainly, in some parts of the layout of the Security Fence, it affects communication between Palestinian cities or it is difficult for the people to have access to areas that are important to them. In several opportunities, Palestinians have defeated the Israeli government in the Supreme Court of Justice in Israel requesting that the part of the fence be modified because the fence unjustifiedly prevents the possibility of working and moving.

Some use the word *ghetto* maliciously to describe Bethlehem's situation as if it was the Ghetto of Warsaw. As if Israel would gather together the Palestinians to assassinate them later. **The comparison of the walls that surround Jerusalem for security reasons to events of the Holocaust, reflects a huge lack of factual rigor and also a banalization of that genocide.**

The association with European *ghettos* may be valuable in Israel's internal speech as a way to warn about the ethical risks of this response to terrorism. However, when used by the anti-Israeli propaganda, it seeks to demonize by producing clearly false associations and ritual blame against Israel.

226. Who is Gilad Shalit?

He was an Israeli soldier kidnapped by Hamas on Jun/25/2006, while he was on duty near the Keren Shalom crossing (the same place where merchandise passes from Israel to Gaza).

Palestinian terrorists of the Izz Adin Al-Qassam Brigades, Popular Resistance Committees and the Islam Army penetrated Israel through an underground tunnel. Two Israeli soldiers died and two others, besides Shalit, were wounded. Two Palestinians were killed. Shalit suffered a fracture in his left hand and a slight injury in his shoulder. The Palestinians took him through the tunnel to Gaza.

Shalit was the first Israeli soldier captured by the Palestinians since Nachshon Wachsman in 1994. Almost in parallel, there was a border incursion by Hezbollah, capturing the Israeli soldiers Ehud Goldwasser and Eldad Regev in Lebanon, the immediate cause that led to the conflict in Lebanon (and also against Gaza) during the summer of 2006.

On Oct/18/2011, Gilad Shalit was freed, after five years in confinement and isolation, in exchange for 1,027 Palestinian prisoners, including some sentenced for multiple murders and attacks against Israeli civilians (the freed prisoners were responsible for 569 Israeli deaths).

During his captivity, he was not allowed visits from the Red Cross or to communicate with his family members (violating his rights according to the Geneva Convention). Ransom was demanded for his return, though not monetary. The only contact between Shalit and the exterior world was three letters, an audiotape and a DVD received in Israel in exchange for 20 Palestinian prisoners.

A commission led by retired Judge Meir Shamgar (Supreme Court), advised modifying the policy of unbalanced exchanges, which began with the Jibril Agreement in 1985, exchanging survivors for survivors and deceased for deceased in similar amounts.

227. How does Israel control the West Bank?

This territory formed part of the British Mandate and from 1948 to 1967, Jordan conquered it and annexed it (only England and Pakistan recognized this violation). When Israel conquered Judea and Samaria in 1967, they took on the humanitarian commitments of the Geneva Conventions, even though they were "in dispute".

Journalist Pedro Brieger (*100 Questions*) assures: "Every settlement built was created in expropriated Palestinian lands without the Palestinians nor the PNA being able to prevent it". **This is not exact. The settlements were located in territories that were dominated by Jordan between 1948 and 1967 and did not belong to Palestinian private owners. Many Israeli houses, which have been effectively built on private Palestinian properties, have been destroyed by the Israeli army.**

On Feb/6/2017, the Knesset approved the "Law for the Regulation of Settlements". If a territory belongs to a Palestinian but Israeli houses are built there, the owner will be compensated with 125% the value of the territory or will receive an alternative property of his election. **This way, the Israeli government intends to "legalize" around 2,000 houses in 25 settlements in Judea and Samaria, which are houses built in Palestinian properties.**

On Aug/17/2017, the Supreme Court of Justice of Israel ordered to freeze the execution of the law to revise it. It is probable that the law will be annulled by a sentence from the Supreme Court.

"There are more than 400 military roadblocks in the West Bank and most of the Palestinians must cross them every day when they go to work in public transportation", affirms the journalist. The number of military roadblocks within the West Bank is fluctuating and depends on the security conditions of the region. The fewer terrorist attacks registered, the less Israeli military presence there will be. Israel also exercises its border control between Palestine and Israel to check the entrance of individuals to its territory. It is the same for most countries in the world.

228. Is it true that Israel steals water from the Palestinians in the West Bank?

The guidelines on the division of water between Israel and the Palestinians were established in Oslo B in September 1995, Article 40 of the Protocols on Civilian Issues (Attachment 3). The guidelines establish that Israel shall use 80% of the mountain aquifer and the Palestinians, 20% (there are 8.5 million Israelis, and about 2.5 million Palestinians in the West Bank. Palestinians will continue to use 118 million cubic meters where they were already extracting, and they will also extract from new non-used wells of the eastern mountain (an additional 70-80 million per year).

The Palestinian Authority needs about 200 million cubic meters of water per year. At present, it extracts 87 million from existing wells, where Israel used 118 million, so they could extract an additional 70-80 million from the eastern part of the aquifers. The problem is that Palestinians do not carry out effective maintenance engineering work. Besides that amount, Israel sells the Palestinians 55 million cubic meters at a price below production costs, and lower than what Israelis pay for the service (20% less).

In the Gaza Strip (where there are no Israelis), Palestinians could easily duplicate the available amount of water without Israel's aid. If Palestinians would build a desalination plant on the coast of Gaza (totally financed by the international community), they would increase the amount of available water in 60 to 100 million cubic meters per year. If they repair the leaks, treat and recycle water and adopt drip irrigation, they could duplicate their water as well. In synthesis, if instead of launching rockets at Israel they would worry more about their civilian population, they would solve the issue.

229. Do Palestinians use their citizens as "human shields"?

Hamas recognizes that it uses its people as human shields and there are hundreds of visual proofs that confirm it, so it would be strange to affirm the contrary. The previously cited Argentinean journalist (question 85) affirmed that "it is false... what happened is that they had nowhere to hide". At the time (2010) this affirmation was incorrect.

In declarations to the Gazan TV, a spokesperson of Hamas, Sami Abu Zuhri, said: "The fact is that people want to sacrifice themselves against the war plans of Israel to protect their homes; I think this strategy is working. And we, Hamas, encourage our people to adopt this tactic".

In 2014, Israel began to develop a technique called "knock on the roof". It is used by the Israeli Defence Forces (Tzahal) before attacking buildings where they suspect there are weapons or other military objectives. A small rocket is launched on the roof of a house, that basically makes a noise to let the non-combatants know that they must escape. In general, between the first "noise rocket" and the actual attack there is a 5 to 15 minute period. Hamas usually orders civilians to stay in the houses to use them as human shields and avoid being attacked. See *Knock on Roof* at https://www.youtube.com/watch?v=H0PgMCpydIo

Besides "knock on roof", Israelis throw leaflets informing the Palestinians where they will attack, sending text messages to those affected in the attack areas. **Military authorities such as Col. Richard Kemp, commander of the British military forces in Afghanistan, affirmed that "Israel is the army with the highest morals of the world" and that it uses techniques as no other army does to reduce the number of innocent victims in conflict areas.**

See below 10 links that show the use of human shields. There are hundreds more at *Human Shields Gaza*.
1. https://www.youtube.com/watch?v=GWQQFJXMrg4
2. https://www.youtube.com/watch?v=fcrWy3PT6zc
3. https://www.youtube.com/watch?v=j3yAYJIhzEA
4. https://www.youtube.com/watch?v=eOU6FYIs5d0
5. https://www.youtube.com/watch?v=O11h1rK5PYU
6. https://www.youtube.com/watch?v=I7M-TCfnZmg
7. https://www.youtube.com/watch?v=lpTZUAkNOUA
8. https://www.youtube.com/watch?v=4cC4jEIpRQY
9. https://www.youtube.com/watch?v=OPpF70eEkog
10. https://www.youtube.com/watch?v=HEUgUtGAmrY

230. What are the selective killings practiced by Israel?

Any human being that carries out military actions, by default, becomes a legitimate target in the framework of war. If a Palestinian from Rafah, dressed in jeans and shirt, smuggles rockets into the Gaza Strip, he violates twice the international laws; he is carrying out war actions, so he should be dressed in a different way than civilians; he is carrying out war actions, intentionally, within civilian structures, so he transforms the home where he enters through the tunnel into a legal military objective.

A terrorist on his way to commit an attack or that organizes terrorists could be detained, but if it is impossible (because he is hiding among civilians), it is totally legal to target him (Bagatz Dec/14/2006). The objectives of selective assassinations are: prevent attacks, intimidate the enemy and weaken its military capacity. **At present, the western armies that are combating Islamists share the legality of "selective assassinations".**

The ex-Chief of Staff of the Israeli Army, Moshe Yaalon, explained the dilemmas of the phenomenon in *Ethical Dilemmas in Counter-terrorism*: "Selective assassinations are not destined to punish terrorists for their past actions, but to prevent them in the future. In the seven years since the beginning of the war against Palestinian terror, there was only one case in which the IDF killed a civilian intentionally, together with a terrorist, during an operation. The cited terrorist had a fundamental role in the planning and execution of suicidal attacks (Palestinian). The first time we had the opportunity to kill him, he was with his daughters, so we canceled the attack and forgave his life. Six months later, we chose again to kill him when he was alone with his wife. Does the fact that his wife died too make our mission unjust? Was the previous decision, which resulted in no Israelis murdered, a correct one?"

231. Do innocent civilians die when Israel kills a Palestinian terrorist?

In 1996, Israel killed Yehi Ayash of Hamas, the engineer that built the bomb-vests of the Palestinian suicide martyrs. They gave him a telephone with a bomb in its battery, killing only him and no one else in his home knew what happened. This "sterile" operation is not very common in this type of attack.

Journalist and military correspondent of the Israeli journal *Haaretz*, Amos Harel, reviewed the proportion of civilian deaths and deaths due to selective assassination throughout the years. Between 2002 and 2003, the proportion was 1:1, which means that for every terrorist killed, there was also a civilian killed.

Yehi Ayash – Hamas
(*Source: Wikipedia*)

Harel called this period the "black days" because of the high proportion of civilian losses compared to other periods. **At the end of 2005, the proportion of civilian victims had decreased considera-bly to 1:28, meaning that one civilian had been killed for 28 terrorists killed.** The proportion increased to 1:10 in 2006 due to a "series of errors of the airforce". In 2007 and 2008, however, the proportion fell again to an unprecedented 1:30. Harvard University Professor Alan Dershowitz stated that the number 1:30 in 2008 is the lowest index of civilian casualties in the history of anti-terrorism. He also affirmed that this number could be tricky, as not all of those presented as civilians were innocent spectators.

According to the statistics of the Israeli NGO Betselem, between 2000 and 2008, the proportion was 1:1.52 (based on Palestinian testimonials, mainly). Investigators such as Jonathan Dahoah stated that the organization usually classified armed activists and terrorist operators as civilians that were not participating in combat.

232. Why do Palestinians and Israelis accuse each other of terrorist practices?

Among western specialists, there are no great differences when defining terrorism. However, the Arab-Islamic block of countries, where most of the terrorism of the world originates, considers that if someone combats against what they qualify as "foreign occupation", the person has the right to use all the possible forms within his reach (including terrorism).

In general, definitions of terrorism in the west include all of the following conditions: 1) killing or threatening, 2) civilians, 3) intentionally, 4) to achieve political objectives, 5) within a propagandist framework. The definition accepted in the academy and in different international conventions is more detailed than the aforementioned here.

People in Latin America who sympathize with terrorism, show it as the "weapon of the poor" when it should be presented as the "weapon of the immoral".

The traditional *modus operandi* of the PLO in the 70s were random terrorist attacks, and at present (2019) terrorists use firearms to shoot against Israeli civilians.

Hamas, on the other hand, launches rockets from Gaza or has executed (2003-2016) 151 suicidal attacks killing 725 people. Hamas tries to argue that what they do is not terrorism: 1) "We try to shoot rockets against military bases but it doesn't come out right, and we shoot civilians", 2) "There are no Israeli civilians, they are all potential military", 3) "Our rockets are so bad that they fall on Israeli cities… but actually, we want to assassinate the military".

If Israelis bombard intentionally the Palestinian population to assassinate civilians, the country would carry out state terrorism. If that were the case, Israelis would be processed in international courts. **To prove the contrary, the Israeli army films its air raids so when irresponsible or malicious accusations come about, they can be defeated easily in a court of justice.**

233. Why did Israel carry out Operation Cast Lead in the Gaza Strip in December 2008?

This was an important military operation (Dec/27/2008-Jan/18/2009). The reason was explained by Prime Minister Ehud Olmert: "No state can tolerate the launching of rockets over its territory".

In January 2008, Hamas violated the border between Gaza and Egypt (the Philadelphia route), smuggling long-range rockets. On Jan/5/2008, a powerful Grad rocket was launched against Ashkelon (Israel) from the neighborhood of Al-Atatra, in the north of the Gaza Strip. **During those six months, they launched 100 rockets per month against Israel.** After a cease-fire mediated by Egypt (Jun/19/2008 – Dec/19/2008), Hamas reinitiated the massive launch of rockets.

The objective declared by Israel was not to destroy Hamas, but to weaken its military capacity (different to what Olmert declared in 2006, when he said that the objective was to "destroy Hezbollah" in Lebanon). Israeli military usually call these operations "cutting the grass", increasing the enemy's dissuasion.

The Israeli casualties were clear: 14 deceased (3 civilians) and 320 wounded.

The number of Palestinian victims varied due to the political explosion of the issue: according to Israeli Intelligence, 1,166 lost their lives (709 combatants, 162 unknown, 295 "not involved"). According to the Palestinian Ministry of Health (in the hands of Hamas), 1,366 Palestinians died, almost all of them civilians. **However, in November 2010, the Minister of Internal Affairs of**

Hamas, Fathu Hamad, confirmed that 700 of its combatants had perished in Operation Cast Lead. This number is similar to the data published by Israel and contradicts those shown by human rights organizations. The proportion of deaths: for each deceased military, 0.51 civilians.

In February 2009, Amnesty International published a report stating that during the operation, Hamas eliminated alleged collaborators with Israel (endorsing them to Israel).

234. Is it true that Israel violates International Law by using "white phosphorus"?

White phosphorus is a common allotrope of the chemical element phosphorus, with wide military use as an incendiary agent. It is also used to create smoke screens; it can produce instant camouflage to cover military actions. **The use of white phosphorus for camouflage missions or to illuminate combat areas during the night is NOT banned by any international treaty**.

In 2005, Peter Kaiser, in an interview for RAI, spokesperson for the Organization for the Prohibition of Chemical Weapons (OPCW), stated that if white phosphorus was used as camouflage "it is considered as a legitimate use within the Convention", but if "the toxic properties of white phosphorus are used solely as a weapon; it is, of course, prohibited".

During Operation Cast Lead Durante (2008-2009) Israel was criticized for "violating" the international law for using white phosphorus. However, its use to mark combat areas, to illuminate or to create smoke screens, is totally legal. Critics argue that it was used in highly populated areas (Gaza) and that it produced severe burns.

The Israeli army understood that white phosphorus "looked bad on film", so they dropped its use at the end of Cast Lead. **Since 2009 Israel has not been accused again for its use. Although it was legal, it looked bad**.

Was any Israeli accused of misusing White phosphorus by mistake? Two Israeli officers were punished for the incorrect use of white phosphorus bombs during Cast Lead on Jan/15/2009. Colonel Ilan Lamka and Brigade General Eyal Eisenberg were investigated and received disciplinary sanctions for ordering to launch ammunitions with white phosphorus to the UNWRA complex in Gaza. Two employees of UNRWA and two civilians were injured.

235. Why was Operation Cast Lead so harshly criticized in the media?

One of the arguments to justify criticism against Israel was the number of deaths. "Over 1,300 Palestinians died, among them, 400 minors, and only 13

Israelis", condemns Brieger. The numbers are different, according to Hamas's confession. Moreover, and considering the disgrace of losing innocent lives, exposing numbers as an argument is an act of manipulation. During World War II, between 1.2 and 2.1 million German civilians died, compared to 60,000 British. **Were the Nazis the victims because more Germans died than British?**

Another partially true accusation is that the media could not cover the battle, because Israel forbade it. **Access to the foreign press was limited from November 2008 via Egypt and from Israel.** On Dec/29/2008, the Supreme Court of Israel ordered that journalists could enter Gaza. The Palestinian security forces encouraged all foreigners (especially Europeans and North Americans), including humanitarian aid workers from international organizations, to leave the land of Gaza "for fear of new kidnappings". For this reason, Israel informed that it could not guarantee the lives of professionals.

From January 2009, the Islamist TV from Qatar, Al-Jazeera, informed that Ayman Mohyeldin and Sherine Tadros were in Gaza reporting before the war. BBC had a local Palestinian producer, Rushdi Abu Alouf. **One of the few "serious" reporters that covered the events from Gaza, explaining the complex situation, was Lorenzo Cremonesi from *Corriere Della Sera* from Italy.**

Another argument was that the United Nations schools were attacked by the Israeli army. The truth is that Israelis were being shot from within these facilities. The terrorists of Hamas transformed the schools into a legal military objective. See https://www.youtube.com/watch?v=P-G5t0_YUQg

236. Why is Israel generally so harshly criticized in the media?

Most of the European and Latin American media defend a clear pro-Palestinian narrative. The reasons that explain this are conceptual and practical.

From a conceptual point of view, many blame Israel for "occupying" Palestinian territories as if there had been a Palestinian state or as if the conflict were about territory. The materialistic influence on media professionals is considerable.

Another conceptual inconvenient is that the Palestinian-Israeli conflict is very complex. TV media usually avoid offering context information arguing that they lack the time. Possibly, something like this would demand more knowledge and preparation. The alternative to the required depth is to present "human stories".

Conceptually, there is a tendency to side with the weak (the Palestinians), without questioning who is the aggressor. When the weak ones and the aggressor are one and on the same side, the media prefer to show David fighting against Goliath.

From a practical point of view, most of the military actions occur on the Palestinian side, with less "pro-Israel" images (such as a destroyed bus after a suicidal attack). The TV companies do not have their own cameramen, so they receive images from the news agencies (AP, Reuters), who use images filmed by the Palestinians that live in those cities. **It is almost impossible to find free-press culture in totalitarian societies such as Hamas in Gaza.**

There is a certain degree of lack of professionalism and the impossibility of wandering around the area. In Gaza, the journalists usually do not move from the restricted area assigned to them by Hamas, and when a TV company films material that discredits Palestinians, they have suffered death threats, like what happened to the RAI cameramen who filmed the savage lynching of two Israeli soldiers in Ramallah (2000).

Finally, not always have the Israelis been able to communicate professionally.

237. Is it true that Palestinians violate international laws with their war actions?

Being a terrorist organization violates international laws. Hamas has been classified as "terrorist" by the US, Canada, the European Union, Jordan, Egypt, Israel and Japan. **At least 16 conventions and protocols have been adopted since 1963 by the United Nations, criminalizing all aspects of international terrorism.**

In the field, Palestinians continuously violate several laws of war: 1) when a Palestinian is disguised as a civilian, even as a nurse, as has happened, to conduct military actions, he is violating international laws; 2) when a Palestinian of Hamas, for example, shoots from a civilian zone, he is violating international laws. The fighter has to act from an area that does not endanger civilians; 3) when a Palestinian uses human shields, he is violating international laws (Article 51 (7) of the 1977 Protocols of the Geneva Convention); 4) when a Palestinian launches rockets intentionally against civilians, he is violating international laws. These are established in the Regulations of The Hague 1907 (Art 25) or Protocol I of the Geneva Convention, 1977 (Articles 48 and 51).

Palestinian actions are crimes against humanity and crimes of war, subject to processing by the International Criminal Court (ICC), as well as in courts of law guided by universal criminal jurisdiction.

A religious holy war with the objective of creating a regional Islamic State and destroying Israel is against the guidelines of the 1948 *Convention on the Prevention and Punishment of the Crime of Genocide*.

According to international law, non-state parties are bound by the guidelines of the customary international humanitarian law when they become a party in an armed conflict. The Special Court for Sierra Leone clearly stated: **"All the parties in an armed conflict, state or non-state, are bound by the international humanitarian law"**.

238. What are the legal approaches to fight against Islamic terrorism (including the Palestinian)?

There are three approaches: 1) **Criminal legislation** – Throughout the 80s and the 90s, the western states understood the need to find a reasonable balance between acceptability and democratic efficiency in the fight against terrorism. They wanted to guarantee the security of their citizens, but at the same time, they were committed to liberal democratic principles in their response to the threat. This way, the states "criminalized" internally the phenomenon of terrorism, and responded through the criminal justice system.

In recent decades, the traditional way of dealing with terrorism has been to consider it as an internal criminal act, to be dealt with via the criminal justice system, just as a robbery, a violation or a murder.

2) **Negotiation and appeasement**- As an alternative, negotiations have tried to be held with terrorist groups and the unilateral political reforms destined to appease them and to reduce their motivation to using violence. In this context, Israel has considerable experience in negotiating commitments with Palestinian leaders, establishing obligations to counteract terrorism. Such obligations have been inevitably violated by the Palestinians; not only do they not avoid terrorism, in many cases, they encourage it.

3) **The need for an affirmative approach** – However, because of the increasingly international reach of terrorism, the ever-growing and available resources for terrorism, its universal dimension and the modern ways to propagate instigation via the Internet, the traditional methods of internal criminalization or appeasement are not enough anymore. The ideology that seeks to widen the Islamic domination over the world, hampers any type of conciliation or commitment. **The states begin to understand the need to combat radical *Dawa* and not only Jihadist actions.**

239. Is it true that Israelis violate international laws by using disproportionate force?

It is common to see accusations among journalists and international organizations, affirming that Israel uses its force "disproportionately", and therefore, violates international law. **These accusations are factual and legally incorrect.**

Proportionality in armed conflicts is a measure established as follows: **The magnitude of the force used by a country has to be proportional to the foreseen concrete and direct military advantage.** For example, if a terrorist carries a nuclear bomb estimated to murder 3 million people, a combat aircraft kills the terrorist and 400 innocent civilians, then such a "selective assassination", according to the international law, is "proportional".

Disproportionality cannot be established by comparing the number of victims of the parties involved and the damages during combat.

This principle is considered part of the customary international law, valid for all states, and has become a part of the positive law of armed conflict via the First Additional Protocol of the Geneva Conventions of 1977. Article 51-5b confirms this.

The tragic and sad fact that there are more civilian victims and damage in Gaza than in Israel does not show disproportionality. The fact is that Hamas intentionally uses civilian buildings for its rocket facilities or exposes Gazans as human shields and shows them cynically as martyrs in the media, increasing the solidarity of the world public opinion with the Jihadist cause. At the same time, Hamas blocks civilian access to its underground network of tunnels and anti-air raid refuges, reserved for the military commanders. Israel has developed an anti-missile system, "Iron Dome", to reduce its victims, and the population is trained to run to the refuges. Logically, these measures result is fewer victims on the Israeli side.

240. What happened with the UN schools (UNRWA) during Operation Protective Edge 2014?

During Protective Edge (2014) Israel attacked seven times UNRWA refuges in Gaza. The incidents happened due to shooting of artillery, mortars or missiles, detonating in or near UNRWA facilities, used as refuges for civilians, and sometimes to hide Palestinian terrorists. As a result, at least 44 civilians, including 10 members of the UN, have died. During the conflict between Israel and Gaza, it was estimated that 200,000 people (10% of the population of Gaza) took refuge in the UNRWA schools. Part of them were terrorists.

On three occasions, Jul/6/2014, Jul/22/2014 and Jul29/2014, UNRWA informed that it had found rockets in its schools. UNRWA claimed that there were groups responsible for "flagrant violations of the neutrality of their facilities".

The Israeli Defense Forces (IDF) declared that "Hamas chooses where these battles take place, and in spite of the efforts of Israel to avoid civilian victims, Hamas is responsible for the tragic loss of lives. Specifically, in the case of UN facilities, we must recognize the reiterated abuse of the facilities by Hamas".

Since Jul/24/2014, UNRWA has closed down 23 facilities in Gaza, and Hamas has taken advantage of these vacant buildings as storage for weapons. Even worse: after discovering the rockets, the UN organization, UNRWA, "returned them to Hamas". Also, Hamas launched rockets and mortars from nearby UN facilities, as the case of the UNRWA primary school for boys, Shahada Al-Manar in the Zeitun neighborhood of the city of Gaza, from the UNRWA distribution center, or from the Health Center in Jabaliya.

241. What is the Human Rights Council of the United Nations?

The demonizing/anti-Semitic condemnations against Israel come mainly from the General Assembly and the Human Rights Council of the United Nations.

The Human Rights Council of the UN (2006) is the continuation of the vilified Commission for Human Rights. Based in Geneva (Switzerland), its creation declared a priority to include those countries that respect Human Rights. At a later date China, Russia, Libya or Saudi Arabia were designated... states that are highly repressive and particularly non-democratic.

In formal terms, a report from the Human Rights Council of the UN could be the basis for a resolution by the UN Security Council.

On June/29/2011 Richard Falk published in his blog an anti-Semitic post that provoked an apology (*Source: Wikipedia*)

Since its origin in 2006, and until 2014, the Council condemned Israel 50 times for alleged "violations to human rights", half of the total resolutions including the rest of the countries together.

In 2009, the Human Rights Council organized the "Goldstone Commission" to investigate "crimes of war by Israel" during Operation Cast Lead. The Council decided that the takeover by Israel of the Mavi Marmara Fleet was illegal because the (legal) blockade was illegal. In 2014, they published another report after Protective Edge, acquitting Hamas by stating that the offensive tunnels of the terrorist group and the launching of rockets by Palestinians (including one that resulted in the death of a 4-year-old child) were legitimate attacks against "military objectives".

One of the most nefarious characters named by the UN Human Rights Council was the denier of the Holocaust and anti-Semite, Richard Falk, an observer sent to Palestine to report on human rights. Among other things, Richard Falk affirmed that Hamas is not a terrorist group, that Israel was carrying out genocide, and that the Hebrew state was planning a Palestinian Holocaust.

242. What is the Goldstone Report?

In 2009, the UN Human Rights Council formed the "Goldstone Commission" to investigate the Israeli crimes of Operation Cast Lead (2008-2009).

Israel decided to not cooperate with the Jewish South-African Judge Goldstone, because it was a commission formed by an organization with such an obsessive anti-Semitic record, and because the mission of the investigation was only about what Israel had done (later they modified its mandate to investigating all violations to human rights).

Richard Goldstone, not counting on the contribution of Israel, decided to publish a report based only on testimonials of Hamas, accusing Israel of committing crimes of war.

A perfect example of this mediocre report is its analysis of the Israeli attacks on the area of the Al-Quds Hospital in Gaza City on Jan/15/2009. The report dedicated over eight full pages (pages 174-182) where it considered the Palestinian testimony that there had not been Palestinian attacks from this area, and on the other hand it cited an Israeli report that reached the opposite conclusion.

The official press release of the Goldstone Commission reported: "There is evidence that shows severe violations of international human rights and humanitarian laws committed by Israel during the Gaza conflict, and that Israel committed actions considered as crimes of war and possibly crimes against humanity".

On Apr/1/2011, Richard Goldstone wrote a column in the Washington Post criticizing Israel for not collaborating with him, but amazingly, he confessed: "if I knew then what I know now, I wouldn't have accused Israel of crimes of war". **Richard Goldstone said that the Council was acting unfairly towards Israel, that Israel had professionally investigated his demands, and Hamas had not.**

243. What was the Flotilla to the Gaza Strip?

It was a media event (May/31/2010) in which six ships (the "Freedom Flotilla") with 670 people, tried to trespass the legal blockade on Gaza. Among the passengers, there was the Israeli congresswoman Hanin Zoabi and the Islamist Shiek Raed Salah, together with 40 unidentified people.

The Israeli forces approached the ships (in international waters, 190 km northwest) and ordered them to navigate to the port of Ashdod, where they would be inspected and their donation would be delivered to the Palestinians via Keren Shalom.

Five of the six ships complied with the international law. The largest ship, "Mavi Marmara", (belonging to the Turkish Islamist group IHH) rejected the order.

The soldiers announced they would take over the ship by force. Huwaida Arraf, one of the organizers of the fleet or someone close to him, responded: "Shut up, go back to Auschwitz".

According to filmed documentation, after descending on a rope tied to the ship (by passengers) to try to bring down the helicopter, the soldiers were beaten, their personal weapons were taken from them and shots were heard. After about 40 minutes, the Israeli soldiers received the order to use real fire. Nine passengers died and 30 were wounded. Ten soldiers were also wounded, two of them in a critical state.

Two Israeli commissions (Ayland and Tirkel) investigated the event. As was expected, the Human Rights Commission sent a commission headed by Judge Carl Hudson-Phillips, who condemned Israel: "it was a flagrant violation of human rights and international law".

In July 2010, the UN formed the Palmer Commission (with the participation of Alvaro Uribe), and they defined that besieging the Gaza Strip was legal, the Flotilla was violating international law, but Israel used excessive force, so they recommended paying compensation to the families of the deceased.

244. What was Operation Pillar of Defense 2012?

An eight-day military operation between Israel and Hamas, the governing authority of the Gaza Strip, initiated on Nov/14/2012 with the selective assassination of Ahmen Jabari, head of the military branch of Hamas. Jabari planned numerous terrorist attacks against Israel, launched rockets against civilians and planned the kidnapping of the Israeli soldier, Gilad Shalit.

According to the Israeli government, the operation began in response to the launch of over 100 rockets against Israel in a 24-hour period and an attack against a military patrolling jeep within the Israeli borders.

The Israeli government declared that its objective was to stop the rocket-launching and interrupt the capacity of the militant organizations. The Palestinians blamed the Israeli government, indicating the blockade of the Gaza Strip and the "occupation" of the West Bank as the reason for their attacks with rockets.

During the operation, the Israelis stated that they had attacked over 1,500 locations in the Gaza Strip, including rocket-launching platforms, weapons storage and government facilities. According to a report by UNHCR, 174 Pa–lestinians died and hundreds were wounded. Some of the Palestinian deaths were caused by their own mis-launched rockets, and eight Palestinians were killed by members of the Izz Adin Al-Qassam Brigades for alleged collaboration with Israel.

During Defense Pillar, Palestinians launched 1,456 rockets, 142 falling within Gaza itself. Six Israelis died and 240 were wounded. Almost 421 rockets were intercepted by the new anti-missile system, Iron Dome.

That year, 2012, Egypt was governed by Muhammad Mursi of the Muslim Brotherhood, the ideological cradle of Hamas. During those months, Hamas increased its military capacity, so Defense Pillar was a limited operation in which Israel tried to avoid direct confrontation with Egypt of the Muslim Brotherhood.

245. What was Operation Protective Edge 2014?

The Israel-Hamas War (26 days, starting on July/8/2014) began because of serious internal problems in Palestine. Hamas was governing in Gaza thanks to the funds they received from countries such as Qatar, and for the taxes they were charging to anything that went through the tunnels connecting Gaza and Egypt.

When the Egyptian president A-Sissi overthrew the Islamist regime from Murci (supporters of Hamas) in July 2013, he closed down the tunnels, accusing Hamas of killing Egyptian military.

Hamas was unable to pay its 42,000 officers; unemployment in Gaza reached 46% and the GDP/*per capita* was only $4 per day. Hamas tried to form a national united government (with the Palestinian Authority) so they could pay for the salaries of their Islamist employees in Gaza.

In order to survive, Gaza required funds urgently and needed to achieve an internal cohesion to distract the latent anger against them; nothing better than to attack Israel by increasing the number of rockets. Also, Hamas was sure that a high amount of Gazan victims would create international pressure and media coverage to force Israel to open a maritime port and an airport to charge taxes (and introduce weapons).

At first, Israel tried to manage the increase in the rockets that were being launched (100 per day) without "escalating". However, the murder of three teenagers by terrorists of Hamas, while they were on a road trip, stopped Israel from continuing its "contention" policy.

In the beginning, the Israeli military strategy was focused on weakening the missile capacity of Hamas. Then, they began a partial terrestrial penetration (3-5 km from the border) to destroy the entrances of 32 tunnels leading to Israel. Hamas and Israel agreed on a cease-fire when the selective attacks against Hamas leaders began.

Hamas did not achieve its strategic objectives, so a new wave of violence can be foreseen.

246. What narrative was imposed during Operation Protective Edge 2014?

Hamas was able to impose several narratives during this war. On Aug/29/2014 Ishmael Haniyeh (leader of Hamas) declared to Al-Jazeera: "Our narrative has taken advantage. Our supporters have become the river in which the global media quench their thirst for information about what is happening".

The media were broadcasting quite unsustainable affirmations: 1) It was assured that Hamas had become moderate, because of its ideology or because it was feeling "isolated"; 2) It was said that Hamas was acting that way because Israel maintained the occupation (?), and 3) The threat against Israel was minimized assuring that Israel was starving the Palestinians in Gaza.

The most important discussion was about the number of civilian deaths during Protective Edge. The UN Human Rights Commissioner, Navi Pillay, vilely affirmed that "about 74%" of the Palestinian mortal victims were civilians. The numbers presented by the UN were based on the information provided by the Ministry of Health of Gaza (offered by Ashraf Al-Kidra), directed by Hamás. The UN and other Palestinian sources stated that 2,100 Palestinians lost their lives.

On Dec/1/2014, the Meir Amit Center for Intelligence and Terrorism Information informed in a detailed analysis, name by name, the 1,598 Palestinian mortal victims during Operation Protective Edge, 75% of all the deceased. Of the victims that were identified, approximately 45% were not combatants, while 55% were.

During Protective Edge 2014 the relationship between civilian and military deaths was 1:1, a noticeably low proportion compared to the somber war standards against terrorists that use human shields or that hide among civilians intentionally. The efforts of the coalition in Afghanistan, for example, result in a proportion of 3 to 1, and 4 to 1 in Iraq.

247. Why is the United States so influential in the Middle East?

Powers can influence any region as long as they have the capacity to achieve two things: punishment and reward. After World War II, the position of the US was almost neutral, condemning European countries for the Sinai War against Nasser and pressuring Israel for its nuclear plan.

The strong Soviet penetration in the Arab countries, with the Egypt-Czechoslovakia (1955) weaponry agreement, pushed the US into the Middle East. At the time, Israel purchased weapons from France and the only aid the US provided Israel was food. During the presidency of Lyndon Johnson, the US modified its posture to strong support to Israel, though not unconditional, because they thought that the Arab countries (Egypt, Syria) were irreversibly pro-Soviet.

For the US (2019) the three main allies in the Middle East are Saudi Arabia, Israel and Qatar. Many times, its allies defend contradicting interests.

The US support to Israel is economic, military, diplomatic and strategic; strong support that has undergone its ups and downs.

After signing the Peace Agreement with Egypt (1979), the US has rewarded Israel with 3 billion dollars a year: 74% must be spent in purchasing goods and services from the US. Egypt also receives 2.2 billion a year. **For Israel, the economic support of the US (2019) is not existential.**

In the diplomatic arena, the US used its veto power in 15 out of 24 occasions, between 1991 and 2011. During the presidency of Obama, this support decreased, and in just days Trump increased it again.

For the US, Israel is a stable democracy, a strategic ally. The deceased Republican Senator Jesse Helms used to call Israel "the United States aircraft carrier in the Middle East", justifying the value of Israel in the region. At present, Israel is a partner of the US in many projects, as Israel contributes to the alliance with its technological capacity.

248. What was the strategy of Barack Hussein Obama for the Palestinian-Israeli conflict?

There are people who affirm that Israel enjoys "immunity" in the US. The registers of Obama (2008-2016) contradict this.

The strategy of Obama in the Middle East was to prioritize the solution of the Palestinian-Israeli conflict mainly by pressuring Israel. It was not the first time this happened (Kissinger in 1975 and George Bush in 1991).

Obama also considered that the Arab countries should turn to democracy, and partially abandoned the US alliance with less radical dictators. This posture was evidenced when they did not support Hosni Mubarak during the revolt against him. Countries such as Saudi Arabia felt betrayed by Obama, and even rejected participating in the UN Security Council.

When he began his mandate, Obama pressured Israel to formally accept the creation of a negotiated Palestinian state (Netanyahu accepted during his speech in Bar Ilan) and to stop the construction of housing in the West Bank for 10 months. As this did not include the construction of houses in eastern Jerusalem and 300 previously approved houses that were under construction, the Palestinians rejected this measure for "being inadequate", and refused to negotiate for nine months.

In parallel to the political pressure on Israel, Obama accepted to sell (2009) anti-bunker bombs to Israel for a possible anti-nuclear attack against Iran. From a military and economic point of view, Obama was very good for bilateral relations.

From a diplomatic standpoint, Obama declared that the US would veto any Palestinian request to enter the UN as members, affirming that "there cannot be shortcuts for peace" (Sep/20/2011). On the other hand, he promoted Resolution 2334 (2016), which undermines Israel.

The tension between Obama and Netanyahu increased when Israel opposed the Iranian anti-nuclear agreement (6+1). The Prime Minister qualified it as a "historic mistake", defying Obama before the two chambers of the North-American congress.

249. What is Resolution 2334 of the UN Security Council? What role does it play in the Palestinian-Israeli conflict?

On Dec/23/2016 the Security Council approved a Resolution that openly condemns Israel, with full force, similar to Resolution 465 of 1980.

The US under Obama, in the epilogue of his period, abstained, although promoted the Resolution from the backstage.

The Resolution was adopted under Chapter VI of the UN Charter and does not include sanctions for its non-application; but its violation could lead to another decision under Chapter VII, with sanctions.

The decision states that the Security Council will not acknowledge any changes on the lines of June/4/1967, including Jerusalem, without consent from the parties, via negotiations (Article 3). The settlements, it affirms, located in occupied Palestinian territory, including eastern Jerusalem, lack legal force, are a flagrant violation of international law and represent a serious obstacle to the solution of two states (Article 1). It also states that Israel is the occupying power and that it should respect the Fourth Geneva Convention.

This Resolution contradicts the previously approved Resolution 242 because it places Israel as a violator of a border that was not acknowledged in 1967.

The declared intention of the US was to stop the constructions beyond the Blocks (see question N° 5), although on paper, the decision does not distinguish between isolated settlements, the blocks of settlements and eastern Jerusalem, nor between construction in State-owned lands and construction in private lands.

The resolutions of the Security Council do not have the legal power to affect international law. **However, it is one of the sources examined to determine international law and can play a role in any legal proceedings related to settlements.**

On Jan/5/2017, the House of Representatives of the US Voted 342-80 in favor of condemning the Resolution of the UN **It is yet to be seen if Resolution 2334 will replace Resolution 242 as a basis for future negotiations**.

250. Are the territories of Judea and Samaria (West Bank) "Occupied Territories"?

The term "occupation" is normally used more politically than legally, and it seems to apply to Israel and hardly ever to other territorial disputes.

Qualifying the West Bank as "occupied Palestinian territories" reinforces the pro-Palestinian argumentation: 1) it justifies violence and terrorism (by the way, before 1967); 2) the demand to "end occupation" outs the possibility of a territorial commitment as established in Resolution 242 of the Security Council; 3) it denies any Israeli historical intention over said land.

Why does Israel argue that Judea and Samaria are territories "under dispute"? **First, customary international law acknowledges only one form of military occupation: belligerent occupation, that is, the occupation of part or the entire territory of an enemy, that is sovereign, at the time of the war.** This is established in the Rules of The Hague and the Fourth Geneva Convention of 1949. According to Articles 42-43 of the Rules of The Hague IV (1907), there are three conditions to establish an "occupation": a) the area must be under the effective control of the enemy army; b) previously, the area had to be a part of the sovereign territory of the other state; c) the occupying force dominates the area in order to return it to the previous sovereign. **There was no such sovereign state in the West Bank**.

Those that reject this form of interpretation of the Geneva Convention, sustain that it is questionable that the signatory has to be a sovereign state, and besides, Jordan "was" a signatory party, with or without sovereignty over the West Bank (it was not).

The strongest argument states that the Fourth Geneva Convention has become customary law, determining that all territories under control after a military confrontation, must be automatically considered as occupied.

Evidently, when the time comes, Israel will invest its best minds to impose its legal vision on the topic.

251. How do the Oslo Accords and the Disconnection from Gaza 2005 coexist with the "Occupied Territories"?

Based on the Interim Agreement between Israel and the PLO of Sep/9/1995 (Oslo B), areas A and B (approximately 40% of the territory) are under the effective control of the Palestinian Authority. Because of the continuous presence of certain Israeli troops in the area, it was agreed and regulated by the Agreement, that said presence should not be considered as an occupation unless the validity of the Oslo Accords B (1995) is ignored.

Despite having signed, Palestinian Authority argues that they continue seeing Israel as an occupying power in their collective imagination. Furthermore, in the absence of a final agreement, the status of Israel has not changed. On the other hand, the Palestinian Authority argues before the US courts that they ARE a "foreign state" and therefore they are protected by sovereign immunity. If they are a state, as they affirm in the US courts, then THERE IS NO occupation, at least not in areas A and B of the West Bank.

Others also argue that Israel is the occupying power in the Gaza Strip, although there is no Israeli presence in the area. However, there is an alternative effective government led by Hamas since the coup of 2007.

In Gaza or the West Bank, 95% of the Palestinians live under a Palestinian government (2019).

Resolution 2334 of the Security Council contradicts the Israeli interpretation of the term *occupation*, and with a political decision, fixed the line that separates the forces of 1949 (Green Line) as a border between states, declaring that all Jewish civilian activities beyond the line are illegal.

Time will tell if all these political decisions have achieved a legal re-interpretation to adapt to the political desires of their promoters.

252. What is the strategy of Donald Trump for the Palestinian-Israeli conflict?

It is complicated to determine if Donald Trump has a clear strategy for the Middle East. **In the Palestinian-Israeli conflict, he thinks that he can make the "deal of the century", a peace agreement not yet developed (March 2019).** In any case, it will hardly differ from what was presented in questions 5 and 6.

Donald Trump bases his policy on the following: 1) North-American neo-isolation: withdraw military forces in the region (Syria-Iraq), because it creates enormous expenses for the tax-payers. 2) strong support to its allies and rhetorical despise for its opponents. In this sense, the Palestinians are part of the axis of evil and the Israelis are their strategic allies. Saudi Arabia also enjoys this after Obama. 3) "Anti-Obama": Donald Trump tries his best to prove that he will promote a different and opposite policy from that of his predecessor.

In order to reinforce Israel, to satisfy the Evangelical and Jewish vote, and to differ from Obama's slightly pro-Palestinian policy, Trump has decided to punish the Palestinian Authority by undercutting the resources donated directly to UNWRA, to Palestinian medical centers, to bilateral encounter projects and closing down the PLO representation in Washington.

In favor of Israel, Trump named a pro-Netanyahu ambassador, David Friedman, and announced in September 2017 that the US would open its first permanent military base in Israel. A short while later, on Dec/6/2017, President Trump acknowledged Jerusalem as the capital of Israel, opened the Embassy of the US in western Jerusalem (while keeping offices in Tel-Aviv) on May/14/2018, on the 70th anniversary of the Independence of Israel.

The reelection of Trump as president of the United States would be terrible news for the decadent Palestinian position in the conflict, especially when the Middle East is disarming after the Arab Spring and because of the need of a moderate Israeli-Sunni alliance against Iran (at the expense of the Palestinian agenda).

253. Why is Jerusalem so important for Jews, Muslims and Christians?

Jerusalem is part of the most basic spirit of the Jewish identity; in its moral-historical book (the Bible) it appears about 850 times. On the other hand, "Next year in Jerusalem" has been the prayer repeated for centuries, to show the Jewish attachment to the city. The Temple was located in Jerusalem; its Western Wall (the Wailing Wall) was part of the external fort built by Herod, which was not destroyed by the Romans in the year 70. Jerusalem has been the Jewish capital city three times, and it was never a Muslim capital, nor does it appear in the Quran.

For Christians, Jesus (a Jew from Judea) suffered the last week of his earthly life there (Holy Week). For 100 years, Jerusalem was the capital of a Crusade kingdom.

The sanctity of Jerusalem has been developed in the Hadiths (second source of Islam) since the year 682. A rebel from Mecca, Abdallah Iben-Zubajer, forbade the leaders of the Omeya Caliphate (Damascus) to do their Pilgrimage (*Hajj*). A revolt that lasted 10 years. During that time, the Omeyas searched for a holy city to do their yearly pilgrimage and opted for Jerusalem, which was already holy for Jews and Christians.

To justify the link between Islam and Jerusalem, wise men and poets based their narrations on Sura 17:1, which tells the nocturnal journey of Mohammed to the Distant Mosque (Al-Aqsa). Historically, Al-Aqsa is located in Jirranah, halfway between Mecca and Taif.

In the same period, the Hadiths speak of the ascent of Mohammed to the seven skies, which ends with him leading the prayer and imposing his superiority over Moses, Abraham, Jesus, John the Baptist, Adam, etc.

Today, Jerusalem is a holy site for Sunni Muslims (far less among the Hanbalites) and among the Shiites only after the Islamic Revolution in Iran in 1979.

254. Does the relocation of the US Embassy to Jerusalem improve or diminishes the peace process?

The Old City of Jerusalem (and part of the eastern side) was in the hands of Jordan, between 1948 and 1967. Jordan did not allow the entrance or freedom of worship to the Jews in their sacred sites. The Knesset and the government were in western Jerusalem, considered by Israelis as their capital city.

Acknowledging Jerusalem as the capital city of Israel evidences a pro-Israeli posture of President Trump. However, we must verify where was the Embassy located. If Trump located the building in eastern Jerusalem, it would mean that the city would continue unified under Israeli control. **The Embassy was located on the western side and the North American administration declared that its decision did not mean that the eastern part could not be, via negotiation, the capital city of a Palestinian state.**

On the other hand, some people believe that the decision of moving the Embassy can result in a religious war in the region. As has been explained at the beginning of this book, the religious motivations already existed and have been exploited by the Arab-Palestinians since the killings of 1920 and 1929.

The main question is if the pressure on the Palestinians, who are witnessing the loss of part of their hopes about Jerusalem, approaches peace or moves it away. From an Islamic point of view, the answer is simple: it approaches an agreement. When a Muslim feels that his rival is stronger, he can sign a truce that can allow him to improve his capacities and position. They base this on the *Hudna*, signed by Mohammed in Hudaybyah (year 628). In 1992, when the PLO was lost after its support to Saddam Hussein in 1991, its weakness led to acknowledge Israel and leave the use of terrorism behind. Maybe, thanks to the pressure by Trump and others, the PLO-PA may decide to end the conflict and acknowledge Israel as the national cradle of the Jewish people.

**PART FIVE
- CONCLUDING...**

255. Who are the Sunni and their most radical referents?

Palestinians are Sunni Muslims and belong to the Hanafi School (less radical than their peers Hanbalite-Malekite). As with other Muslims of the world, among the Palestinians there are radical, less radical and moderate Sunni.

Among the Islamic fundamentalists, there is Al-Qaeda and ISIS, which differ in their policies to impose *Shaarya* to Muslims. There is also Boko Haram, acting in mid-west Africa.

Among the Palestinians, Hamas wants to impose a caliphate governed by the *Shaarya*, inspired by the Muslim Brotherhood, destroying Israel, while the Islamic Jihad is inspired and receives support from Iran.

They are all Sunni (Palestinians) and combat the *Yahilyah*. Some see Israel as their main objective to be destroyed and others consider that by cutting the head of the viper (the west, USA, Europe), the rest (Israel) will die by itself.

The Sunni are the majority of Islam, 85% of nearly 1.6 billion people. The main Sunni powers are Saudi Arabia, Egypt, Turkey and Qatar. They believe in the teachings of the Quran and in the traditions and laws that derive from the life of Mohammed, the Hadiths. The Sunni Hadiths are adamant about confirming that the authority of Islam comes from the tribe of the Quraysh. After the death of Mohammed (632), four caliphs succeeded him (called the Rashidun), belonging to the tribe of the Quraysh: Abu Baker (632-634), Omar (who conquered an empire 634-644), Othman (who had the Quran written 644-656) and Ali Ben-Talib (cousin of Mohammed 656-661). The Sunni believe in the legitimacy of all four.

The Sunni Muslims fulfill the five premises of Islam: the *Shahada*, or declaration of faith, the prayer five times a day, the pilgrimage to Mecca once in a lifetime, the *Sadaqah* or charity acts, and the fasting during the sacred month of Ramadan.

256. What is Qatar and to what extent is their radicalism influencing the world?

It is one of the smallest, richest, and most Jihadist states in the world. They have acquired their fame by advertising themselves in the Barcelona and Boca's soccer team shirts and for "achieving" the organization of the 2022 World Cup. **In the Palestinian-Israeli conflict, it provides financial support to Hamas with cash contributions and hosting its leaders in Doha.**

The Al-Thani clan governs Qatar stably. They are a Bedouin family settled in Doha, called Banu Tamim. After being allies to Great Britain, the Al Thanis were granted their independence in 1971.

Their vast wealth (oil and gas) creates a 500,000 dollar *per capita* income, five times more than the second richest country, Luxembourg. As in Saudi Arabia, the Wahabi extremist ideology dominates Qatar. They support Jihadist groups in Iraq (Al-Qaeda), Syria (Ahrar al-Sham, Jabat Al-Nusra), Gaza (Hamas) and Lybia (Benghazi Brigades). Islamist Luminaries, such as the spiritual leader of the Muslim Brotherhood, Yusuf Al-Qaradawi, and the head of Hamas, Khaled Mashaal, have established their residences in Doha for decades.

The enormous Qatari television network, Al Jazeera, has become one of the best-known in the world. Its English language stations produce clever propaganda against the enemies of Qatar, disguised in western liberal rhetoric. The latest adventure of Al Jazeera, its social networks, AJ+, is directed to progressive youth and it is also in Spanish.

Doha also influences western educational institutions. Qatar Foundation, controlled by the regime, provides millions of dollars in grants to schools and other educational institutions of the world. Qatar is the largest foreign donor to US universities (2019).

Many Sunni governments have threatened to attack Qatar, who feels safe after financing the construction of the US Base in El-Udeid, for 2 billion dollars (the only US base not paid for by the US).

257. Why has Israel approached the non-radical Sunni Muslim countries?

In the Middle East, there are several conflicts explained in order of importance. The first one is the radical Muslims and those who are not. This conflict has led to the death of at least 20 million human beings. Although Saudi Arabia is a pioneer instigator of the *Wahabi* radicalism, it tends to maintain its Islamism within its kingdom. Among the non-radicals, there is Egypt, Jordan and the Emirates. The radicals include Iran, Qatar and increasingly, Turkey.

The second conflict, almost as important as the first, confronts Shiites against Sunni. The Shiites (15%) have always felt threatened by the Sunni majority (85%), and after the Islamic Revolution in Iran (1979) and their military victory against Iraq (1989-1988), they have promoted their policy of Shiite revolutionary expansion as a way to survive. During the last decade, Iran has become a regional military power (although weaker that Israel), threatening the Sunni regimes. It has achieved an indirect dominance over Iraq after the fall of ISIS, it has strengthened its domination over Lebanon via Hezbollah and has rescued its Alawite ally, Bashar El-Assad, placing a new base in Syria. **The Iranian euphoria, encouraged by the nuclear agreement they signed with the west, awakened deep concerns among the Sunni (except Qatar and Turkey)**.

The third conflict is the one between Palestinians and Israelis. This confrontation was used by many to hide the deep tribal-religious conflicts of the region. Israel and the Jews served as a way to escape and to distract the attention.

There are other minor conflicts such as the one between Muslims and Christians (who are disappearing from the Middle East), or among Arabs and non-Arabs (Turkey-Iran versus the rest).

In a reality such as the one here explained... Israel has approached, for common interests, to the non-radical Sunni.

258. Who are the Shiites and how do they express their radicalism?

After the death of Mohammed (632), the followers of his son in law and cousin, Ali Ben Abu-Taleb, demanded that he be named the first Caliph. For them, the succession had to be by blood lineage. They were called in Arabic *Shiat Ali*, deriving in *Shiite*.

Among the Shiites, there is a unique or centralized leadership function in the person of the IMAM. The Imam is infallible and must be a direct descendant of Mohammed (Hussein, the third Imam, was the son of Ali and Fatima, the daughter of Mohammed). However, because the Imam is concealed, the members of the community are free to govern themselves on earth.

Within the Shiite Islam, 12 wise men are elected, called in Arabic *Ulemas* and in Persian *Ayatollahs*. At present, the supreme leader of the Shiite, Ali Khamenei, governs Iran and is the successor of Ayatollah Khomeini.

Large concentrations of Shiites can be found in the south of Iraq, sponsored by Iran. After the fall of dictator Saddam Hussein (who was Sunni), they have governed Iraq scaring away the Sunni minority. Those who left decided to rebel and joined tribal Islamists creating ISIS.

In the south of Lebanon, there are many Shiites, representing at least 30% of the population, although they have their own army which is financed, armed and trained by Iran: Hezbollah.

The Shiite country, Iran, with 95% of the Shiite population, instigates risings against the Sunni in several countries, such as their support to the Huti Shiites in Yemen, or instigating the Shiites in Bahrein.

The Shiite theology included five religious principles, three of them similar to the Sunni. The fundamental difference is the *Imamah*, meaning leadership and guidance, in religious and mundane affairs, following the Prophet of Islam.

259. What is the influence of the Shiites on Latin America?

The Iranian penetration in the Spanish and Portuguese-speaking continent is manifested in five different forms.

In the first place, in order to expand the revolution and to recruit new followers, Iran maintains a propaganda and assistance network (*Dawa*). Iran-Hezbollah has been operating in Latin America since the 80s. They have taken over mosques, schools and cultural institutions. In 2012 there were 32 Iranian cultural centers in Latin America, with the purpose of facilitating the expansion of their Islamic revolution. Today they have over 100.

Second, to expand its influence, Iran has Hispan TV, broadcasting in Spanish for all Latin America, and give themselves away with one of the manifestations of Islamism; anti-Semitism.

Third, Iran has understood that it doesn't need to convince large public opinions to penetrate a country... It is easier to buy a politician that becomes the promoter of its interests. Its "natural" allies can be found among the extreme left. The most notorious case is Spain, with the political party Podemos and Pablo Iglesias. The Iranian Mahmoud Alizadeh is pointed out by Javier Negre of *El Mundo* as the person to hand 2 million Euros to Podemos for installing Hispan TV in Spain with a program conducted by Iglesias: "Fort Apache". From 2013 to 2015, Mahmoud contributed through his company 93,000 Euros to Iglesias for directing a program that is still broadcasted in Hispan TV. In Argentina, for example, Judge Daniel Rafecas said that Iran pays the Kirshnerist and anti-Semite leader Luis D'Elia, highlighting that "at the doors of the courts of Comodoro Py, where I work, there are people handing out money to others to insult the State of Israel, and side with Palestine"

Fourth, the alliance Iran-Hezbollah feels comfortable joining irredentist ethnic nationalists movements such as the Ethnocacerism in Peru, or Araucania in Chile.

260. Is there a relation between Hezbollah in Latin America and drug traffic?

The fifth penetration tactic is through drug trafficking and diverse criminal actions. No Latin American country has cataloged Hezbollah as a "terrorist organization", so they can operate with relative impunity. Furthermore, as Venezuela has become a spring-board for the documented arrival of hundreds of Shiites, their movement throughout the continent has become quite easy.

In April of 2017, an officer of Hezbollah, Mohammed Hamdar, was absolved in Peru on accusations of terrorism The court considered that his role in Hezbollah was not considered as terrorism. **This legal void on Hezbollah can also explain why the links between Islamic terrorism, drug traffic and organized crime throughout the region are underestimated.**

"In some countries of the region, such as Venezuela, the advances of Iran and Hezbollah have been promoted by the political elites. The Venezuelan vice-president, Tarek El-Aissami, a descendant of Syrians and Lebanese, with links to Hezbollah and to cocaine traffic, supervised the illegal sale and distribution of at least 10,000 passports and other Venezuelan documents to individuals arriving from Syria, Iraq and other countries of the Middle East. Among them, there are terrorists from Hezbollah and members of the Iranian Islamic Revolutionary Guard Corps. Over a decade ago, a report of the US Congress warned that "Venezuela is providing support – including supplying documents – to radical Islamist groups" affirmed Judith Bergman (Gatestone).

In 2008, the US started the secret plan, "Cassandra", to stop the activities of Hezbollah in Latin America. According to a report by *Politico*, the Obama administration obstructed the action, in order to maintain the good climate after the nuclear agreement with Iran.

Iran has found in Latin America (thanks to countries like Venezuela and Bolivia) a way around the sanctions imposed against them.

261. Why are there few doubts about the responsibility of Iran for the attack on AMIA?

When the authors of the terrorist attacks are questioned (or the murder of Prosecutor Alberto Nisman), it is not so important who pulled the trigger or activated the bomb. The volunteer/hitman is less important than who sent him. The more effective questions would be: Who is interested in committing the attack?, and Who has the capacity to do it?

Iran had already attacked in Argentina with a car bomb in 1992, murdering 22 people, and Hezbollah declared it was their revenge for the selective murder of their leader Abbas Missawi a month before. **The *modus operandi* of the car bomb was classic Hezbollah. If they attacked in 1992, it is believable that**

they kept in Argentina their capacity to attack again in AMIA, especially as they see the case remains unpunished.

According to Argentinean intelligence, the attacker was a 25-year-old suicide Lebanese, Ibrahim Hussein Brou, who exploded a 400 kg device in a car bomb, in front of AMIA. He had arrived in the country a week before the attack through the triple border, with local Hezbollah agents. **This could have been revenge for the cancellation by Argentina of the nuclear technology and nuclear materials contracts, signed two years before with Iran.** There is still no DNA evidence proving that this was the person who carried out the suicide attack.

The Iranian representatives registered signals of changes in their routine. At the moment of the attack, the Iranian ambassadors of Argentina, Chile and Uruguay were away from their posts. In the days before the attack, many phone calls were registered between Iranians and Hezbollah in Argentina, Lebanon and Iran. After the attack, the second in command of operations of Hezbollah, Talal Hamia, was recorded celebrating with his leader, Imad Mughniyeh, for the success of "our project in Argentina".

262. What were Israel's complaints about the 6+1 agreement with Iran?

If a state wishes to develop nuclear weapons it must have two things: intentions and capacity. Intentions translate into an investment of great amounts of funds and capacity into having the people (hired or local) to carry out such a mission.

From a practical viewpoint, it must have three capacities: 1) the capacity to produce fissile material (enriched uranium or plutonium); 2) having exact missiles with the capacity to carry nuclear warheads; 3) knowing how to build nuclear warheads.

On one side, Iran assured that its nuclear program was peaceful (without war intentions) but on Apr/29/2018, Netanyahu presented documents stolen by the Mossad proving a secret military program called "Project Amad".

In relation to the capacity to enrich uranium, the 2015 agreement with Iran (the Vienna Agreement) required Iran to dismantle temporarily over two-thirds of its 19,000 centrifuges to enrich uranium. During fifteen years, it was only authorized to use 6,104 and it could enrich less than 3.67% (a bomb requires 15 kg of 100% uranium U235). **However, this didn't prevent that during these years they will research how to enrich uranium more rapidly and with fewer centrifuges.**

The signing of the Vienna Agreement Jul/14/2015 (*Source: Wikipedia*)

The agreement with Iran did not prevent either the development of more exact missiles with greater accuracy and scope. In this sense, Iran could concentrate more energy on improving this essential capacity.

Taking into account that Iran trains, pays for and executes terrorist actions throughout the world, the agreement also did not control its world-wide activities, freeing millions of dollars instead in exchange for a limited time pact, that could be reinvested in more terrorism.

Donald Trump (and the leaders of the intelligence agencies of Europe) applauded the information revealed by the Mossad, and it was one of the reasons for the withdrawal of the US from the 2015 agreement, reinstating sanctions. This action was not copied by the European Union.

263. How did the civil war in Syria favor the penetration of Iran? Can we assume that there will be confrontations there?

The Alawite region (of the Syrian president, Bashar El-Assad) has been recognized as part of the Shiite although the Sunni consider them as non-Muslims. When the uprising against Assad began, he was rescued by the Shiite government of Iran and its Lebanese satellite, Hezbollah.

While Russia was shooting against ISIS from the air (the US in IRAQ), someone had to conduct the operations on land. Besides the Lebanese of Hezbollah, Iran organized groups of Afghan Shiite soldiers with hundreds of members of the Pasdaran or the Revolutionary Guard. The Shiite dream was to create a Shiite half-moon, from Teheran, passing through a Shiite Iraq, following to Syria, now in their hands, and Russia, for existential needs, ending in Lebanon, already an Iranian satellite with Hezbollah (2019)

With Bashar El-Assad remaining in power, Iran continues its intentions to build precision missile factories in Syrian territory to provide to Hezbollah, to open another front against Israel on the Syrian side of Golan Heights and to use the national platforms of Assad to deliver weapons to its ally.

In order to frustrate Iran's plans, Israel has executed dozens of attacks against Iranian capacity in Syria, coordinating with Russia and trying to avoid the death of Russian soldiers (not always with success). Moreover, Israel has modified its ambiguity policy, recognizing that in many cases the authorship for these attacks possibly to provoke an open confrontation with Iran.

Probably, Israel prefers a confrontation now, when Iran is not totally settled in Syria, and while Russia does not act to defend them. If a conflagration occurs, it is probable that Israel will also attack infrastructure in Lebanon, a country that allows the action of those who govern the country *de facto*: Hezbollah.

264. Did the Arab Spring favor the Palestinian national aspirations?

The "Arab Spring" resulted in profound damage to the Palestinian position. In the first place, in a Middle East region with dozens of failed countries unable to confront popular protests and demands for democracy, these regimes had to undergo terrible internal pressures, putting aside the Palestinian agenda. Let's think about the case of Muammar Khadaffi... was his last intention surviving or supporting the Palestinian cause?

The harsh threat of ISIS also hurt the Palestinian cause. Suddenly, Jihadism became a central topic in the world news, and in the concerns of the citizens. Although in Europe Palestinian terrorism resulted in sorrowful impunity, the multiplication of attacks in Paris, London and Barcelona awakened the interest to learn about the country fighting against radical Islam for years: Israel. It was easier for Israel to explain that Hamas and Al-Qaeda or ISIS were after the same objectives, especially when European terrorist were copying the *modus operandi* invented by the Palestinians (cars launched against civilians, or sudden stabbings).

The spring (actually, the Islamic winter), allowed the expansion of the Shiite colonialism, awakening sudden fears among the Sunni. There are not many possibilities that a country like Saudi Arabia would sacrifice Palestinians to sign a separate peace agreement with Israel, unless it needs the Israeli army to maintain the regime, as happened to Jordan in the mid-70s. However, collaboration in topics such as intelligence, for example, has increased the "sympathy" of Sunnis such as Emirates, Egypt or Oman with the Jewish state. This approach reduces the belligerent rhetoric that favors the Palestinian cause.

Obama, in his eight years, was not able to reach a solution in line with the Palestinian desires and was replaced by Donald Trump, who has undermined them severely since taking office.

265. How has Donald Trump punished the Palestinian intransigence?

The Palestinian president, Mahmoud Abbas, has repeated emphatically that he will not support the "Deal of the Century", presented by Donald Trump, assuring that the "conspiration" that began with the Balfour Declaration (1917) is not over yet.

Trump has placed the Palestinian Authorities among his enemies, he recognized Jerusalem as the capital city of Israel and moved the US embassy there.

In September 2018, the US government announced the closing of the office of the PLO in Washington, accusing it of not moving forward in "direct and significant negotiations" with Israel. This is how Trump reacted to the fact that Palestinians had decided to address the International Criminal Court (The Hague), to accuse Israel of alleged violations.

Previously, the US had announced that it would cut all funding to the UN Palestinian Refugee Agency (UNRWA). Moreover, the US requested to drastically decrease the number of people considered as Palestinian refugees, adapting it to universal parameters. The real refugee number could be around 20,000-50,000 people.

At the beginning of 2018, the US delivered only 65 of the 360 million dollars (of a total of 1.1 billion). This was the last grant by Trump. Previously, the State Department announced another cut to the aid to Palestinians, by canceling a 200 million dollar donation destined to finance humanitarian aid programs in Gaza and the West Bank.

Meanwhile, Abbas was filmed yelling (about Trump) "may his house burn!", he rejected the North American mediator and requested different mediators other than the US alone, (they preferred the Quartet established in Madrid 20002: UN, US, EU and Russia). Without a doubt, the Palestinians are reading Trump wrongly.

266. Who are the so-called "new Israeli historians"?

The new historians (a term introduced by Benny Morris, one of them) came about to rethink if the national myths were true or if they were just as they had been told by the officialism. For example, studies by Morris showed that Arab-Palestinians were expelled from some places in 1948.

In 1994, historian Benny Morris told a newspaper: "they lied to us, they hid the truth, they swept data under the rug (...). They knew that there had been massive deportations, massacres and violations, but they suppressed what they knew and divulged lies".

All nations have fundamental myths. The Palestinian foundational myth is by far more imaginative. A few years ago in times of Arafat, the Palestinian Embassy in Buenos Aires, published in its website the "history" of Palestine and the conflicts, with statements such as that the Palestinians are descendants of the Philistines and the Jebusites (coincidentally, the founders of Jerusalem) or that the Ashkenazi Jews descend totally from the Khazars and that they have no link to Palestine. They have also affirmed that Jesus was Palestinian, that there was never a Temple in Jerusalem, or that all was harmony in the Middle East until the arrival of Zionism...

If the Israeli historiography of the first stage omitted the flight of the Palestinians, as if the Israelis were anxious to retain them, this new wave – sometimes – does the opposite. This way, it is not possible to group together Benny Morris with others like Ilan Pappe and Shlomo Sand.

In this specific case, the mainstream Israeli historians deny the existence of a massive expulsion, as there is no documental evidence of a preconceived plan; there are no important testimonials or programs of the Mapai Party or speeches by Ben-Gurion on this issue.

267. Why are there people who cite Ilan Pappe or Shlomo Sand?

Anti-Zionism extracts arguments written by these new historians and raises them as trophies, "because this is said by the Jews-Israelis themselves". Among the cited pro-Palestinian anti-Semitic historians, Ilan Pappe and Shlomo Sand stand out.

The prestigious historian, Ephraim Karsh, accuses Pappe of misrepresentation, distortion and falsehood. "He tells readers about events that never happened, such as the inexistent 'massacre' of Tantura (May 1948) or the expulsion of the Arabs in the twelve days after the Partition resolution. He claims to know about political decisions that were never taken, such as the Anglo-French plan of 1912 for the occupation of Palestine or the preparation of a 'master plan to free the future Jewish state of as many Palestinians as possible'".

Historian Benny Morris analyzed in *The New Republic* the book by Pappe, *History of Modern Palestine: One Territory, Two People*. "Unfortunately, much of what Pappe tries to sell his readers is a hoax (...). This book is flooded with mistakes, never seen in serious historiography. (...) For those in love with subjectivity and dependent on historical relativism, a fact is not a fact and precision is unattainable".

Shlomo Sand usually argues that the Romans did not expel the Jews and that there was never a Jewish people, that it was made up. He even stated that there is no relation between the ancient Jews and the current ones (they descend from the Khazars!), even though genetic testing proves the opposite. Prestigious historian Anita Shapira criticizes Sand harshly, for "taking a theory that is, at the least, not very orthodox" in a study area, to later stretch it out "to the external limits of logic and beyond, and Sand does it throughout the 3,000 of history he tells".

268. What is BDS?

BDS are the initials for Boycott, Divestment and Sanctions, and it refers to three different punitive measures against Israel. Boycott means the rupture of relations with Israel as a means of protest, punishment, intimidation or coercion; cultural, commercial, sports and academic boycott. Divestment is the withdrawal of investments in Israel by banks, pension funds and others. Sanctions are punitive actions adopted by governments and international organizations including commercial sanctions or prohibitions, the embargo of weapons and ending diplomatic relations.

The three declared and official objectives of the BDS campaign (founded by the Palestinians in 2005) are:

1) Ending Israel's occupation and colonization of all Arab lands and dismantling the Fence; sometimes the leaders of BDS state that their goal is to achieve the total retreat of Israel towards the Green Line, but many others clearly state that the goal is all of Palestine, in other words, the disappearance of Israel. What does it depend on? The public. If they clearly state their goal they will scare people with morals.

2) Recognizing the fundamental rights of the Arab-Palestinians of Israel to full equality - that means a bi-national state. They argue that there is no equality for them in Israel, even though there is. "Inequality" means that there is a law of return for Jews and that the flag and the national anthem mention Israel as the national cradle for the Jews (who are 80% of the population).

3) That Israel grants Israeli citizenship to 5 million Palestinians. They demand a national suicide.

Two of the three demands have nothing to do with the consequences of the

Six-Day War of 1967; they are related to the independence of Israel of 1948. In fact, the three conditions can be understood as "promoting the dissolution of the State of Israel as a democratic Jewish state".

269. How was BDS born?

Although it may sound contradictory (it is), modern BDS is the result of the UN World Conference against Racism, Durban 2001. The "pro-human rights NGOs", with help from Arab states and Iran, ensured including a final declaration that stated: "[We call upon] all the international community to impose a full isolation policy over Israel as an Apartheid state, similar to the South African case, meaning sanctions and total embargos, the cease of all links between all states and Israel".

One of the public figures of BDS, Omar Barghouti, is the author of *The Declaration of a State* (November 2007), as a result of several conferences he held in London and Madrid. He stated in *Nueva Republica* that even if Israel would cease its control over the West Bank, his calls to boycott would continue: "Most of the Palestinians do not suffer because of the occupation, they suffer from their impossibility to return to their homes". In other words, he wants Israel to absorb what he calls refugees (5 million) in order to destroy the current structure of Israel as a Jewish democratic state.

At present, BDS is supported by a varied alliance. A small and loud group of anti-Zionist Jews (having Jews brings "legitimacy"), radical Muslims and some churches are part of this alliance. In the west, some elements of the extreme left are their notable partners. In general, they sustain post-colonialist/ post-imperialist theories (inspired by intellectuals such as Edward Said and Noam Chomsky), in which Israel is perceived as the imperialist enclave of the Middle East. Since the collapse of the Soviet Union, extreme-left groups have proposed the political Islam (Islamism) as the only organized force able to resist North American hegemony and its perception of "empire".

270. Why has BDS been forbidden in so many democratic states?

Several countries have forbidden BDS because they oppose anti-Semitism and believe it should be fought legally.

BDS is being used as a platform to destroy Israel as a nation-state of the Jewish people. Michael Gove, leader of the Conservative Party of Great Britain, tagged the European calls to BDS as a "resurgent, mutant and lethal virus of anti-Semites," that reminds the Nazi boycott against the Jews in the eve of the Holocaust. Why does Gove say that BDS is camouflaged anti-Semitism? Because as clearly stated by its organizers and ideologists, there is ONLY ONE country in the world that deserves to be boycotted, and that country is the national cradle of the Jewish people: Israel. The Pro-BDS believe that there is only one people in the world that cannot express itself nationally (Zionism), the Jewish people. This is discrimination against Jews: anti-Semitism.

These same people do not make an effort to verify if their Apartheid accusations against Israel are real but use them in their demonizing rhetoric.

In several states of the US and in Europe, there have been laws enacted against BDS. In April 2015, Tennessee approved a resolution condemning BDS as well as the governor of New York, Andrew Cuomo, who signed an administrative order to boycott any business that boycotts Israel. In February 2016, the House of Representatives of Canada approved a measure officially condemning the BDS campaign. In March 2017, the Swiss Parliament approved a resolution prohibiting the state from "financing any organism that supports racism, anti-Semitism and BDS" In December 2017, the Municipality of Munich approved a law against BDS, forbidding the boycott to Israel and prohibiting financing the campaign.

271. Who promotes BDS in Spanish-speaking countries and what have been the judicial issues?

There are two main focuses of propagation of the anti-Semitic BDS: the leaders of Podemos in Spain and the radical Palestinian community of Chile (see question 285).

There has been a lot of evidence of financing by the Venezuelan dictatorships and Iran to the extreme-left party Podemos. Not to be forgotten, the disproportionate funds received by Pablo Iglesias for his TV program "Fort Apache" on Hispan TV. The Judeophobe thinking of Podemos is not only sustained on their wish to return what they received from their sponsors, but it is also about pure conviction "We need to act more firmly against an illegal state such as Israel", stated Iglesias during an interview on RTVE (June/12/2018).

As Podemos takes control of the main Spanish cities, such as Madrid, Barcelona, Zaragoza and Cadiz, it has had access to multiple resources: financial, human and organizational. The local administrators (provinces, municipalities) basically joined the BDS movement and declared their territories "free of Israeli Apartheid" (imitating the Nazi *Judenfrei*). They distributed stickers

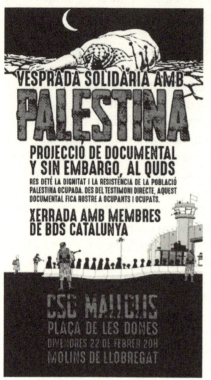

to exhibit in stores and offices, and ordered public companies to avoid working with Israeli individuals or companies, and asked the Spanish citizens that are suspected of associating or sympathizing with the Jewish state to repudiate it publicly so they would not be excluded from social networks.

In Spain, the declarations by BDS have been repudiated by the judiciary, over and over again, due to the legal actions by the organization ACOM.

Anti-Semitism by BDS was clearly exposed when they demanded and achieved the cancellation of Jewish-North American singer Matisyahu in the summer of 2015 in Valencia. Although he was invited again because of pressure, the nature of BDS provoked, among other things, that the people responsible for the cancellation are now facing personal trials. The tendency is that anti-Semitic people become economically sanctioned for spreading hate.

272. What is the relation between the BDS members and terrorist groups?

The BDS campaign is directed by a network of NGOs, some of them linked to terrorist organizations such as Hamas and the Popular Front for the Liberation of Palestine. These terrorist groups understand that armed struggle is not so popular in the west, and concentrate their efforts in apparently innocent civilian actions. Besides, the terrorist organizations use these NGOs to raise the funds they cannot obtain in another way.

A detailed investigation by the Ministry of Strategic Affairs and Information of Israel was able to identify 42 NGOs of a total of 300 organizations in the world that promote delegitimation and boycott the State of Israel. These links can be seen in several levels: joint campaigns, shares operations and financial and logistic aid, among others.

This method that hides the linkages between the NGOs and terrorist organizations has allowed western authorities, mainly in Europe, to consider past and present terrorist operators and these boycott actions as legitimate forms of civilian manifestations.

Here is a concrete example. Mohammed Sawalha (alias Abu Abada) was a member of the political branch of Hamas between 2013 and 2017, and a senior military agent of Hamas in Samaria at the end of the 80s. While being investigated by Israeli agents, he flew to Jordan with false documents and then to Great Britain, where he currently lives. Sawalha founded the Muslim Association of Britain (MAB) and later the British Muslim Initiative (BMI). He had a central role in planning the Mavi Marmara Flotilla in 2010.

An example of a pro-terrorist NGO is the British Friends of Al-Aqsa (FOA). The main headquarters are in Leicester, with branches in London, Bradford and Glasgow. The founder of this NGO was in the Mavi Marmara, at the same time he was leading land-based campaigns to move funds to Hamas in the Gaza Strip.

273. What are the six modern techniques to demonize Israel and promote its destruction?

It is impossible to affirm that all of those who wish for the destruction of Israel or the disappearance of the Jewish people follow the same pattern. These are varied organizations and people that opt for different destructive tactics.

The first technique has been physical force, the prime option of the Arab/Muslim states up to the War of 1973. Since then, countries that do not dare a direct confrontation (for example, Iran), train, finance and arm terrorist proxies.

The second approach is the diplomatic strategy. After the failure of the Arab oil boycott post-1973, an alliance was formed between Islamic-Fascist dictatorships, the communist block and "third-world" countries, who use international organizations to transform Israel into a "systematic violator of the international law".

Third, the journalists: the exploitation of the structure of media chronicles and the lack of depth of professionals to promote victimization.

Fourth, the BDS tactic: its goal is to "starve" the State of Israel by isolating its capacity to produce and sell merchandise throughout the world. They also promote cultural isolation.

Fifth, the dialectic "reasoning", used successfully by the Nazis. Before annihilating six million Jews, they were able to impose the conviction that the Jews were a sub-race, a virus, which had to be destroyed to save humanity.

Zionism equals everything bad, known and unknown. Israel is Nazi, practices Apartheid and it is Zionist... the important thing is to create the legitimacy to destroy Israel.

The last one is "clepto-history": steal from Jewish history, because if they do not have it, they do not exist: affirming that the Temple of Jerusalem did not exist and that the Palestinians are descendants of the Natufians (a pre-Canaanite culture of 12,000 years ago), or that Jesus was "Palestinian". Several university academics stand out in this category.

274. Can the treatment of Israelis to Palestinians be compared to the treatment of Nazis to Jews?

This is an immoral comparison that banalizes the Holocaust and it is also a resource for those who want to weaken Israel dialectically, because if Israel acts like the Nazis... can negotiations be held with Nazis? No, Nazis must be destroyed because they represent absolute evil! The accusation is frequently used by anti-Semites by projecting "seeing in their victims what they are", or they do it to feel that what they have done or supported in the past is now done by the Jews, so they can live better with their dark past.

Here are seven fundamental differences to actually see the ridiculous comparison. First, the nature of the conflict. The Nazis wanted the total extermination of the Jews, while the Israelis state over and over again that they are at war only with Palestinian terrorism.

Second, the conception of the enemy. For the Nazis, Jews were a sub-human race that had to be destroyed. For Israelis, Palestinians are a people with whom they have a territorial and ideological dispute. There are no radical conceptions as in the Apartheid.

Third, the nature of the camps. The Nazi concentration camps were built to harm the victims. The Palestinian camps are refugee camps, they were not built nor are they managed by Jews or Israelis; they were built by Arab regimes aided by UNWRA.

Fourth, the forms of combat. The Nazis developed well-oiled machinery to exterminate civilians. The Palestinian civilians are not the target of Israel, and Israel has developed techniques to reduce the death of non-combatants used as human shields.

Fifth, the capacity to negotiate. When the Nazis decided to execute the Final solution, there was no possibility of negotiation. Israel has always offered to negotiate solutions.

Sixth, the Nazis received support from actions or omissions of practically all the German population. In Israel, there are constant debates when innocent Palestinian civilians die.

Finally, the numbers. The Nazis exterminated 6 million Jews in a planned and premeditated way. There is no possible moral comparison.

275. Can it be said that Israel conducts an Apartheid policy?

As has been previously expressed, the comparison between Israel and the Apartheid imposed in South Africa is an insult to those who actually suffered that regime, and it is a technique to delegitimize the existence of Israel.

South Africans feel offended by such a comparison. This can be read in *Do Not Rob Us of the Word Apartheid*, by Nkululeko Nkosi, or expressed by Kenneth Meshoe (South African congressman): "Comparing Israel to South Africa is to insult our suffering with lies". In a television interview, ex-President Frederik de Klerk (South Africa) strongly affirmed: "Israel is nor an Apartheid state". However, journalists like Pedro Brieger affirm on the radio: "Israel enjoys the impunity of being the eternal victims of the Holocaust to carry out an Apartheid regime with Palestinians" (2013).

The Israeli Arab-Palestinians (20% of the population) do not suffer Apartheid and they are citizens with full rights but without the same obligations (they are exempt from the three-year military service). They have representation in the Knesset, they are judges. A Palestinian judge of the Supreme Court of Justice (Salim Giubran) even sentenced an Israeli president to prison. **Is there discrimination in Israel? Of course there is, just like in almost all societies of the world**.

Palestinians that live in Territories A and B are living under the Palestinian Authority or under Hamas in Gaza (95% of the Palestinians). **In that case, if the Palestinians of Gaza and A and B are not Israeli citizens, saying that Israel does "Apartheid" is like accusing Argentina of imposing "Apartheid" on Scotland.**

Is the strong affirmation of Apartheid based on Palestinians living in Area C (non-citizens), or that enter Israel to work, or that circulate in the roads of Territories B or C? It doesn't seem too serious.

276. I don't hate Israel or the Jews. Why is the Israel-Apartheid comparison misbegotten?

Status of the territories. During the South African Apartheid, "all the territory was sovereign South African territory". All of South Africa and Namibia were governed under a discriminating policy towards colored people. In the case of Israel with the territories of the West Bank, these territories do not belong to Israel, and there is hardly any Israeli presence there.

Civil rights. During the South African Apartheid, the citizenship of colored people was annulled. These people did not have the right to vote, "mixed marriages" were forbidden, there was no freedom of movement and there was physical segregation. The Palestinians of the West Bank were never Israeli citizens nor do they wish to be.

Public Services. During the South African Apartheid, the discriminating regime reduced its civil responsibility. In the Israeli case, 95% of the Palestinians live under the Palestinian Authority. Public services must be claimed to their government.

Focusing on the freedom of movement. During the South African Apartheid, the discriminating regime established segregated Bantustans. They imposed restrictions for the black, they could not live in "white" areas, except with a work permit. In the case of Israel, the restriction to enter Israel, including the Security Fence, is linked to security reasons, not racial.

The important ideological aspect. During the Apartheid regime in South Africa, the black people were considered a primitive race, inferior to the whites, and the whites had to dominate and "civilize" them. In the Israeli case, Zionism does not believe in the domination of other peoples, nor does its vision consider Palestinians as "inferior".

Why such a far-fetched comparison? Think... what to do with an Apartheid regime? It must be isolated, sanctioned and boycotted. That's the objective.

277. Is Israel the only democracy of the Middle East?

The quality of democracies is measured with academic variables and statistics. For example, the democracy index developed by the Intelligence Unit of *The Economist* determines a ranking for 167 states. This scientific study is based on 60 indicators, grouped in five different categories: Is there an electoral process and pluralism? Are there civil liberties? Does the government work effectively? Is there political participation and political culture? Is there freedom in the media?

According to *The Economist* (2017), Israel ranks 31st in the list of the best democracies of the world. It is at the same level as Portugal, Chile, Italy or Poland... all imperfect democracies. Israel scores a noticeable 7.79 while a perfect democracy such as France scores 7.80. All states that live under a dire threat - and Israel is at war since its foundation in 1948 - tend to reduce individual liberties in order to protect its citizens. The war situation has a negative influence on the results of Israel.

Does the fact that 20% of the population is Arab, make Israel less democratic? It is irrelevant. All national states can have different percentages of citizens that are not part of its ethnicity or culture and will be, objectively, in a relatively disadvantageous situation, because the official language, the dominant religion, the festivities of the official calendar, will relate naturally to the main national group.

As a reference, never in the history of mankind has there been a war between two democracies. Wars have always occurred between a democracy and a non-democracy, or between two non-democracies. In the case of the Palestinian-Israeli conflict, it is a war between a demonstrable and calculable democracy (Israel) and two non-democracies (Hamas and AP - 110th The Economist Democracy Index).

278. What type of modern polyarchy is Israel?

Israel is a parliamentary democracy that differs from a presidential system common in America. The executive power is not elected directly, but citizens vote for the main political power, the Knesset (the parliament), and from within this body comes the executive power.

There are four powers in Israel: President, Parliament (legislative), Executive (government) and Judicial

In an election, Israeli voters elect one of the political parties (in 2019 there were 47 options) and the votes are distributed proportionally among all the political parties that have received at least 3.25% of the votes. The Parliament has 120 seats.

After the results are known, the President of the State, a protocolar figure that represents the virtues of the people, convenes all the elected forces and consults about who they recommend to compose the government of Israel. The President then turns the power over to the candidate with better possibilities to present a government after 28 days (with the possibility of 14 additional days). The candidates must negotiate with close and allied political parties (never has a political party obtained the absolute majority, 61 representatives). If the candidate is able to achieve a majority, he or she addresses the Knesset requesting a "vote of confidence" to form the government.

The government must be formed by at least half of the ministers that must also be elected parliamentarians. The Prime Minister must be a parliamentarian. The Israeli government has a four-year period, unless the representatives approve a "vote of no-confidence" (61 representatives) to end the government, but this also leads to their own self-dissolution.

The Judicial Power of Israel, separate from the others, is elected by a special commission of parliamentarians, judges, the Minister of Justice and the Lawyers' Guild of Israel.

279. What does being right- or left-wing mean in Israel?

Since the creation of the State of Israel, there were two parties with different political right- and left-wing tendencies. For example, two tendencies originated from the governing socialist party, Mapai: that of David Ben-Gurion, who was an activist (this group included Moshe Dayan, Shimon Peres and Ygal Alon), while the moderate wing was represented by Moshe Sharett.

After the Six-Day War of 1967, the "Foreign Policy and Security" axis, the same that divides the Israeli political map between "left" and "right", became the main one when defining the national elections, relegating other sectors. It is not the only factor that defines the Israeli vote, but it stands out above the others.

The terms used in Israeli politics are "Hawks" (right-wing) and "Doves" (left-wing). A Hawk (extreme) is a person who believes that there is no Palestinian party to negotiate a peace agreement, who does not want to give the territorial control over Judea and Samaria, does not want to divide Jerusalem, does not want to give up to the Golan Heights, and does not accept the return of Palestinian refugees to Israel. A Dove (left) thinks the opposite. In Israeli politics, most of the political parties accept one or several premises of Hawks or Doves, and very few people are in the extremes.

For example, most of the left-wing Israelis are in favor of maintaining control over the territorial blocks. They are not in favor of returning all territories. On the other hand, a good part of the Hawks accept giving up territories and they are willing to co-exist with a Palestinian state.

In Israel, left and right are political-security concepts and not socio-economic differences.

280. What other topics are crucial to understand the political map of Israel?

The Spatial Theory explains that if we put all the political offers in an imaginary axis based on a central topic, then voters will elect the party or candidate that best approaches the voters' posture. In Latin America, the dominating axis includes the differences in socio-economic topics, and that is a dominating vector.

In Spain, for example, there are two vectors. It is a bi-polar parliamentary system. A vector divides the parties based on socio-economic topics (for example, PSOE tends towards the left and PP more to the right) although there is another vector: those who believe that Spain must be a unified state and those who wish for more autonomy or independence for the regions.

Israel is an extremely multipolar parliamentary system. The most important vector divides the map between Hawks and Doves (see 279). The second relevant topic is the different socio-economic positions. The Likud, for example, offers less state intervention than the Labor Party (Avoda). The third axis divides the parties according to their religious tendency. On one end there are the Jewish orthodox parties that wish to live according to the *Halaha* (the Jewish law), while other forces, such as Meretz, promote a secular state.

The fourth parameter divides the political parties that want Israel to be a state in which the Jewish people can be "well" represented. On the other side, there are parties (such as Arab-Israeli parties) that want Israel to not be the cradle of the Jewish people (canceling, for example, the Law of Return, that favors Jews or changing the national flag). The last axis divides the political parties that represent Sephardic (coming from Arab countries or Spain) and Ashkenazi (European) Jews.

With these five axes, the possible combinations offer multiple political options.

281. Do the Palestinian Authority and the Gaza Strip live in a democracy?

Using as a reference the continuous studies by *The Economist* (2017), the representation pattern for the countries in the Middle East is a dictatorship or totalitarian regimes. Israel's (position 31) neighbors in the Middle East rank as follows: Turkey 97, Lebanon 102, Palestinian Authority 110, Iraq 114, Jordan 117, Kuwait 121, Egypt 133, Qatar 135, Sudan 151, Iran 154, Saudi Arabia 159 and Syria 166. All these Muslim countries are hybrid (they have elections but not democracies), or are terrible dictatorships.

For a democracy to exist, there are specific needs: 1) democratic culture, 2) post-industrial revolution countries to create a middle class, 3) post-French Revolution countries to elevate the unalienable qualities of the human being. The eminence in Middle East affairs, Bernard Lewis, understood the limitations of imposing a democratic regime in the region when it has not gone through the three factors named above. In its place, he proposes a representative parliament of *Jamula* (clans-tribes).

Palestinians live in a dictatorship in Gaza under Hamas. It must be considered that the concept of democracy is negative for an Islamist, as it represents western *Yahaliya*, foreign to the nature of Islam. What right does a human being have to dictate laws when there is a sole law, the *Shaarya*? There is no other Constitution than the law of Allah!, an Islamist would say.

The situation of the Palestinian Authority is that they have elected their president (2005) and since then, Mahmoud Abbas holds the power illegitimately (his period should have lasted 4 years). The latest serious Parliament election was in 2006, with victory for Hamas. However, the PLO rejected granting them the means to govern the Palestinian Authority in a civilized way, and it all ended in a coup in Gaza (2007). Since then, the Prime Minister (who should be the administrator of the Palestinian Authority) changes quickly and unstably.

282. What is the Basic Law of the Jewish State?

In the previous questions, the importance and function of the Basic Laws of Israel were explained (question 118). The *Basic Law of Israel as the Nation-State of the Jewish People* is one of the 14 basic laws approved in Israel (2019). The novelty is that the only people with the right to declare its independence within Israel (the West Bank is not part of Israel) is the Jewish people. All Israeli citizens have the same civil rights, but the Druse, Arab-Palestinian, Bedouin and Circassian minorities cannot declare their independence within Israel. Article 1 states: "The right to exert national self-determination in the State of Israel is exclusive to the Jewish People".

The government of Israel did this to eliminate the possibility that after signing a peace agreement with the Palestinians, the Arab-Palestinian mi-

nority would come up and propose "Now we, the "other people", demand the right to self-determination in the regions where we are the majority!"

There are national minorities within other states of the world, for example, can Peruvians declare their independence in Argentina? No, only the Argintinean people can do such a thing.

The democratic values and defense of the rights of citizens must be considered an integral and fundamental part of Israel, and are included in the *Basic Law of Freedom of Occupation* (1992 and 1994), and especially The Respect for Human Dignity and Freedom (1992).

The law is innovative in its Article 4: "The language of the State is Hebrew. Arabic has a special status in the State". Up to now, the official languages of Israel were Hebrew, Arabic and English.

The political context of the law is the desire of the Israeli conservative government to reduce universal or transnational conceptions, reaffirming its desire to continue being a state-nation.

283. Is it true that there is an alternative to the principle of "two states for two peoples"?

In the framework of the Palestinian-Israeli conflict, arguments are usually heard that affirm or threaten that there are alternatives to the physical separation between Palestinians and Israelis. On one side, Hebrew political forces assure that if Israel does not disconnect (agreed unilaterally), creating effectively a Palestinian state, Israel will become an Apartheid state or a bi-national state. The bases of the argument are that there will be no other alternative than to grant citizenship to 2.5 million West Bank Palestinians, dismantling the Palestinian Authority, and corroding the Zionist ideal of being the "national cradle of the Jewish people with a Jewish majority". It would be a bi-national state with 7 million Jews and 4.2 million Arab-Palestinians (adding West Bank plus those with Israeli citizenship).

The alternative to bi-nationalism is to forcefully maintain the Zionist dream by imposing an Apartheid regime, where Arab-Palestinian citizens are legally discriminated. While transiting this way, a democratic regime should be imposed by force as well, as this spirit and customs are not abundant in the Palestinian Authority.

For this to happen, an Israeli government would have to decide to "suicide" the Zionist dream, annexing all territories of the West Bank and their citizens. Naftali Bennet (one of the main nationalist leaders), for example, proposes to annex only territory C (60% of the territory and 5% of the Palestinians).

Every now and then, Palestinians threaten to close down the Palestinian Authority and "hand over the keys" to Israel. The truth is that the Palestinian leadership will not detach easily from power and the economic benefits derived from this authority. It is not believable either that Israel will accept to re-impose a military government on the Palestinians like before Oslo.

There are two real alternatives to the current situation (2019): 1) creating two Palestinian states, one in Gaza and one in the West Bank; 2) a Palestinian state in Gaza and another confederation, West Bank with Jordan.

284. How is anti-Semitism expressed in Spain?

Judeophobia is an essentially Christian-Catholic-European phenomenon. There is a difference between government, institutional and social anti-Semitism.

In Spain, democratic governments have developed correct relations with Israel, with more anti-Israeli rhetoric during the governments of PSOE (Zapatero, for example). There is compassion for the Jewish victims of the past, and much less for the present ones (Israelis).

The decision to grant the Spanish nationality to the descendants of the Jews who were expelled from Spain coexists with a cold-hostile attitude towards the Jewish state (Israel), seconded by the "traditional Arab-Spanish friendship".

Years of education under Franco against the "Jewish-Masonic" influence and the Catholic tradition in Spain, has kept Judeophobe remainders even in their language. The terms in Spanish *judiada* and *sinagoga* continue to be used as insults.

According to a survey by the Ministry of Foreign Affairs 2010, 58.4% of the Spanish people believe that "Jews have a lot of power because they control the economy and the media". It must be reminded that Jews are 0.05% of the Spanish population. Specialist Gustavo Perednik qualifies Spanish anti-Semitism as "phantasmal".

The two institutions where anti-Semitism is mostly expressed in Spain are the press and in extreme-left political parties (the extreme-right party Vox defends Israel).

The Spanish media (with some honorable exceptions) demonize Israel, presenting it as an intolerant theocracy financed by an international hidden power (*El Pais* stands out for its outreach and influence). The expected result: the average reader will confirm his prejudice thanks to his media, and if he does not suffers from them, he will understand that there is no other solution that does not imply the destruction of the only Jewish state of the world… "such an imperialist one"

Modern Judeophobia in Europe is usually instigated by Muslim immigrants. In the case of Spain, this influence is felt in Catalonia, but in general, it is felt less than in other countries of the EU.

285. Why is anti-Semitism in Chile a matter of concern?

The Chilean ex-senator of Palestinian origin, Eugenio Tuma, affirmed that Israeli backpackers were mapping Patagonia as part of the Plan Andinia. Such anti-Semitic nonsense would destroy many political careers. Not in Chile. **In Chile, the law that criminalized instigation to hate is still locked up and those who oppose it are precisely the parliamentarians that support instigation.**

Several causes for Chilean anti-Semitism can be pointed out. In the first place, Chile is a European-Catholic country in which the Protestant forces (more conciliatory towards Jews) are increasing, but are still a minority group.

Second, Chile has been a refuge for Nazis since the 1930s decade. Historically, Nazism also had opponents in Chile (telegram from Salvador Allende to Hitler after *Kristallnacht* in 1938, denouncing persecution to Jews).

The third reason is the blatant Judeophobia of the extreme left, which in Chile is an important group.

The main instigator of anti-Semitism and promoter of hate in Chile is the Palestinian Federation of Chile. For example, in 2017 the Federation headed a protest in front of the US Embassy in Santiago against President Trump's declaration about Jerusalem, behind a flag that asked for "death to Zionists", a politically correct euphemism for "Jews".

Palestinians (about 360,000) arrived in Chile after World War I, escaping the Ottoman Muslim recruitment. They are descendants of Catholic Arabs, especially from Bethlehem, a city where Catholics are persecuted and humiliated, representing 8-10% of the population (in 1920 they were almost 70%). Although Palestinian-Catholics of Bethlehem requested Israel to annex them in two opportunities (1976 and 1994), their Chilean brothers seem to have more in common with Islamist Hamas than with the Palestinian Authority. The Chilean Palestinian Federation promotes BDS in municipalities (such as Valdivia, declared illegal) and in universities.

286. How is anti-Semitism expressed in Argentina?

The largest Jewish community of the continent lives in Argentina, about 185,000 people (2019), the seventh country with the largest Jewish population.

Anti-Semitism in Argentina began at the end of the XIX Century, expressed in the anti-Semitic libel "La Bolsa" by Julian Martel, published in *La Nación*; or in 1919 during the "Tragic Week" when 150 Jews were murdered. The Nazi-Argentinean party flourished during the days of Hitler and Argentina hosted Nazi leaders (one of them, Eichmann). Judeophobe diaries such as *Clarinada* incited anti-Semitic hate.

Cover pages of *Clarinada*...
Roberto Noble may have inspired by them for his *Clarín*

With the return to democracy in 1983, anti-Semitism was reduced. The State enacted the Antidiscrimination Law in 1988 (Ley 23592) and created INADI (National Institute against Discrimination, Xenophobia and Racism) in 1995. The other side is that the two most important Judeophobe attacks of the continent (Embassy of Israel 1992 and AMIA 1994) remain unpunished.

A report by the University of Buenos Aires (and DAIA) of 2011 revealed a prejudiced and stigmatizing attitude against the Jewish-Argentinean population. Of the respondents, 45% would not marry a Jew, 39% rejects Jews in political positions, 82% affirms that Jews are only interested in making good business deals and making money, 49% feels that they are more loyal to Israel than to Argentina, 49% believe that they talk too much about the Holocaust and 23% believe they are responsible for the death of Jesus.

In the recent years, the anti-Semitic rhetoric has increased by spokespeople linked to the K government (such as Luis D'Elia), especially after the Jewish-Argentinean rejection of the Memorandum of Understanding with Iran and the murder of Nisman. President Cristina Kirchner had no doubt in expressing anti-Semitic condemnations comparing the "vulture funds" to Shylock from the *Merchant of Venice*.

287. What is Plan Andinia?

Plan Andinia is the South American version of the anti-Semitic *Protocols of the Elders of Zion (1905)*. It is one of the theories about Jewish conspiracy published in 1971 by an economy professor of the University of Buenos Aires, Walter Beveraggi Allende, the same person that later published *The Argentinean Inflation* with a cover page showing Argentina crucified by a Jew using Stars of David instead of nails.

Investigator Ernesto Bohoslavsky believes that Plan Andinia was written previously (1965) within the small Nazi party "Argentinean National Socialist Front", created by the sons of Adolf Eichmann after the kidnapping (1960).

According to this conspiracy theory, the plan was a complot to dismember the Argentinean and Chilean Patagonia to create another Jewish state. The attempts of Baron Hirsch (at the end of the XIX Century) to help Jewish immigration with the support of the Argentinean government are considered the first attempts to seek the creation of a Jewish state following the guidelines of Plan Andinia, although Jews settled in Buenos Aires and not the Patagonia.

Those who sustain this theory affirm that the creation of

Plan Andinia in the Patagonia would be carried out thanks to the "same methods" used for the creation of the State of Israel.

Journalist Jacobo Timerman stated that when he was interrogated by the military dictatorship in the 70s and 80s, they demanded details of Plan Andinia.

An Argentinean police officer by the name of Jose Alberto Perez infiltrated in the Jewish community in the 80s to find out how the plan was to be carried out.

At present, the main divulger of this anti-Semitic theory in Argentina is Adrian Salbuchi of the *Proyecto Segunda República* (Project Second Republic).

In Chile, there are abundant spokespeople of the Palestinian Federation that usually recite the Protocols and Andinia.

288. What does it mean that peace is not possible but a Hudna (Truce) is?

In the year 628, the Prophet Mohammed decided to conquer his birth city of Mecca, expecting to defeat the Quraysh tribe. Mecca was the commercial and religious center of the Arab Peninsula and the Quraysh tribe were important regional merchants. Mohammed, who had been expelled from Mecca in 622, arrived in the city with 1,000 men to attack and found 10,000 enemies. Realizing his inferiority, Mohammed proposed the Quraysh a *Hudna* (truce) of nine years, nine months and nine days (10 years) during which he could not attack the Quraysh merchants in exchange for allowing him to express his ideas in Mecca. **Within Islam, this is known as the *Hudna of Hudaybiah.***

After two years, Mohammed violated the truce and conquered Mecca. In the traditional Islam all Mohammed's actions are perfect, therefore, if the great prophet of Islam signed and violated intentionally the truce with non-Muslims, "it is imitable".

Yasser Arafat, for example, after signing the Oslo Agreement, declared publically in a Muslim protest in Johannesburg (1994) that "no one could criticize him for signing with Israel, as he (Arafat) had only done the same thing Mohammed had". Arafat broke the truce of 2000 with the Intifada of Al-Aqsa. When Anwar El-Sadar signed a peace agreement with Israel he requested the "thumbs up" of the influential University of El-Azhar, which approved the political pact as a *Hudna*, like the one Mohammed had done.

In traditional Islam, peace only exists within Islam (*Sulha*). Truce or *Hudna* can be agreed on, but violated if it favors Islam.

So... why Egypt, Jordan or the Palestinian Authority do not violate the Truce? Because Israel is far stronger than the Quraysh were for Mohammed.

289. What has been the role of Europe in the Palestinian-Israeli conflict?

Post-war Europe is not the same one that created the European Union. While it was being reconstructed and during the Cold War, the role of Europe was minor. After the Six-Day War (1967), the positioning of Israel before the eyes of the new European left deteriorated up to the point of reaching the current manifestations of anti-Semitism. The action of the Palestinian terrorism in European soil during the 70s decade creates a partial understanding of the Israeli dilemmas.

Today Palestinians prefer more participation of Europeans in future peace negotiations while Israelis feel a profound distrust towards the European Union, although bilateral relations, among states, are usually better than with the community representation.

Europe is still trapped in the perception that the Arab-Israeli conflict is the key to achieve stability in the Middle East, allowing the return of refugees. They believe that only if the Palestinians are satisfied, the situation will calm down. Therefore, for Europeans, the politics of Israel sabotages their efforts and undermines "protecting Europe".

For decades, Israel exported mainly to Europe, but at present, the Old Continent receives 35% of the Israeli exports. This situation reduced the possibility of Europe pressuring economically.

A problem to mediate in the conflict is that Europe is known in Israel as a financer of organizations that foster Israelophobia. A report of the NGO Monitor reveals that between 2012 and 2016, a total of 39 Israeli NGOs received 142.6 million dollars from foreign donors, mainly from Europe. These NGOs are politically active in the Arab-Israeli conflict, and several of them are involved in the BDS campaign (Boycott, Divestment, Sanctions) against Israel. Some examples of these organizations are the Coalition of Women for Peace and the Sabeel Ecumenical Liberation Theology Center.

290. What has been the role of Russia in the Palestinian-Israeli conflict?

Relations between the State of Israel and the Soviet Union ceased in 1967 after the Six-Day War and were reinstated 24 years later, in October 1991. **Tra-**

ditionally, the Soviet Union, as a power with interests in the Middle East and within the framework of the Cold War, has systematically defended its interests by providing military, financial and political support to the Arab countries, hostile towards Israel. The same support has been received by the Palestinians.

At the start of the 90s decade, Israel and Russia enjoyed renewed relations. It must be considered that the founding fathers of Israel came especially from the ex-Soviet Union. Currently, over a million citizens of the extinct Soviet Union live in Israel, many of them from Russia. It is the largest Russian-speaking diaspora in the world.

Under the leadership of Putin (elected in 2000), Russia became a friend of Israel, and at the same time, it is one of the countries that contributes largely to the instability in the Middle East. On one side, it stands out for its military and political support to Arab countries and to organizations considered by Israel and the West as terrorist organizations. For example, during the Second Lebanon War, most of the rockets launched by Hezbollah were made in Russia. Furthermore, Russia was the first country to recognize the regime of Hamas in the Gaza Strip and its representatives were invited to Moscow for an official visit. On the other hand, Russia coordinated with Israel its attacks on Syrian lands (against Iran) to avoid the death of Russian soldiers.

Given this situation, Russia lacks the capacity to pressure and reward Palestinians and Israelis, and its mediation capacity is low.

291. What has been the role of Latin America in the Palestinian-Israeli conflict?

The vote of the Latin American countries during the Partition (Declaration 181) was of fundamental importance. Of the 33 countries that voted in favor, 13 were Latin American.

After the independence of Israel, the institutional instability, the abrupt changes between democracies, dictatorships and the third-world tendencies of certain countries, making it difficult to explain the conduct of the region as a whole.

In 2006, Costa Rica and El Salvador (moved by the Second War of Lebanon) decided to relocate their embassies from Jerusalem to Tel-Aviv.

There are countries whose Foreign Affairs Ministries maintain significant postures contrary to Israel. The most evident examples are Brazil and Mexico. On Jan/22/2015, the UN General Assembly held its first meeting dedicated to the fight against anti-Semitism. Fifty states signed a declaration, and among those who refused to sign (although they participated) were Brazil and Mexico. **In recent years, Venezuela and Bolivia have emerged as countries that promote the most surreal (and anti-Semitic) condemnation ever heard in the UN institutions.**

Israeli Ambassadors usually affirm that they maintain a warm relation with their Latin American peers in the UN, although this is not always reflected in their votes. Among the diplomats who stand out negatively, there is the President of the General Assembly, the Nicaraguan Miguel D'Escoto Brockmann, who during the 63rd Assembly (2008) stood up to applaud the gross anti-Semitic speech by the Iranian president Mahmoud Ahmadinejad.

Societies in countries such as Guatemala (who relocated their embassy to Jerusalem) or El Salvador admire Israel profoundly. There are also governments who have adopted very pro-Israel policies such as Colombia, Horacio Cartes in Paraguay and at present, Jair Bolsnaro in Brazil.

In the recent years, when a Latin American country is governed by socialists or Chavistas, they usually adopt a clear anti-Israel position (Kirchner, Lula, Maduro) while more conservative governments usually approach Israel (Macri, Uribe).

292. Why does Israel mistrust the United Nations?

The influence of the UN in the Palestinian-Israeli conflict has been particularly negative. Since the mid-70s, the Arab-Soviet-Third World block united around a pro-Palestinian and anti-North American front. As it was difficult to criminalize the US, they opted to attack its regional ally, a declared enemy by the Arab countries. **Since then, the General Assembly of the UN is used to erode the legitimacy of the existence of the Jewish State, undermining a diplomatic solution to the conflict. The General Assembly has contributed to sustaining a policy of non-direct negotiation, but one of internationalization, of the Palestinian-Israeli conflict.**

In 1988 the Assembly designated the PLO as "Palestine". Years later, with Resolution 67/19 /Nov/29/2012) they agreed to admit Palestine as a non-member observer country (maintaining their rejection of negotiating with Israel).

When the peace process was realized, with the Oslo Accord (1993), the condemnations against Israel were reduced in the UN. For the first time, the Human rights Commission condemned anti-Semitism as a form of racism. Later, in 1994, when the Israeli Minister of Foreign Affairs, Shimon Peres, addressed the General Assembly, the only country that was not present was

Iran. In October 1993, for the first time since 1981, the Arab countries of the UN did not question the 'presence of Israel in the General Assembly. **In 2000, everything changed. After the Intifada of Al-Aqsa, the demonization of Israel began again.**

The destructive role of the UN stood out again when the UN World Conferences against Racism was organized in Durban, South Africa 2001. The conference was monopolized by NGOs and the Arab-Muslim block to delegitimize Israel and promote anti-Semitism, Forums such as the Human Rights Council and UNESCO have been sequestered by the same agendas, deteriorating their prestige.

293. Are there specific numbers to justify Israel's lack of trust in the UN?

The infamous treatment against Israel in the UN, especially in the General Assembly, is indisputable. **Five out of ten emergency sessions of the General Assembly throughout its history attacked Israel. In comparison, the Assembly did not hold not even one emergency meeting on the genocide in Rwanda or Sudan.**

The analysis of all the Declarations of the General Assembly (from January 1990 to June 2013) evidences that Israel is involved in 65% of all Resolutions that criticize a country, while no other country appears in more than 10%. **A democratic state, the only one in the Middle East, is the target of most of the criticism. Sounds strange, right?**

Between January 1990 and June 2013, 1676 voted Resolutions were issued by the UN General Assembly. Of these resolutions, 744 did not refer to a particular country, 932 mentioned one country, 646 criticized a country and 272 praised a country; 480 resolutions involve Israel, directly or in relation to neighboring countries. **Of the resolutions involving Israel, 422 or 88% criticize it, explicitly or implicitly. Countries that really destabilize world peace such as North Korea receive 38 criticisms, Palestine (29), Iran (22) and Sudan (10).**

During the period between 1990 and 2012, there were 5,400 casualties in combats related to Israel, meaning 13 deaths in combat for each resolution that criticizes Israel. In the same period, 65,507 people died in combat in Iraq, but Iraq only received 22 criticisms from the General Assembly (compared to 422 of Israel).

In the period 2015-2016, during the 70th session of the General Assembly, 20 condemnations against Israel were adopted, and only 3 against the rest of the countries.

294. What Declaration compares Zionism to Racism?

Among the resolutions against Israel, one of the most shameful ones was Resolution 3379 of the General Assembly (November 1975, 72 votes in favor and 35 against) that compared Zionism to Racism. It declared that it was a type of racial discrimination, a threat to peace and world safety. The resolution was seeking to deny the legitimacy of Israel attacking the moral base of its existence. It was maintained for several years, until finally, it was rejected in December 1991, without the Arab vote.

The Spanish and Portuguese speaking countries that voted in favor of the anti-Semitic Resolution 3379 of the General Assembly were Brazil, Mexico and Portugal. Among those who voted against, Costa Rica, El Salvador, Honduras, Nicaragua, Panama, Dominican Republic, and Uruguay stand out. In the revoked declaration, Resolution 4686, the Latin American countries approved its annulment, with the exception of Cuba.

Although the Arab-Israeli peace process, which began in Madrid in 1991, is structured on the base of direct negotiations between the parties, the UN constantly undermines this principle. The General Assembly usually adopts resolutions that intend to impose solutions for critical issues, such as Jerusalem, the Golan Heights and the Jewish settlements. **Ironically, the most accepted resolutions of the Security Council, 242 and 338, propose bi-lateral negotiations continuously refuted by the General Assembly**.

The Palestinians have been treated as de-luxe members, even when they were not part of the UN. Since 1975, the General Assembly granted the PLO the status of permanent representation. Frequently, special committees of the UN with apparently harmless names become obsessively anti-Israel forums. In March 2006, the only resolution by the Un Commission on the Legal and Social Status of Women condemned Israel for abusing women.

295. Why do countries that are close to Israel vote against it in the United Nations?

In general, there is a reality: the less democratic a country, the more it tends to vote in favor of all resolutions that demonize Israel. Maybe, because these countries do not wish to be spoken of and their every-day human rights violations.

There is a second explanation: the vote in the General Assembly is an expression because resolutions are not binding, they do not compel to actions. Votes are generally in blocks. The block of the autocracies and the "weak democracies" has an automatic majority and those are the ones who vote against Israel. An explanation of this conduct is the theory of "decoy voting" (Schelling 1978) for criticism. Decoy voting distracts the attention of the repression acts that autocrat or not very democratic rulers carry out against their people. **In other words, if they criticize Israel, which is free, no one will pay attention to them**.

A third explanation suggests the following: there are personal benefits for career diplomats, by representing and increasing activity within international organizations if they support crusades of dictators against Israel. A diplomat votes for Syria and Lebanon together, and in exchange, he is voted for X position. National politicians can also dictate guidelines for the vote for UN delegations, and they benefit personally from the sympathy in the relations with these dictators.

"The UN has an image of a world organization based on universal principles of justice and equality. The reality is that the die has been cast: it is nothing more than the executive committee of the dictatorships of the third world" (Jeane Kirkpatrick, ex-Ambassador of the US to the UN).

Discrimination against Israel has been acknowledged by ex-Secretary Generals Kofi Annan and Ban Ki-Moon. Unfortunately, they acknowledged it after leaving their positions.

296. What is the peace initiative of Saudi Arabia? Do the Arab countries want peace with Israel?

The Saudi Initiative is a proposal to end the Arab-Israeli conflict approved by the Arab League during the Beirut Summit (2002) and reaffirmed in the Riyad Summit (2007). The Initiative proposes 1) the normalization of relations between the 22 Arab states and Israel; 2) the withdrawal of Israel from the territories conquered during the Six-Day War (1967), dividing eastern Jerusalem, surrendering all the Golan to Syria and all of the West Bank to Palestine (there can be an exchange of minor territories, a point accepted in another summit in 2013); 3) a fair solution for the problem of the Palestinian refugees, based on Declaration 194 of the UN General Assembly (traditionally, the Arabs interpret this as a "right": descendants of refugees "return" to their homes in Israel; 4) Israel accepts a Palestinian State with eastern Jerusalem as its capital.

The proposal was made by Prince Abdallah Iben Abdul-Assis and was interpreted at the time as an attempt to improve their position in front of the western world, especially after the attacks against the World Trade Center. The Arab Peace Initiative arrived on one of the bloodiest months of the Second Intifada. On the same day of the Summit, there was a Palestinian attack at the Hotel Park in Netanya, which took the lives of 31 civilians during the Passover festivity. The increase in violence made the Arab Peace Initiative weaken.

The Israeli government, led by Ariel Sharon, rejected the Initiative arguing that the Arab countries were asking Israel to "pay" beforehand (acknowledging its principles) and then the normalization would come. Besides, he said that the Initiative contradicted Resolution 242. **For a part of the Israeli political map, the Saudi initiative is a good basis to negotiate both a regional and a final solution.**

297. What "bottom-up" peace initiatives can be highlighted in the framework of the Palestinian-Israeli conflict?

There are hundreds of extraordinary projects for co-existence and mutual acknowledgment, which seek to demystify the parties involved in the conflict and to help develop a positive disposition to peace from civil society.

The project Women Wage Peace, created by Israelis in the aftermath of Operation Protective Edge 2014, has involved their Palestinian peers, inspired by similar movements in North Ireland and Liberia. They have over 20,000 members working to promote peace.

The beautiful project *Hapoel Katamon* (2007) was born as a club of members for all Jerusalem citizens; Arabs and Jews, Once a month they unite the 50 neighborhoods of the city to play soccer and support students with their school work. Imitating this spirit, *Beitar Nordia* was created in Jerusalem (2014), a soccer team that encourages the participation of Arab players.

One of the most noticeable projects is "Roots of Peace" (2015), which gathers settlers of Gush Etzion with the Arab population to foster joint dialogues in plantations of the area. In the same topic, the project A New Way (*Efshar Acheret*) seeks to develop a long-term association between Jewish and Arab schools in the region, in order to change the attitude among youth and adults. The movement "Marching Together to a Shared Future" is trying to strengthen coexistence with joint meals between Jews and Arabs.

Medical projects could be described in which Palestinians are treated in Israeli hospitals or in Palestinian cities, or the production of sneakers with decorations made by families of deceased Palestinians and Israelis.

The main problem of all these projects is that the participation of Palestinians is less popular than Israelis. In any case, these are noble initiatives that must continue multiplying.

298. Why has Israel become a creative power?

In recent years, Israel has been recognized throughout the world for its inventions and developments in almost all fields. The high technology companies created in Israel (Start-ups) have transformed into a source of important income for the State of Israel.

The reasons that explain what has happened are varied (national *per capita* income 41,000 US dollars a year). Above all, the "adversity" of not having richness or natural resources; this forces Israel to be very creative in order to survive. For example, if it is not possible to depend on ships to transport products because others may organize a boycott, then it is preferable to create cyber programs to sell via the Internet.

The second reason is the influence of the army. Units such as Talpiot or the 8200, produce hundreds of specialists that acquire knowledge that they later invest in civilian actions.

An Israeli is usually considered as a *Chutzpan* (audacious – from *Chutzpah*), that does not pay respect hierarchies or forms, and doubts everything, no matter the status of who issues the opinion. If you add to this that they study more than one career, being multi-disciplinary fosters creativity.

Israeli society was born from immigrants, who by nature are risk-takers, as they have not much to lose. The government has intervened to promote Start-Ups, with incubators and financial facilities and with the advisory of creative directors in each ministry to approve projects with potential.

The universities have developed departments that commercialize the inventions and research of their teachers, reinvesting their capital in new research. There is also a healthy failure culture, that doesn't hide but considers it a learning experience for the "next adventure".

As was correctly stated by the eternal Shimon Peres: "Israel has not received water or oil, but it has received something more valuable: its non-conformity".

299. Is the implosion of Iran possible (2019)?

At present, there are more possibilities of Iran imploding than its fall because of a western or Sunni attack. **The decrease of the Iranian threat would be good news for the Middle East, although the Iranian reform forces nowadays lack the strength to produce a real change.** It must be kept in mind that traditionally, Iranians have been the most pro-west and progressive among the Muslims, even though they have been subject to a religious dictatorship since 1979.

The latest surveys in Iran show an increase in the public frustration: 85% of the respondents expressed their sense of despair for the future and their mistrust in the capacity of the government to provide solutions for the citizens. The surveys also show the acceleration of the process of secularization in the Islamic Republic: approximately 50% of the respondents admitted that they had not fasted during the month of Ramadan.

Part of the severe economic crisis (2019) is due to structural problems in the Iranian economy, such as the dependence of the state income on oil, the weakness of the private sector and the general corruption. In November of 2018, the Central Bank of Iran estimated inflation in 18.4% and the IMF estimates that inflation in Iran will increase by over 34% in 2019. The unemployment crisis may also worsen as a result of the significant decrease in economic growth and foreign investment. Unemployment is already 12%. Among young people under 30, unemployment is nearly 30%, and among young people with higher education, it is over 40%.

One of the main arguments that have been heard during recent protests indicates that Iranians are tired of having their funds invested in international adventured to expand the revolution instead of investing capital in the population and their problems.

300. Does time play in favor of Palestinians or Israelis?

For Palestinians, there are four reasons to believe that time favors them: 1) the increase in the Iranian military capacity may weaken the spirit and military potential of Israel; 2) the increase of anti-Semitism in Europe and the US may weaken the position of the Jews, especially when neo-anti-Semites declare themselves as anti-Zionists; 3) the separation of the US Democratic Party from Israel; a president with a profile such as Bernie Sanders could severely damage relations with Israel; 4) the internal socio-political disputes in Israel and the distancing from the Jewish communities of the world could increase the gap and weaken the capacity to sustain the conflict for more decades. The Happiness Index of the Palestinians (2018) is in the 104th place of 156 countries.

Israelis have reasons to believe that time plays in their favor: 1) a significant reduction of the importance of the Palestinian agenda. It seems that the Palestinian-Israeli conflict IS NOT the main one of the region, although it comes afloat on certain periods; 2) important Sunni states require Israeli support to stop the main enemy (Shiite Iran); 3) *Jihadism* nurtures with funds from oil, the black gold that is losing its power of cohesion.

Israel is the main power of the world in two essential topics for the Middle East: it knows how to desalinize water at marvelous prices and specializes in agriculture in impossible conditions. Leaving behind its military capacity, Israel has much more to offer in the technological-material sector than its neighbors; 4) one of the most hostile fronts against Israel, Europe, is having severe difficulties to stay as a Union. In parallel, bilateral relations with the EU countries are improving. The Happiness Index of the Israelis (2018) is in the 11th place of 156 countries.

Made in the USA
Middletown, DE
26 November 2024